# Chasing Horizons

Jon Lakin

Copyright © 2022 Jon Lakin
All rights reserved.
ISBN: 978-1-7396535-0-7

FOR ISABELLE AND GEORGE

# CONTENTS

Part One
| | |
|---|---|
| Into the Night | 3 |
| Talisker Whisky Atlantic Challenge | 6 |
| Signing Up | 9 |
| Learning to Row | 11 |
| Out on the Water | 14 |
| Hatching a Plan | 17 |
| Boatyard | 21 |
| Thirty-Six-Hour Rowing | 24 |
| The Gym | 28 |
| Back on the River | 30 |
| The Hull | 33 |
| Bristol Thirty-Six-Hour | 35 |
| Emily | 40 |
| The First Few Sponsors | 42 |
| Birmingham | 47 |
| Bristol Sport | 52 |
| Bristol Harbour Festival | 54 |
| Balloons | 61 |
| Race Entry | 66 |
| Scotland | 71 |
| Bristol Black-Tie | 78 |

Part Two
| | |
|---|---|
| La Gomera | 85 |
| Unfinished Business | 90 |
| Into the Water | 93 |
| Race Start Day | 97 |
| Sea Rescue | 102 |
| The Final Hurdle | 106 |

Part Three
| | |
|---|---|
| The Launch | 111 |
| It's Brutal | 117 |
| Vomit and Routine | 123 |
| Monstrous Waves | 131 |
| The Drogue | 136 |

## Chasing Horizons

| | |
|---|---|
| Team O2 Recovery | 141 |
| Team Tenzing Recovery | 145 |
| Navigation Problems | 150 |
| Christmas Day | 154 |
| Impact | 158 |
| Surfing | 161 |
| Exhaust Fumes | 163 |
| The Super Yacht | 168 |
| Power | 172 |
| Broken Seat | 176 |
| Sunrise | 179 |
| Shock | 182 |
| The Tropics | 185 |
| Debt | 189 |
| Failed Interview | 192 |
| Into the Blue | 195 |
| The Nutilus | 199 |
| Fungal Infection | 202 |
| Flat Waves | 206 |
| Water Maker | 209 |
| Radio Interview | 212 |
| Lost Electricals | 216 |
| Flood | 220 |
| Flying Fish | 225 |
| Night Theatre | 228 |
| New Moon | 232 |
| Autohelm Disaster | 235 |
| Manual Steering | 240 |
| Misinformation | 243 |
| Whales | 247 |
| Sleep Deprivation | 253 |
| Frigatebirds | 257 |
| Autohelm Fix | 260 |
| Flights | 264 |
| Caprice | 267 |
| Near Collision | 272 |
| Sargassum | 274 |
| Suntiki | 276 |
| Out-voted | 279 |
| Letters | 283 |
| Full Moon | 288 |

Chasing Horizons

| | |
|---|---|
| Almost There | 290 |
| Slow Progress | 291 |
| Countdown | 293 |
| Necessity | 294 |
| The Last Twenty-Four Hours | 296 |
| Journey's End | 299 |
| Part Four | |
| Antigua | 307 |
| One Year Later | 310 |
| Acknowledgements | 315 |
| About the Author | 317 |

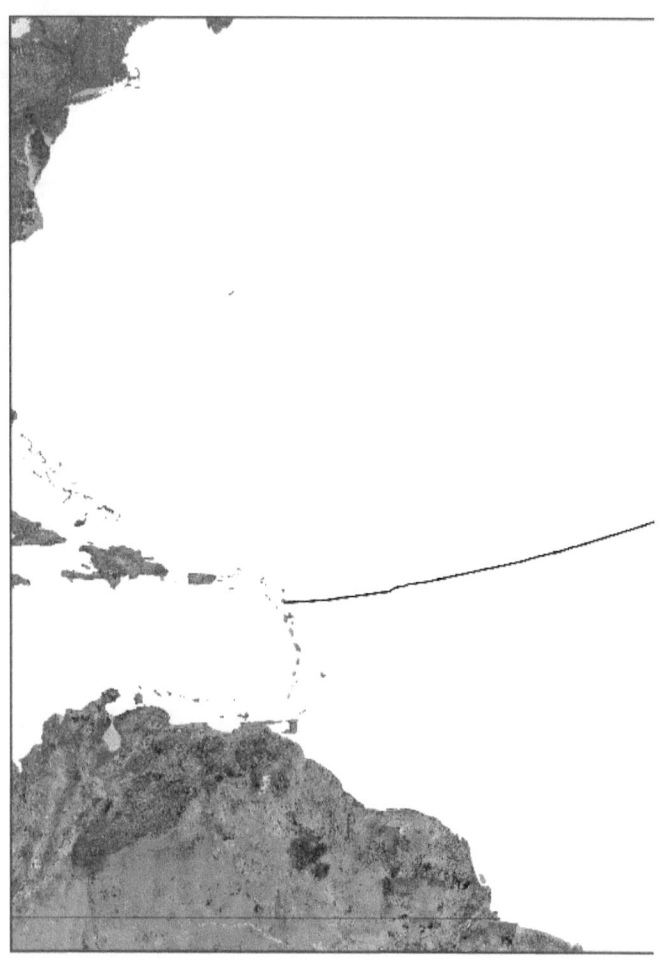

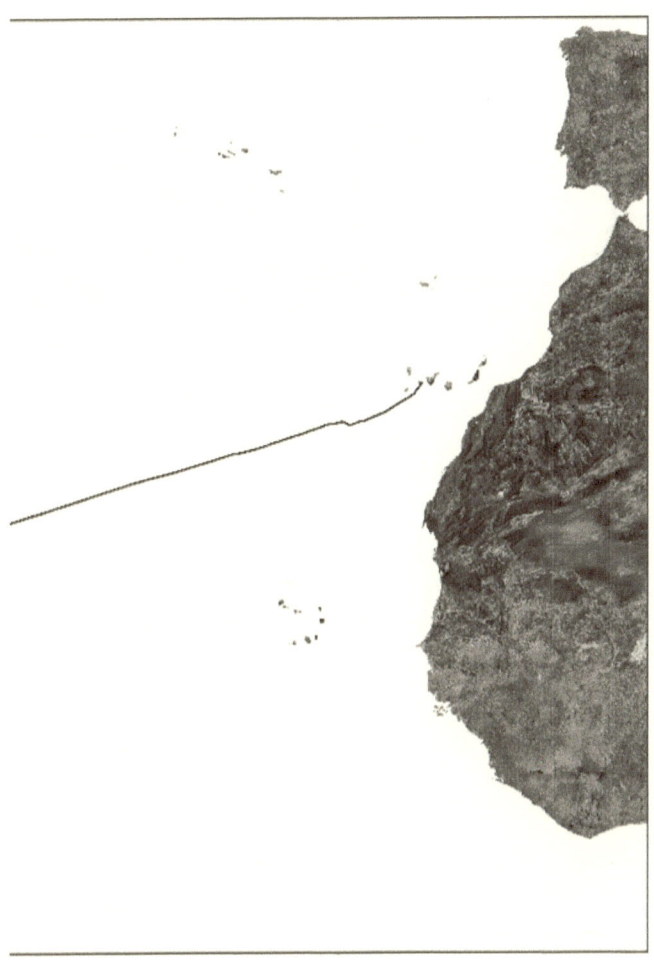

# PART ONE

# GETTING TO THE START LINE

# INTO THE NIGHT

The rain lashed down, adding another layer to the already harsh, unrelenting chilly night. My hands were clawing from holding on for hours, and it was hard to straighten my back from being in this position for so long.

The middle of the night drew in, daytime shoppers long gone, leaving the Saturday night drunks stumbling past. Late-night fast-food packaging scattered the paved ground, and bars thumped on a nearby street. Despite continuous exercise and layers of clothing, I couldn't shake off the cold of the night. The chill was biting through to my bones. The lights from Brighton shopping centre sparkled invitingly, taunting us from our now drenched marquee. We thought we'd get a decent footfall outside a shopping centre. How wrong had we been?

With the torrential rain now horizontal, I longed to be in the tent. I dreamed of my break; two hours of glorious but temporary comfort. But I still had 45 minutes left of my own two-hour hell. I gritted my teeth and dug deep.

The rain had well and truly set in. We decided to put the side of the marquee up for a little relief. We wouldn't get any punters now at 03:00. No-one would know if we were completing this or not, but we knew. We had to keep going.

If we couldn't even get through this weekend, then who were we to think we could wrestle an ocean?

My sodden hands were lazy, my brain slow from the lack of sleep, yet I couldn't get this side protector up quick enough. Each fumble just meant longer in the rain. Finally, the side was on. Now to get back on the rowing machine. I sat down, everything sore. I extended my arms and accepted the next 30 minutes. Not long to go. These mental games would serve me well on the ocean, I thought.

If we even get there. How on earth would we get there?

At last, the time came. I called out to the tent.

'You're up, guys…'

Selfish, overwhelming relief swept through me. The tent would be dry. I would be warm in my sleeping bag. My aching muscles would have time to rest.

Crawling in, I collapsed on my roll mat. The next time I'd be out, it would be daylight. Everything gets better in daylight. I gave way to an instantaneous, deep sleep, in whatever position I happened to lie down in.

We were halfway through a thirty-six-hour row and doing our best to look like we knew what we were doing. It was a dry run to experience the sleep pattern we would have to adopt out on the ocean, and to raise our profile. Secretly though, we were so far from rowing an ocean it was laughable. There was no money. There was no boat. There was very little chance of us even making it to the start line of the Atlantic Rowing Race.

But we had a goal, and we were going to do anything to make it happen.

There was a noise from beyond the flimsy tent wall.

'Your turn now!'

My two-hour off shift had evaporated in an instant; time seemingly not obeying the usual rules. Surely not already? I had only just closed my eyes. Unzipping the tent, I checked I wasn't dreaming. I wasn't. Head dazed, reddened eyes, limbs tingling with fatigue, it was time to haul my body back out into the driving rain.

This time there would be people. Any of them could be a potential lead, a potential sponsor, a contact or media opportunity. I tried to appear less grumpy.

'You'll get there,' a passer-by called out.

It was nice to hear her optimism, but it was an optimism based on her perception of our determination. Surely, we couldn't believe our way to the start line, and yet a part of me thought we must. If we didn't believe it was possible, then what would we be basing the foundations of our campaign on? We didn't have long to go. I was doubtful we would pull this out of the bag, but a fiery determination not to quit burned within me. Quitting was not an option. People achieved this. This was possible. There will be a way.

# TALISKER WHISKY ATLANTIC CHALLENGE

Over a year prior to the Brighton rowing marathon, I was lazily scrolling through expedition blogs on a crisp autumn Saturday morning, clueless that this moment would change the course of my life.

Steam rising from my cup of tea, the tick-tick-tick of the scroll button spoiling the music I had on, my eyes scanned down the familiar screen in front of me.

Safe. Comfortable. Easy.

But this was the opposite of what I was craving. I was addicted to consuming articles and videos of what seemed like other worlds; other people living completely different lives to mine; a life of expedition and adventure; a life trajectory not explained as a career option at school, yet achieved by some; the path less trodden.

I sipped my tea, a subconscious sigh looming in the back of my head. It would be Monday before I knew it. I had such ambition, but I was conflicted, overridden with conformity.

Then I spotted it. A post caught my eye. Someone was looking for a partner to join him in a row across the Atlantic.

## Chasing Horizons

My mind was instantly blown. I had no idea it was even possible to cross an ocean in a rowing boat. It had me captivated more than any other expedition. Devoured by the sheer thought of it; a seed planted that I couldn't suppress. I could never unthink this.

Pouring tea down my neck, I ingested information on this alien concept, oblivious to the outside world. Cemented firmly in my chair, I binged video after video on ocean rowing. Every new bit of information drawing me further into this inescapable thought vortex. I clicked through a couple of links and glared at the statistics.

> A distance of 3,000 miles across the ocean from La Gomera to Antigua.
> Rowing in two-hour shifts, 24 hours a day.
> Rowers are unsupported, generating power and making water.
> On average, each person on the boat will lose 12 kilograms in weight.
> Boats are nine metres long, with a cabin at each end.

I sat back, basking in optimism and a nervous excitement. Could I row an ocean? Who was I even to think this? I wasn't a rower. I wasn't rich. Could I do it regardless?

I was instantly within its inescapable grasp. It was a challenge unlike any I'd seen before. Rowing an ocean. I knew in that instant I had to do it.

Monday soon came round. Although functioning at work, my subconscious mind was racing with ideas. My eyes uncontrollably glanced at the clock at the bottom right of the screen again. It was now late afternoon. I was sitting at my desk, the working day nearly over. The winter's gloom seeped into the tired office, the whites and greys of the walls and desks now tinged with a yellow from the harsh ceiling lights. There was a small group of us in our isolated little room.

I had consumed so much information on the subject I

was incapable of keeping it to myself. As fast as I had gulped down information, I vomited it back up.

'I saw a few videos of this ocean rowing race. What do people think……?'

With a certainty I didn't question, my friends at work, Steve and Mark, responded.

'This sounds incredible. I'm in,' said Steve.

'Rowing across the Atlantic Ocean? Yes!' said Mark.

It was so definite, as if it was obvious this was what we would do.

Work disappeared.

The prospect of achieving this captivated me. Having no funding or rowing experience, I loved the idea of pulling the impossible out of the bag. It obsessed me.

Around a month later, Steve's brother Dan was on board. We had a team, but little did we know what we were letting ourselves in for.

# SIGNING UP

Now a team, the campaign was rapidly moving from an idea in my head to making physical strides forwards in reality. I returned to the laptop and eagerly leaned in to research how to achieve this, rather than just watch the well-edited marketing videos. It was as if the initial excitement had been reorganised to fuel more useful thought patterns. The general advice was that funding and building a campaign takes around two years to achieve. We planned for the December 2017 race.

When choosing a charity to row for, there was only really one choice. Other members of the team knew people affected by the causes Movember fights for - testicular cancer, prostate cancer, mental health and suicide prevention. This, together with their annual moustache-growing and hipster brand, Movember seemed like the perfect fit. The decision was made.

With the charity chosen, it was only a matter of time before we had an awesome team name. 'Nuts Over The Atlantic' was perfect. We were crazy to think that we'd be able to complete this massive challenge, and we wanted to highlight the principle aims of the charity.

The initial thrill and excitement had subsided to a

persistent quivering, deep in my stomach. I needed to understand how to achieve the massive logistical and financial challenge that lay before me. The numbers and time frames were daunting, but I was as enticed by this challenge as much as I was by the ocean row. I felt a willingness to do whatever it took to make this happen. I could almost feel my mind narrowing with a hyperfocus on this one goal. Now I must orientate everything in my life towards this. Nothing else mattered.

Daunted and drunk with anticipation, we filled in the forms and signed up. This would be a formative, all-encompassing two-year journey. We were committed.

I must admit, I had my doubts. Funding was a massive problem. I had no issue with putting in the effort and time, but it was such a vast financial mountain to climb. I was hesitantly reassured by the rest of the team's confidence in achieving this monumental ambition.

Signing up committed us to be in La Gomera for the start of the race in December 2017. We would have to pay the £20,000 entrance fee by September 2017 and raise an eye watering sum of money circa £100,000 to fund the campaign.

People said that getting to the start line is as hard as rowing the Atlantic. We had two years to find out how true this statement was.

# LEARNING TO ROW

Fresh spring air accompanied the glistening water of the docks. The warm sun beamed down and reflected off windows as we strolled along the harbour, desperately trying to look as if we belonged there. A bundle of nerves twisted in my gut.

We walked towards the clubhouse, where a huddle of people stood awkwardly by the water's edge. As we approached, we spotted a scattering of rowing machines next to the slipway. The clubhouse came into view, boats carefully stacked outside like a fortress, barricading it from the outdoors. A few confident people strode around, tall, athletic, with broad shoulders and branded gilets. Clearly, they were members of the club and knew what they were doing.

We were at the Bristol Rowing Club for our first ever row. Judging by the shuffling feet and stilted conversations, several other nervous newcomers joined us.

Across the sparkling water were the familiar colourful houses resting on the hill in the centre of Bristol. This city I knew so well, suddenly felt unknown. The rowing club was a place I had walked by countless times but had never paid much attention to. My experience with the docks had stopped firmly at the beer garden of the pub nearby, having a cold glass on a sunny day and watching other people out on the water.

The invisible barrier between land and water was now disappearing. I was in the hazy no-man's land between solid, reliable ground and the uncertain, alien water.

I felt like an undercover operative hiding my true intentions. We weren't supposed to be here.

Other people were looking for a new hobby. It was a taster session. People were here to see if they enjoyed the sport and, if they did, they would sign up to the Learn to Row course and then, maybe, the Novice Squad.

We needed to learn a skill to help us on the way to becoming ocean rowers in less than two years.

I looked around the group of newbies. There were people of all ages and walks of life. Steve, Mark, Dan and I fitted in seamlessly.

Suddenly, a tall man in a thick Bristol Rowing Club jacket came towards our small, tense group.

'Ok, we better get started. We're going to be working in two groups. One half on the ergs….'

He pointed at the collection of rowing machines.

'….. and one half on the pontoon.'

We were on the ergs.

I wanted to keep our plan quiet. It seemed ludicrous that four slightly unfit blokes had already signed up to row an ocean, and were about to attend a beginner's rowing class. I didn't want the experienced coaching staff to think that we were a joke.

'So,' said the coach, as we began strapping our feet into the rowing machine, 'what made you want to take up rowing?'

'Well,' said Mark, 'we're rowing the Atlantic next year. Can you teach us to row?'

Eyebrows raised.

'Oh! You're the Atlantic rowers, are you? We'll see what we can do.'

# Chasing Horizons

I felt unnerved. We couldn't even row and here we were at a club on a taster session, asking someone experienced to get us across an ocean. Surely this is not how it's done?

I suddenly became conscious of everything I was doing. It was as if the coaches were assessing me even for standing, judging me on my posture, evaluating how I retied my shoe lace. I so wanted to please these athletic men and women. I wanted them to see that we had potential; that rowing an ocean wasn't completely out of the question. That we were serious.

Almost without realising it, the session on the erg became transactional. We needed to achieve a certain level of aptitude to pass some unspoken quality assessment exam. We needed to get into the club, and the watching eyes of the coaching staff held the entrance key.

With aching limbs, I stumbled off the erg. The session was complete. A weight seemed to lift from my shoulders.

We'd made a big step on our rowing journey. Now we just needed to find out if were in.

## OUT ON THE WATER

We slung the boat above our heads, each person now looking like a leg of a beetle with the boat making the body, as we scuttled down the pontoon. The sun remained strong into the weekday evening, and a refreshing breeze brushed over the water. People's laughter travelled from bars on the other side of the docks.

Tonight, we would attempt to row as an eight. With each step drawing us closer to the water, I recalled the journey we'd been on in a relatively short time.

After learning the basic technique on ergs, we'd been allowed on the water for a few brief sessions.

The first time we'd awkwardly climbed into the slim boat, it was immediately unsteadied, rocking uncontrollably under us, threatening to throw us into the icy water. To counter this, four rowers placed their blades flat on the water to steady the boat, while the other four practised technique and timing. We got to grips with how the boat handled, working as a team, rotating between steadying and rowing on the cox's call.

With every session that went by we gained in competence, from four rowers steadying the boat to two, and now, here we were about to try all eight of us rowing.

We lifted the boat from our shoulders, pushed it above our heads, and slung it down onto the water. I stepped into the boat with slightly more confidence than before and sorted my oar and footplate. We pushed off and gently edged our way out into the harbour to the sound of the cox's command.

The regular drills began, with only a few of us rowing whilst the others steadied the boat. Silent concentration saturated the team. A slight breeze wrapped around our faces. Our muscles were like coiled springs. We were ready.

Gradually, we built to six rowers. As the speed, technique and resultant balance increased, the cox gained in confidence and so did we.

Then, without warning, the call came.

'OK, seven and eight ready to row and… stroke, and… stroke, and…'

We were off! The boat swayed from side to side, like a spinning top losing energy on the verge of crashing out of control. With razor sharp focus, I examined each part of my stroke, not wanting to be the one that toppled us. Focusing on the rower's head in front of me, I feathered the blade, getting the catch dead on and putting power down to propel us forward. Perfect timing was crucial.

It was difficult with eight people rowing. I hadn't realised the nuances involved in trying to keep your stroke balanced, being in perfect harmony with the rower in front of you. The slightest change to your stroke would send the boat off balance. The steadying rowers had previously absorbed any mistakes with their blades flat on the water, balancing the boat. With all oars pulling, there was nowhere to hide, but so much to gain.

We were flying!

The less I concentrated, the better I was. Air rushed into my lungs, legs pushed down onto the footplate, my body temperature rose rapidly. The sound of my breath and beat of my heart tried valiantly to keep pace with the demands of the exercise.

This was exhilarating!

Buzzing and exhausted, we slowed it down. Relief, pride, and triumph filled the boat. At a gentle pace and with the boat steadied, we made our way back to the pontoon.

I gazed up at people in bars enjoying a sunny evening after work. I'd been oblivious to the unexpected spectators a few moments ago. The extreme focus had overwhelmed my senses. I wondered if any of the people in the bar knew that I'd been one of them just a few weeks before.

Back on the pontoon, we hauled the dripping boat back over our heads, and rested it on the trellis to wash before returning it to the boathouse. My body was still rushed with endorphins and I buzzed with optimism. Working as a team against the elements was on another level. Everyone was on form, and we could only improve from here. How would this feeling compare to rowing an open ocean? What an evening it had been!

## HATCHING A PLAN

As strange as it sounds, it never actually entered my mind that I wasn't capable of rowing an ocean, not egotistically. I think I was so obsessed with the image of us crossing the finish line that there wasn't an alternative.

I could, however, see us failing to make it to the start line. The monumental financial challenge, and lack of traction with sponsorship, weighed heavily at the back of my mind. This was the crux of the entire project and the only real obstacle between us and rowing an ocean.

I didn't know how to raise this enormous sum of money. To pull off something on this scale we needed to plan an entire campaign with a marketing strategy, branding, and relatable message, whilst offering value to investors. We needed all this in place immediately.

It was a weekday evening. Having just fought through a dimly lit rush hour in the city centre, I was ready to crash out in my flat. I slumped down, clunking my phone by the side of my laptop, and wearily dialled into the weekly call with the team.

Blue light strained my eyes as I battled to keep them open. I searched for the extra gram of concentration I desperately needed. With so much to keep track of and plan, the weekly meetings had quickly become essential. We would aim to finish in a reasonable time but, from experience, I knew the call would go into the early hours.

It had been a long day at work, and I had barely had time to chuck some food down my neck. However, an underlying sense of anticipation was present. Tonight was the night we would launch our campaign.

After researching other teams' sponsorship plans, we tried to emulate their ideas using our own angle. We then designed our own sponsorship brochure. This is the part of large expeditions that you never hear about; the hours behind the computer; the graft behind the scenes.

My eyes scanned the brochure for what seemed like the thousandth time. It had to be spot on, look slick and be professional. Branding, logos, colours and messaging were all carefully talked over. This would be our hook for discussing investment in the future meetings we would hopefully have.

To secure these important meetings, we planned to use social media, distribute flyers, and send emails to as many companies as possible. We even used a professional email signature. The complete image mattered. We wanted to look as if getting to the start line was inevitable. People wouldn't invest if it didn't look serious.

Tonight, the brochure would be available online for the first time. Anyone could stumble upon it and want to back us. My eyes ran to the bottom of the PDF. I was happy. The other guys were happy.

As part of the launch, we'd put together a competition with merchandise we had received from Movember. Hopefully, this would encourage the post to be shared and gain interest outside of our direct social circles. Everyone likes free stuff. Movember also had links to several major companies. If we raised enough money for them, they may use their leverage with these big corporations and lend a hand with sponsorship. We knew this was how other teams landed deals. Being at the foot of this financial mountain, we had to explore every avenue, every trail, every track, and every battered road sign possible.

Some hours later, the call ended. It was time to launch our campaign into the world. I closed my laptop with a satisfying thud, stretched out my back and walked to the kitchen to boil the kettle again. The next stage of the evening was about to begin, and I craved sustenance.

Time had raced by. It was September 2016, much to our frustration. We would have loved to have launched earlier. The deadline to pay race entry hadn't moved and was looming on the horizon. We were still nowhere near having the funds. Having worked round the clock for six months, things were not going to plan. Aspects of the launch, such as the website and sponsorship brochure, had taken longer than expected.

Lying on my sofa, full of unease, phone in my sweaty hand, I exhaled. The automated launch would be in any second. It was a moment I was not looking forward to, but understood it was necessary. We needed sponsorship, donations and funds. We had to get the word out there. I just hated social media, and this launch would be that, times a million. I dreaded the potential attention it would draw, and was worried what people would think. Not even my friends knew about the row. I would have preferred to get on with things quietly.

My stomach churned. I found this worse than signing up for the actual event. If there was a route to financing our expedition that did not involve social media, I would have taken it in a heartbeat. I would have been more than happy not posting a single photo online and just getting on with the row, leaving the story for close friends and family at the pub. The days of anonymity were over. I needed to grapple with the anxiety of selling my soul to social media.

Finally, we launched. My phone instantly lit up, sounding like I'd just hit the jackpot on a slot machine. I was pinged with more messages than I could keep up with. People meant well, but it felt like more admin on top of our already huge list of things to do. The guilt of not replying meant I spent the rest of the evening on my phone. I wanted to know people's reactions to our big reveal, and yet I didn't want to know at all. A small egotistical part of me craved recognition, while the rest of me would have preferred to stay quiet.

My heart raced, my fingers frantically tapping away to keep up with the influx of messages. This was quite an announcement to make with no prior warning.

Movember shared the post, and we gained immense traction. I couldn't believe it. The competition had actually worked! Hopefully it didn't matter that the followers were mainly from Movember's share of the post and just wanted to win free stuff.

# BOATYARD

Boats chimed as they gently swayed, welcoming us into the marina. A fresh salty sea breeze invaded our noses. The gravel crunched beneath our feet as we walked up and gave the door of the boatyard reception a firm knock.

'Hello chaps. Here to look at the Pure hull?' said Chris, welcoming us in.

We had learnt that there are two types of ocean rowing boat, Pure Class and Concept Class. The Concept design made the most of the wind and was, therefore, the faster boat. Pure Class was slower, but less susceptible to capsize, which was definitely a plus.

Having discussed getting a second-hand boat, it seemed a better plan to buy an empty hull. We could then negotiate with equipment manufacturers to complete the boat build. This way we would have a newly built boat at a discounted rate that we could sell on after the race. Hopefully!

A fumbling round for keys ensued before we left the building and made our way round to the warehouse. Walking by the side of the building, the sight of an ocean rowing boat greeted us as if it was a normal thing to see. This secret world was slowly unveiling itself.

No one would guess this understated vessel could ferry

four people across an ocean compared to the yachts in the marina. The white paint glistened in the sun as I gazed down the side, the curve of the hull leading my eye along the entire length.

'Come on Jon, let's look at the one we're here for!' said Dan.

The owner herded us to the warehouse to look at the hull we were there to see. The heavy door crept open, letting the sunlight beam through, highlighting the dust in the air. A handful of sleek ocean rowing boats in various stages of construction were balanced on trailers.

We walked up to the hull in the centre of the room. Chris hauled the dust sheets off, revealing a pristine white, half-finished boat. A previous team had bought this hull but had pulled out of the race because of financial reasons.

'Well, I'm sure that's not going to happen to us,' said Mark, as he ran his hand along the smooth lines of the craft.

Despite his confidence, I still felt a twinge of concern in my gut. What if we didn't raise the money in time? What if we couldn't even afford to buy a boat?

Pushing this dark financial cloud to the back of my mind, I jumped on deck.

The boat wobbled erratically on its trailer. I stumbled, clutching Steve for support. How on earth would I fare on the vast ocean if I couldn't even handle the boat on dry land?

Even with no rowing positions, it was a struggle to manoeuvre round the deck. Clambering over each other, I reached the aft cabin and buried my head in. It was tiny and claustrophobic. Scraping my shin on the cabin frame, I lunged forwards into the cabin. It felt snug, tucked away, and secure from the outside. Currently empty, this small space would reduce further once we had decked it out with equipment.

I gazed through the hatch along the deck towards the forward cabin at my teammates. Instantly, my imagination transported me to the sea. I could see the waves lapping over the deck, the spray lashing the oars, and the wide, open sky.

## Chasing Horizons

We exchanged knowing looks with each other. The weight of the campaign momentarily evaporated as we were lost in our own imaginations. Suddenly, the whole adventure felt very real.

# THIRTY-SIX-HOUR ROWING

The year was drawing sharply to a close. Mark and I were sitting in the pub, catching up over a much-needed pint. Christmas decorations bombarded my eyes, festive music was playing, and the feeling that there wasn't long until the break from work saturated the air. People having one too many drinks filled the main room next to us with a loud, merry buzz. In stark contrast, we had located ourselves in the smaller quiet room next door. Our laptops sat on the sticky table; our beers precariously balanced beside the keyboards. There was work to be done.

Tainting the festive spirit came one sobering and all-consuming fact. We now had half the time to ascend this financial mountain. Despite researching hundreds of addresses on Companies House, hand-writing letters to directors, and sending out flyers, we had no traction. We weren't getting anywhere with sponsorship.

With one year to go, no way to pay for the boat or equipment, and £20,000 race entry due in September, we had to regroup. We also needed a better way of producing social media content, as well as raising money for charity and, hopefully, getting some training in. Now, sat in the pub, we were desperately dreaming of ways to make this work.

'Let's go back to basics,' I said, stretching my aching back from being huddled over the laptop.

'We've researched every team, past and present. What have we missed?'

A silence fell over the pair of us like a heavy mist. We had gone over fundraising strategies countless times. If there was an easy answer, we would have sussed it out by now.

Mark looked up.

'Wasn't there a team last year that did well out of a thirty-six-hour row in a shopping centre, or something? Maybe we could do that.'

My hands subconsciously had the YouTube video up on my screen quicker than I realised. It looked doable, and they had a well-produced promotional video off the back of it to send to potential sponsors. Without another word, we both knew this was it.

Part of the issue with our sponsorship strategy was that we didn't have an interesting story compared to other teams. We were four normal guys in their late twenties. Not the oldest, not the youngest. We were all fit and healthy. To get press coverage we thought we needed to do something extreme, something that no one could ignore.

'Let's do a tour of thirty-six-hour rows, then.'

Just like that, the next year was decided. We'd go to city centres around the UK. At each event, we would contact local press, undertake interviews, hopefully get on TV and build a following. The final event was to be in London, in November, to coincide with Movember, and just before we left for La Gomera, the start line of the race. We would professionally film the first event for a promotional video. By the end of the tour, the aim would be to break the national press as other teams had, and with coverage and a following, would come potential sponsors. Genius!

Before this idea, we were struggling to get everything done. This would solve everything. It would get us noticed by the press, give us publicity, cover our training, provide social media content and raise money for charity.

## Chasing Horizons

The plan was simple. Drive to a city on Friday evening, set up the marquee, feather banners, two rowing machines and a tent, and then rotate rowing for two hours, with two hours off, for 36 hours until Sunday. Then drive back to Bristol, crash out and go to work Monday morning. It was brutal. But so brutal it must get noticed.

After a lot of debate, we decided on Bristol, Cardiff, Brighton, Newcastle, Birmingham and London, calling it our 'Nuts Go Row' tour. With this, we committed ourselves to an enormous amount of additional organisation, extra meetings, logistics and emails. We now had to find time in our already busy schedules to speak with every council and agree on locations. We needed to buy and design the marquee and feather banners, and blag as much equipment as we could for free.

My phone buzzed on the table. I picked it up and gazed at the message. I'd been moaning to a friend about our financial worries and our plan for the coming year.

My friend simply said, 'You have to do this. You're lucky enough to have the opportunity.'

In my mind, this sentence was the wrong way round. We weren't lucky. We had worked hard and there was no guarantee we would do this. The more opportunities we could give ourselves, the more chance there would be of having some luck and success. But we had to engineer those opportunities ourselves. We were quite far into this campaign. We'd done a heck of a lot of hard work to get to where we were. Luck had nothing to do with it.

In fact, I now felt that people were rarely lucky. Maybe some were, but I felt I just hadn't seen how many times they had failed, and only judged them on their successes.

Maybe doing the thirty-six-hour rows would maximise our opportunity and maybe we'd get some sponsorship. But it wouldn't be luck that got us there. It was us, putting ourselves out there and making the opportunities happen.

Restless optimism filled my brain. Maybe this would work. I was itching to get to work on the logistics. With that,

## Chasing Horizons

I downed my beer, eager to get stuck into this new challenge… after another round, obviously.

# THE GYM

With our new chaotic lives in full steam, we still needed to train to get our bodies ready. Unsurprisingly, there isn't much literature on how to train to row an ocean! However, there are a few fundamentals to a successful crossing. Being strong and heavy is key. We needed muscle mass. We had to have enough weight to lose weight. We wouldn't eat enough during the day to replace the calories spent. Extrapolate this over several weeks at sea and the weight will drop off. Added to this, building mental endurance was vital and, of course, learning to row.

It was now time to hit the gym.

We decided to go before work. Only people with a reason to be out on the road accompanied my journey at this hour. Bleary-eyed and half asleep, I transported my body to the gym. As I pulled up, I saw that Mark and Steve's cars were already in the car park.

My stomach fluttered. I'd never been to a gym before. I stepped inside, intimidated. This was not an environment I relished. I prefer to be outdoors, exploring the world in combination with exercise, rather than exercising for the sake of it. Our gym routine comprised of lifting weights. Exercises that strengthen the postural chain were essential.

I found Steve and Mark in the changing rooms, already chatting excitedly about the upcoming exercise session. Enveloped by the usual clammy faint smell of sweat in the changing rooms, I quietly got myself changed.

Out on the gym floor, they encouraged me to go first on the weight machine. I sat on the sweaty seat before me, looked up at the shiny metallic bar, stretched upwards and clasped the grips ready to pull down.

'Jon! You're on the seat the wrong way round!' laughed Mark.

I couldn't believe it. I recoiled my clumsy, now self-conscious hands, and repositioned myself on the seat. At least the gym was relatively empty, I thought. I had a lot to learn on this journey.

Suppressing his laughter, Steve updated us on gym sponsorship; a welcome distraction and a key deal we were after. He'd been going back and forth with David Lloyd for a few weeks now.

'David Lloyd are interested lads,' he said, scrolling through his phone as I pulled down on the weighted bar.

'Gym membership, in return for social media content, it is! They want to meet this week after work to formalise it.'

Although it wouldn't be a huge injection of cash, free gym membership for social media content was an obvious deal that would help.

It was now late November 2016. We had exactly one year to pull this out of the bag, and the biggest sponsorship we had was free gym membership.

We had such a long way to go. My dream of an ocean row seemed such a long way off.

With an injection of impotent rage, I yanked hard down on the bar.

# BACK ON THE RIVER

It was now winter. The nights were dark and cold, and there was a damp musk in the air that only comes with the season. We were still attending weekly rowing sessions at our local club. I had a strange relationship with these rowing sessions. Because of the ever-present weight of campaign admin, I struggled to justify the time. Yet when we were out on the water, I got a sense of peace that I couldn't find elsewhere.

Readying the oar, sliding it through the oar gate now had a ritual feeling about it. An air of anticipation loomed as nine individuals and a boat were about to become one functioning machine. I gripped the cold oar to the ripping sound of Velcro, as everyone strapped their feet in. Pushing off the pontoon, we edged our way to the centre of the water, now feeling separated from the chaotic city.

Days in the office were temporarily forgotten. Worries drained away. Peace filled the boat. The background noise that constantly buzzed around my brain slipped into silence, as if it knew it wasn't important, and I needed to focus. Then we were off.

Our oars in unison took command of the water, slicing through and catching it. Our fatigued quads propelled us forwards, the boat gliding along the surface. Blood rushed through my body and cold air hit my face. The oars obeyed the cox's call in a trance-like rhythm. All senses disappeared as my focus narrowed. I was only aware of the cox's call, my pounding heart, and the form, timing and power of my stroke. With no chance to think of anything else except gasping for air, I lost myself in the mesmerising rhythm.

Winter rowing in Bristol docks was wonderful. It was freezing cold, but the atmosphere was incredible. On a crisp winter evening, the water would be like glass. Lights from pubs and restaurants glistened off the water like decorations. Fog hovered over the water, adding to the film-like scene.

We would row through tunnels, embracing the instant darkness and echoing calls from the cox. We would row slightly out of the harbour but still within the city centre. It felt like a complete wilderness with the foliage and trees overhanging. Other times, the weather was horrid with cross winds, and cold torrential rain. I loved this too. It meant a hard-fought session both for boat control and warmth.

My legs would go numb during rowing. Within 15 minutes I'd lose all feeling from my calf down. When it was brutally cold and wet, I would step off the boat onto the icy, slippery pontoon, onto what felt like nothing.

I never regretted a rowing session. It was great headspace and gave me no option other than focussing one hundred per cent on the exercise. However, the campaign was snowballing. With under a year until we were due in La Gomera, our time was more precious than ever. As much as I enjoyed the rowing sessions, there were a few things that needed balance. We were there for a purpose, to learn to cross an ocean, not to become river rowing athletes.

The two disciplines were like night and day. Having spoken to some ocean rowers, we now understood the requirements of training and the expedition itself.

River rowing is about precision, timing and accuracy; the blades feathered in an elegant, well-orchestrated dance.

Ocean rowing is just a battle where anything goes, as long as progress is being made. The two most important things are to be as efficient as possible and avoid injury. Keeping blades square would help prevent repetitive strain injury. We were told that we should expect periods of time rowing full pelt with just one oar, simply to keep the boat on course.

There was also a sense of guilt. We were already slacking, missing sessions and just not being very committed members to the club. It made little sense to most people. To row an ocean, you need to learn to row, surely? Coaches assumed we needed more practice. Friends would ask how learning to row was going. The reality was we needed money. It was like starting a business. Learning to be a river rower wasn't contributing to this. We needed more gym time, packing on muscle, doing deadlifts and eating.

All of us had the basic rowing stroke down and, as much as I loved the rowing sessions and the headspace, it was time to move the campaign forwards. The cold hard fact was that money had to be our number one priority; without the funding, everything else was pointless. An evening spent perfecting our rowing stroke was not an evening sat behind the laptop working on sponsorship.

With the basics learnt, we continued on with the rest of the campaign.

## THE HULL

It was now February 2017. The year was settling in faster than I thought necessary. The September race entry deadline, and the expedition itself, felt closer than was comfortable. Although a way off, we could feel it looming.

Still with no boat, we had been in regular contact with the boatyard, discussing the hull we had seen five months before. We had minimum funds, so a deposit was a big ask. But with less than a year to go, it wasn't only funding that was becoming an issue. We needed a boat, not only for the expedition, but also to get some much-needed practice on the water and achieve the mandatory qualifying hours.

Walking under the burnt orange light cast from lamp posts, back to our cars after a gruelling gym session, we had our inevitable impromptu meeting. The heat from my body rapidly escaped, and the chill of the night, that exercise had temporarily masked, made itself known.

'So, the Pure hull,' Mark prompted. 'What are you guys thinking?'

My mind was sinking slowly back to reality from the short escapism that came with exercise. We had to commit if we were serious; we needed a finished boat after all. The boatyard had confirmed the hull was ours if we wanted it, and they'd be able to finish it by the end of July, providing we supplied all the equipment on time. They also confirmed there wasn't enough time now to build a boat from scratch.

'July would be ok,' said Steve. 'We'd still have enough time to get some practice in before we row the ocean in December.'

Dan smiled his usual grin.

'Yeah, I'm sure we'll find sponsors soon. What do you think, Jon?'

A tenseness ran through me, and a heaviness sank in my stomach. I fought to suppress my negative instinct, trying desperately to feel the confidence that the rest of the team felt. We still had time for sponsors to get on board, and with our thirty-six-hour row tour looming, we had more confidence in our strategy.

As desperation and determination were ramping up, my mind-set had shifted. Before, it had been 'We can't afford this!' Now, it was 'How can we afford this?' The money existed. It was out there somewhere. We just needed to shift some of it in our direction.

'Ok, let's do it,' I said. 'We'll put the deposit down tomorrow.'

The heavy feeling in my stomach lifted slightly, but was most definitely still there, too deeply embedded to shift with one conversation. But we could do this. We had to do this. We had to make it work.

I got back in my car, blasted the heating on full whack and drove home for the evening. Mind now drained and muscles fatigued, I immediately collapsed on the sofa. Progress was being made, and we had time. This was possible, I reminded myself.

# BRISTOL THIRTY-SIX-HOUR

'Ouch!'

I missed the pin and whacked my thumb again. Punching holes in a marquee roof was not how I planned to spend the night before our first thirty-six-hour row. There were a lot of last-minute jobs to do. Artificial light flooded Steve's living room. It was now the early hours of Friday morning. We had a full day at work ahead of us before we started our rowing challenge.

'This is ridiculous!' said Steve, his exasperated face laughing in acceptance of the situation.

'I know, people wouldn't believe the last-minute panics we've had. Getting thrown around in the back of the Transit with that picture board wasn't on my to do list!' I said.

Earlier that evening, we had carted it across Bristol. I was in the back of the van, holding it up. Every corner we went round, the board would fall on me. We had to transport it somehow but didn't have time to think things through.

'Let's crack on. We'll get there if we keep at it.'

I punched another hole. Hopefully, I was doing this right. I'd hate for mine to be the one that ripped and caused rain to get in. My mind wondered. At least I thought this campaign could work. We'd discussed this with Nikki, the

Atlantic Campaigns representative. She confirmed no one had done anything like our thirty-six-hour rowing tour before and seemed keen on the idea. Despite how chaotic and under-funded we were, we looked as if we had it together and had a strong campaign planned that should generate funding.

Finally, we punched the last hole, and with that, the marquee was ready. I said bye to the guys and went back to my flat to catch a few hours' sleep. When I woke, it would mark the start of a long three days.

Work came and went in the blink of an eye. Everyone knew what was in store for us over the weekend. All the conversation and expectation added to my nerves, but I had greater things to think about. I left and was immediately in 'getting things done' mode. A keen stride set in as I marched to my car. The static pit of nerves in my stomach during work was now being put to use, and I felt it.

I parked up and walked towards the plot that would be our home for the next 36 hours. I could see Mark organising kit that scattered the ground, and a huge van parked alongside. Pedestrians wandered past, oblivious to what we were doing, stuck in their own worlds, as was I. Time was limited.

I jumped in the van and drove to the university gym to collect the rowing machines, about an hour's round trip.

Returning, my nerves soared. People were watching us set up. We needed to look confident despite not having done this before. We had never rowed for more than about 15 minutes, and here we were about to attempt 18 hours each, combined with no proper sleep, in public and in February. If we couldn't do this here, then we'd never manage an entire ocean.

I didn't think about this too much. I knew I'd get through it somehow. I was more concerned that we got media coverage and, hopefully, a few sponsorship leads out of it. It appeared like an endurance event, but to us it was a means to an end; the end hopefully being the race start in La Gomera.

I looked back and admired our setup. Atlantic row aside, I was quite proud of this individual event, let alone the entire tour. We'd taken an idea in our heads and turned it into reality. I realised I was so focused on the end goal of rowing to Antigua, that I hadn't thought about the logistical accomplishment that this minor event was. I hadn't given it much consideration. If this was in isolation, I would have been proud and content, but in reality, it was only a stepping stone. The overall campaign dwarfed it.

Our first thirty-six-hour rowing setup was now waiting to become part of our campaign. Framed by our blue marquee sat two rowing machines. On either side of the marquee stood two feather banners gently swaying in the wind, with key messaging that echoed the text of the marquee itself. To one side, we had our cut-out board of a rowing boat which had all our contact information on and a sneaky hashtag. People could pose behind the cut-out to become the rowers. A great selfie opportunity and excellent way to send out our information. Next to the selfie cut-out was our leader board. We planned to run a 500m sprint competition for the public on the third rowing machine, which sat beside the other two. To round things off, we planted buckets for collecting Movember donations on each corner of the marquee and a speaker hung from the frame.

We switched on the music, stood back, and admired our achievement. We were ready to go.

Darkness prevailed on this cold, wet winter's evening. Music from nearby bars thumped, lights lit up the rain, and the cold seeped in. Groups of people, ready for a night out, passed by. Loud and excited, not caring about the rain, as they stumbled into the refuge of warm bars with steamy windows.

With the setup complete, my stomach turned once more. This being our first event, and in our home city of Bristol, we had arranged for press coverage. We had a few radio shows who would cover us over the course of the weekend. The most impressive one, however, was the BBC news. This would be our first appearance on TV and first press coverage to launch the event and campaign. This was really happening now.

The BBC van drove around the one-way system and onto the pedestrianised area next to our marquee. A huge mast extended into the sky ready for broadcasting, and the crew and presenter hopped out. People were staring even more now that the BBC was here. Something interesting was going on.

'So, I'll row whilst interviewing one of you and the other guys can be in the background of the shot,' the presenter said. 'Remember to get everything in the answers you want to say, what you're doing and why, and feel free to sneak in that you're looking for any potential sponsors.'

Before we knew it, we were live on the local news on Friday night and as quickly as they came, they left. We felt elated. We were finally getting coverage and, hopefully, looked more professional.

The evening drew in and with it, the start of our thirty-six-hour row. I sat down on the cold plastic seat, which felt like it had a solid permanence about it.

The real challenge started. Hordes of drunks stumbled by. Overly competitive stag-dos had a go at the 500m challenge and crumpled into the hard ground. Groups of people talked loudly in our faces about their lives, while we rowed and politely listened. I already craved crawling into the relative warmth and anonymity of the tent.

In the early hours, Friday-night stragglers stumbled towards us through the cold and wet. Looking worse for wear, they embarked on long, drawn-out conversations I could barely follow.

Sunrise broke after what seemed an eternity. Warmth gently restored. Fresh golden light bounced off the cobbles, revealing a scene that looked as if a litter bomb had exploded after a Friday night binge. My face felt weathered. A still peace fell over the city centre. It was the empty transition between night and day and we had the place to ourselves. We had completed one night, and I now felt a tired, relieved sense of calm.

After another radio interview and a steaming hot coffee, we wandered around trying to spark interest in our cause. Armed with flyers, brochures and stickers, we went into as many shops and businesses as we could, hoping it would lead to funding. Every stranger that engaged with us while walking by, was a conversation approached with full attention and optimism. We never knew who they might be or know.

The end of the long second night eventually came as the warm sun heated us up again, signifying that shelter and rest were near. Friends and family were there to see us finish. We had managed 36 hours of rowing together. This was a triumph. We had emulated the pattern of the expedition and survived. My mind felt callused. We had built collective mental strength and confidence. The ocean felt more tangible.

The rest of the tour awaited. Although we didn't have any strong funding leads this time, we had many events lined up. The more we did, the more our name was out there and the more people we would meet. It had to be a numbers game. Surely, we were onto something. We simply had to put the hours in.

# EMILY

I stood in the smoking area with my friends, escaping the music and mass of bodies in the small club. Music thumped in the background and the back of my mouth had a regretful taste due to my friend buying rounds of shots that no one had asked for.

I had sneaked home for a rare weekend off to celebrate my friend's birthday, and everyone was going.

'You should meet Emily,' my friend shouted rather loudly in my ear.

Before I had a chance to respond, it had happened.

'This is Jon. He's rowing the Atlantic.'

I winced. I didn't like people saying this. In fact, I really hated it. I just thought it sounded like bragging, and with the entire project all over the shop, it didn't feel like this was certain. Time spent at home, listening to what my friends had been up to and enjoying normal life, was a treat. I didn't particularly want to talk about the row.

'Well, can I swim it? I'd have a go. Someone's swimming it now, aren't they?!'

No one had ever responded like this. Usually, the whole idea of the adventure left people amazed and confused. I regularly encountered a perplexed expression and a moment of awkward silence while they tried to comprehend such a vast activity.

Emily just looked at me as if it was a normal thing to do. She completely got it. She responded how I had when I signed up. She didn't need any more information. Clearly it was an awesome idea, and no more questions were needed. We were wired the same way.

We hit it off, and the direction of both our lives changed instantaneously.

# THE FIRST FEW SPONSORS

Buzzzzzz….

My finger pressed into the cold, hard metal button. The little intercom seemed to have more power than it should have. It was as if the person on the other side of the intercom was the guard in charge of a castle drawbridge, deciding whether to let me in.

I buzzed again, pressing harder, as if that would make a difference. I stood there with a handwritten letter and sponsorship proposal flapping in the wind under one arm.

'Hello.'

'Hi, my name is Jon Lakin. I'm part of an ocean rowing campaign. We have a few investment proposals to offer. Is it possible we could speak to a director or the person in charge of the Corporate, Social and Responsibility budget?'

Declined. In fairness, this one was a punt. I didn't know their names or have a tailored proposal. I turned round and caught Mark's eye. He'd clearly just had the same experience.

An overcast day awaited us. A hint of grey seemed to tarnish the surrounding office blocks. We'd taken a couple of days off work to go round company to company, knocking on doors, attempting to get in front of someone who was in charge of the budget.

Sometimes we had a target, a person we'd researched and who we had handwritten a letter for, hoping we could give it to them in person. Other times, we just left a generic letter and flyer at reception explaining what we were up to.

Midway through the second day, the usual tired, irrepressible doubt was setting in. Currently, it was being overruled by forced optimism. Only determination allowed us to put one foot in front of the other and continue dropping off these letters to companies.

It might not work, but we had to try. Alongside emails and badgering on LinkedIn, we had allocated these dreary days for physically getting a presence out there. We must continue, despite the odds. I couldn't let myself rest until I knew that we'd got our information to as many companies as we could manage. Every industrial estate, every business, every hotel, every shop, big or small, in Bristol city centre and surrounding towns. Repeating the same thing over and over. It was exhausting and soul destroying.

In parallel, we were expanding the list of companies to approach. The spreadsheet was vast, each company falling into a category based on how we aligned with them and the approach used. Targeting everything we could think of, from men's health to nautical themes and engineering. We looked into companies that push the boundaries of what's possible, or supporting local endeavours, or even just a gamble on a company. We then emailed a specific contact we'd researched, or if not, a generic email address, and attached our proposal. Or we'd post a handwritten letter with our flyer attached. Usually, we did both.

Learning as we went, we'd rebranded our entire Nuts Go Row tour with fresh messaging on our marquee and feather banners. We also redesigned our sponsorship proposal to align with Corporate, Social and Responsibility budgets. This re-design took time and money, but it was worth the risk… we hoped.

On the way to the next set of offices, we took our chances with a tile shop on the side of the road.

The sliding doors offered a more welcoming entrance. A solitary man stood next to the checkout.

'Hi there. We are an ocean rowing team and have some great investment opportunities.'

'Sorry, mate. A Welsh team came in here a few months ago, and we're already sponsoring them. We can't do another.'

I looked at Mark in disbelief. They were from miles away and had beaten us to our local tile shop and been successful! A shop that sold tiles! They were way ahead of us. How many more businesses had they got to? A tile shop was the least likely of places I'd have expected, and yet they would probably have sponsored us if we'd been earlier.

It was now past five o'clock, and many places were closing. In a last-ditch attempt, we decided to just post a flyer and letter through the doors of the remaining companies in this industrial estate and go home. The clip of the metal letter boxes rang round the industrial estate for another five minutes, and with that, we brought the two days to a close.

Work soon came round the next morning. Refocusing was always hard. How could I think of anything else but how to get this enormous sum of money? To make things harder, everyone was constantly asking about training and the boat, which seemed irrelevant in comparison. After a couple of days' holiday dedicated to trying to find funding, it was hard not to think of how we could have done things differently.

I looked at my phone for relief. Steve had texted.

'Alright guys. Great news. BMT are in!'

My mood changed in an instant. BMT was the company Steve worked for, and he'd been trying to get them on board for a while. Not only was it much needed cash, but with each new logo on our website and displayed at events, we looked more credible to potential sponsors.

Unable to think of anything else, time vanished at my desk. Another text, this time from Mark.

'A company called Arc Monitoring from yesterday's drop of letters is interested. Can you get to their office at three o'clock for a meeting?'

I couldn't believe it. What a day!

The usual conflict of work against the rowing campaign came hurtling back. I had just had two days off, and the first day back I was going to ask to leave early for a meeting.

I parked up outside their office, took a deep breath and walked to the door, this time buzzing the intercom with enthusiasm.

I walked into the modern glass container-like office and sat next to Steve and Mark. I still hadn't got my head round this. This one was an impersonal letter simply posted through the letterbox of an office, and they were interested in sponsoring us. It was unbelievable.

'Hello. You must be Jon. I'm Jonathan Sturley. Great to meet you. These chaps were just telling me about the incredible expedition you have planned.'

Mark and Steve sat opposite his desk, obviously trying to look confident, but I could tell they were considering every word they said. Our budget rested on a knife's edge. Incredibly, things seemed to be going more than well. He was sifting through our large sponsorship brochure and talking about a reasonable sum of money.

I hid my sweaty palms under the desk and was conscious my posture was overly bolt upright. The silences between talking dragged out and exacerbated my already dry mouth. I caught Mark and Steve's eye, but didn't want to look excited.

The booklet landed on the desk with a thud.

'We're in, but we'll be in contact in a day or so to work out the details.'

We stood up, shook his hand, and pushed the glass door open. Standing tall, we tried not to grin too much when catching each other's eyes. Things were happening.

# BIRMINGHAM

July, and the Birmingham leg of our thirty-six-hour rowing tour had come round in a flash. Fatigued, Steve, Mark and I crammed into the front of the van on the drive up, with our equipment in the back. Dan would get the train from London and meet us there. We were now used to what it entailed, and the buzz of it all had worn off. Packing the equipment in the back of the van was now slightly more organised, in contrast to the panic that was Bristol.

The dashboard rattled in response to the vibrating engine. Warm air came out of the air vents, attempting to cool us down. The summer heat had brought with it a weary nostalgia. We reminisced about the previous legs of the tour.

'The onslaught of rain in Brighton…'

'Remember the brutal cold of Newcastle?' Steve said.

It felt so far in the distant past. An unbearably frosty night. It was here we realised that sleeping in the van was toastier and felt more secure than the tent. Once ensconced in the warm van, we forgot about the stag dos, drunken chanting and competitive idiots falling off the rowing machines.

'And the mini raves!' added Mark.

We'd learnt from Bristol that our setup was loud from music blaring from the little speaker, but completely dark.

To combat the darkness, we had dressed the marquee with fairy lights to accompany the late-night, drunken dancing. It was amazing for morale whilst rowing, but made the van even more appealing at the end of your shift.

'At least today isn't as hot as Cardiff,' said Steve.

Headaches and dehydration were our enemies at Cardiff. A busker accompanied us in the square on the Saturday, attracting hordes of people, making it feel like we were rowing in a summer festival.

We agreed the biggest take away was the education in UK night life. We could have made a documentary on what we'd witnessed. The 05:00 shift was the worst. This was when the inevitable stragglers would stumble past and start monotonous conversations that seemed endless.

'Hopefully this weekend will go without a hitch,' Mark said.

None of us were convinced.

We had received a warning about an organised protest near the pitch we had negotiated and paid for. However, with this warning also came reassurance that it would be peaceful and under control.

We pulled up in the square. The van jolted our heads in synchronisation as we went up the curb. The protest hadn't started yet.

I jumped out of the van and surveyed the area. My shoulders slumped. I instantly realised the weekend would be pointless.

Before me in the square was a lovely flat area where we would be rowing. Steps led down to the main street. Thankfully, the pavement surrounding the square was also the route into town to get to bars. However, there would be no reason for the public to walk up the steps, and being such an enormous square, we would be out of sight. It would isolate us with nothing but our thoughts for the whole weekend and little chance of passing foot traffic.

It was hard enough doing these weekends in busy areas, but at least you would see the point in it. There was hope in anonymous strangers walking past. They were all potential leads. But with no footfall, it left us with 36 hours of rowing by ourselves, and our internal demons telling us we wouldn't raise the required funds.

We set up in sombre silence. Reluctantly, we lugged the rowing machines across the paved area, their small caster wheels getting stuck in between paving slabs. After the initial rush of getting things off the ground, the Nuts Go Row tour wasn't reaping as much benefit as we'd hoped, and they were exhausting. The marquee, feather banners, and tent all came together silently; it was second nature now. We were like aging members of a band standing next to each other, ready to face the music once more.

With no more excuses, we began the row. With no traction, we continued to post on social media, pretending everything was fine. The day passed without event, going through the routine of our two hours on, two hours off shifts, discussing the campaign and future plans. Darkness fell and an oddly quiet night passed without event.

Saturday came quickly, and with it, the protest. A small group of people mingled the other side of the square. The crowd grew, as did the atmosphere. Transformed, the now swarm-like mass gradually engulfed us. The sound of the megaphone and chanting was deafening. People dwarfed the area. A riot van stealthily came into view, just waiting, making its presence known.

I looked up at Dan, his face saturated with disappointment. Our bodies slumped, seemingly about to fall off their skeletal frames. Our heads hung low as acceptance crept in. We all knew it. There was no way we could fundraise for Movember in these conditions. We tried to keep a brave face on social media. At least we could pretend we were doing okay, and that it was going well. But it just got worse and our motivation plummeted further, inversely correlating to the energy of the crowd. What was the point in being here doing this if no one around cared?

The distorted voice pummelled out of the megaphone, making communication strained as I feebly pulled back on the rowing machine.

'What do you reckon then, guys?' Steve said, a question that probably meant more than just this event.

The whole Nuts Go Row campaign was not going as we'd hoped. People didn't know the truth. Although we had been saying on social media that we needed help, conveying the extent and gravity of the situation wasn't easy. Our social media and Nuts Go Row campaign painted a different picture. We were touring the country, rowing for 36 hours at a time, raising money for charity and rowing the Atlantic in December. It all sounded great.

But there was a huge underlying issue. With all the expenses, such as paying for the slot, renting the van and the marquee, we were losing hundreds of pounds each month. Not only were we not gaining sponsorship, we were moving further away from our target.

On top of this, each of these weekends raising money for Movember was hard. Nobody seemed to care, and when they stopped to speak to us, they thought we were having a laugh.

'Of course, you're not actually rowing the Atlantic. You're just doing this weekend, right?'

Maybe our messaging was off. Maybe the scale of rowing the Atlantic didn't translate to passers-by who saw us rowing on ergs. Something was wrong. Our message and branding were not clear.

We were also learning more about marketing. The original plan was to get on the local press at each event, eventually breaking national press and gaining sponsorship as our following grew. Although we gained press at each event, it was not as much as we needed. We were learning the hard way. If you are not from the area, it is very difficult to get the public and the press engaged. A local campaign was the way to go. People need to see things multiple times before absorbing the message. With each event, people may see our messaging once and never again. A national campaign was not the way to do this.

Protesters inundated the square. The riot van rolled in like a weary parent attempting to prevent mischief with their very presence. The background noise made sure my thoughts started from a rocky foundation, and a hard truth bubbled away under the surface. This weekend had cost us a lot of money and we were gaining nothing from it. We were in trouble. With six months to go, now we were looking like the charity.

'This isn't working. We can't waste time doing this anymore.' I said, now regressing from a weak row to a firm stop.

I sat slumped on the seat, looking up at the guys for inspiration. We didn't want to call off the event. Movember were watching online and offering support. Despite abortive thoughts, and fatigue, we felt we had a duty to continue. But with no footfall and with the losses we were making, it was a better use of time to go home and get behind the laptop to raise funds.

On paper, the entire tour provided so much - our social media, our training, charity fundraising and hopefully sponsorship. No team was doing anything like this. But we were failing, and it was hard to take. We had to have a rethink.

'Let's call it a day,' I said.

The others agreed.

We packed up the van. It rocked with the slam of the door that resonated on a disappointing level. Dog-tired and with heavy hearts, we hit the road.

# BRISTOL SPORT

It was a sweltering hot day. The sun reflected off the white clad stadium and made my eyes squint. I had negotiated a longer lunch with work to slot this meeting in. The work shirt and heat not being a wonderful combination; dark stains appeared under my armpits.

Today was our meeting with Jon Lansdown, the owner of Bristol Sport; the umbrella company for Bristol City Football Club, Bristol Rugby and Bristol Flyers Basketball Team. We had been trying to arrange this meeting for a while through a mutual friend. This was our first contact made through a mutual friend, and we had heard repeatedly that most sponsorship comes from people you know. Having had so many failures from cold emails and knocking on doors, we knew this was a big moment.

'Hi, you must be the ocean rowers? Let's grab a seat.'

I scraped the chair back with an ear wrenching noise. I felt clumsy. We sat on metal chairs around a table outside the stadium. Passers-by to the café had no way of knowing that a potential deal was about to happen to part fund an ocean rowing expedition. With a hesitant and dry throat, I began talking through our proposal.

Jon was very humble, and straight away gave some

advice that we needed to hear. He contemplated his words.

'I think it's going to be difficult to raise funds outside of November. Movember as a charity is synonymous with that month.'

He hesitated.

'And………..,' he paused to choose his words.

'What's the principle message of the flyer?'

We took deep breaths. Our messaging on our new flyer still wasn't on point, despite this being our second attempt and having thrown money at it.

'But we can certainly help you out, and we can help you out with more exposure, too.'

I caught Steve's eye. This was huge. We now knew that we needed a local campaign. This was a key sponsor in Bristol with great links. In addition, we had two huge local upcoming events, the Bristol Harbour Festival and the Bristol Balloon Fiesta. If we could put their logo on our boat by these two events, and make connections, it just may all come together.

# BRISTOL HARBOUR FESTIVAL

My fingers nearly tore as I made my third attempt to open the cabin hatch. The boat, along with others, sat in a row on some grass at the back of the boatyard, appearing as if someone had just left it to find its own entertainment. Memories of our first visit flooded back as the boat rocked on its trailer. But this was different. I ignored the rocking. I was under pressure to get this boat back to Bristol. My fingers slipped off again as I failed to prize the hatch. Nobody had opened it for quite some time. It was stuck fast.

Mark shouted up to me.

'Come on, Jon! Use those new muscles you found in the gym!'

Then it went. I was flung back onto the wet deck as the damp, mildewy cabin revealed itself. A pile of rowing equipment lay in a heap, as if someone had dumped it in a rush.

We had driven from Bristol to Christchurch after work, to pick up another team's boat and bring it back ready for the Bristol Harbour Festival. The event attracts thousands of people each year and was an absolute must for us.

We had little time to complain. We needed the boat to be in the water by 21:00 tonight in Bristol and only had a few hours to get back.

'I'll reverse the car up and let's attach it,' said Dad, who had kindly driven down to help.

We attached the trailer to Dad's car and strapped the boat down. Mark and I jumped into a separate car and we were off.

Being in the car and only able to sit, forced me to calm down. My mind wandered. Although it was July, work to get us a spot at the festival had started in January. Contacting the organisers had not been easy, but an Atlantic rowing team at Bristol's maritime festival was an opportunity we had to capitalise on. When negotiating this, I was confident we'd have a boat for the event half a year later, but our boat was nowhere near ready. It was still just the hull. So here we were, frantically towing someone else's boat back to Bristol to borrow for the weekend.

We needed this boat. With a boat, we looked credible, ready for the ocean. Without a boat, we looked like dreamers with a couple of rowing machines and an idea.

Dad had been direct with instructions and careful when loading the boat. He clearly knew time was of the essence and that he was about to tow something worth a lot of money that wasn't ours. I looked up and saw the white boat with Dad's car in front, bobbing up and down along the unmaintained road.

'We're on the road, guys!' I texted Steve and Dan.

One hurdle down.

After a while I looked up again, and gazed out of the windscreen. I couldn't see the boat. The road was straight and neither of us noticed when or if Dad turned off. We kept going. Dad knew the way.

An hour passed. Not concerned that he'd taken a different route, we called him.

'Hi, Dad. How's it going?'

'Err... not so good, son. I went for the A-roads. I thought it would be better than the motorway. Anyway, a wheel has come off the trailer. I'm currently at a farm and walking to the nearest place to, hopefully, get spare parts to fix it.'

I couldn't believe it. My mouth went dry. Every sound seemed to disappear apart from the voice coming out of the phone. I felt awful for him. He knew what this event meant to us. We didn't have long to get the boat in the water, and he was stuck in the middle of nowhere.

'It's ok. There's nothing you can do. Carry on and I'll fix it.'

Miles apart and helpless, all we could do was to continue on the motorway to Bristol.

'Hey, buddy!' Dan gave his usual happy greeting, as we met up at Bristol harbour, now rammed with all sorts of boats.

'How's it going?'

It was immediately obvious there was no boat. Conversation continued as we began assembling our usual marquee setup for another weekend of rowing.

Time ticked by as we busied ourselves.

And then we saw it. A stealthy, large black car rolled round the corner, behind it, a long, white ocean rowing boat. Dad grinned from the driver's seat. He'd triumphantly turned up just one hour before the boat had to be in the water.

Immediately into action, my fingers tried to smooth down the expensive logos we had paid for. My inexperience causing regretful bubbles to form but, as with everything in this campaign, we just had to wing it. I stood back. Bristol Sport and BMT, our two largest sponsors, looked prominent. On the aft cabin a huge 'Your Logo Here?' stood out. With thousands of people this weekend, we were hopeful it would catch someone's eye.

The light had faded. An empty sky stretched above us, pinpricks of stars shining, and a bitter wind whipped through the harbour. We threw on our warm jumpers.

'You need to be in the water now!' The event organiser said frantically down the phone.

They were looking to close up for the night and needed us in the water so everything would be ok in the morning. We'd have to finish the rest of the logos tomorrow morning before everything started.

We launched the boat down the slipway and into the dark water, jumped in, and looked at each other in disbelief. There was something missing.

It was suddenly so obvious! Where were the seats and lights?

Mark opened the cabin hatch to grab the oars, cursing in the process as it took several attempts.

We plunged into the silky black water. A panicked conversation ensued as we gradually drifted out, leaving Dad and the trailer on terra firma. Our first time in an ocean rowing boat and I was on my knees, along with Steve to my left, one oar each, trying to row. Mark was at the back steering and Dan was forward, watching where we were going.

'Get some lights!' The harbour master called.

We were already annoying people.

'One more stroke. Steve, Jon, hold!'

The boat steered into the pontoon. We'd done it. We moored the boat. With the thirty-six-hour row already set up, we called it a day.

I glanced at my watch. It was nearly midnight. We needed to get home and get some sleep. Tomorrow was Friday and the start of the three-day festival. We would start our row that evening.

Exhausted from yesterday, and a full day at work, the evening came round quickly. I would do the all too familiar two hours on, two hours off regime from now on. We had a few people pass by, but it would be Saturday and Sunday when the real crowds came along.

The pontoon shook from side to side. I looked up and saw ITV News marching down towards us.

'Hi chaps. Would you mind if we did an interview with the boat being rowed in the background?'

'Of course,' we all said.

A knowing look exchanged instantly between us. We'd only rowed the boat once, and that was extremely sketchy.

And now we were about to have our debut on TV – rowing without seats!

Steve, Dan, and Mark boarded the boat. I drew the straw for the interview. They rowed out whilst I began answering questions, facing the other way, oblivious to what was going on, desperately trying to remember the key points…

'… yes, it's a 3,000 mile rowing race from La Gomera to Antigua…'

'… we're currently looking for support, so if anyone would like to sponsor us, please get in touch…'

An embarrassing firm clunk reverberated on the pontoon as the guys collided with the wood. ITV packed up.

'Thanks, chaps. That was great. We'll see you over the weekend.'

'That was awful,' said Dan, his usual smiling face lost in a frustrated frown.

'With that wind, we were completely out of control. We couldn't even time our strokes. It was a disaster. They'll never use that footage,' said Steve, head drooping.

Saturday came and, after some reassuring early morning practice on the water, we were more ready for our slot today. We were due to row up and down the docks twice each day. A team member was to disembark to do a live interview broadcast on loudspeakers, whilst the boat circled in the water.

I stepped onto the boat, my legs shaking. This would be in front of the public in choppy waters. Although we now had some rowing experience, this was something else altogether. The boat was much larger than the river boats we'd been learning on. Its size made it hugely susceptible to getting blown around by the wind. It felt a completely different concept to master. It was like learning to drive a Mini and then being forced to drive an articulated lorry in front of an audience.

We edged ourselves out. Steve and I synchronised into a rhythm. We concentrated on our every move, trying to avoid obstacles whilst blocking out the noise from the surrounding crowds. The harbour master pointed us to the side of the docks, the holding area. We had not discussed this, and it was a tricky manoeuvre for our limited experience. We scrambled through and sat ready for the next instruction.

The signal came. We engaged our legs and launched the boat into the middle of the docks. This was it. Our 'Your Logo Here?' was now in front of thousands of eyes, along with the huge Bristol Sport and BMT logos showing that people were already investing. Mark steered the boat towards the pontoon, preparing for Dan to disembark. The wind picked up. We were getting pushed sideways into a huge boat. Steve and I rowed with everything we had. We couldn't crash someone else's boat in front of thousands of people. Our oars scraped the side of the boat as we got pushed sideways. Our boat edged round the corner, allowing us to put some power down and thrust our way out of the situation and towards the pontoon, and the interview.

Not having practised disembarking, this would be the next first. We edged as close as we dared, starboard oars in, and Dan leapt off the boat onto the pontoon. Done.

Now to complete another couple of circles without crashing. The loudspeaker was now just a buzz. I couldn't concentrate on anything else but rowing round in this choppy circle unscathed.

After a couple of sketchy circles, the interview ended, and we rowed back. Now in a straight line and the spotlight off, our nerves settled. We think we pulled it off! All we had to do was repeat the same action several times over the weekend.

Back at our marquee, with the boat safely moored to the pontoon, we relaxed. Despite the terrible winds and choppy waters, we had succeeded. We knew we could manage the weekend. We went straight back to the rowing machines and engaging the public in what we were trying to achieve.

It was Sunday, and we were in the swing of things when a rumour circulated that Carol Vorderman was chilling out a few yachts down the pontoon. This was an opportunity we couldn't miss. Getting a picture of the Countdown celebrity on the boat could get more attention. She may even post us on social media.

I gingerly trotted down the pontoon to see for myself. It was true. I could see her auburn hair and instantly recognisable face, laughing and enjoying her time aboard the swanky yacht. I edged closer. I couldn't miss this.

'Hi! Sorry to interrupt. I'm part of the Atlantic rowing team over there, and I just wondered, if I bought you a coffee or something, would you come and take a selfie with us on the boat?'

'Of course!'

Result. What a change this was. We'd gone from having no boat, to a wheel falling off the trailer, to a failed TV interview, and now Carol Vorderman was clambering onto our boat. Coincidently, The Bristol Post was wandering by and immediately took a photo of Carol with us and the boat.

Riding on this luck, I grabbed a different ITV reporter as he wandered by and secured an interview, which was a success. Later, The Bristol Post did a full interview on the boat with us rowing. Amongst other bits of press, and what seemed like an engaged public, the weekend had been a success. Hopefully, someone had seen our 'Your Logo Here?' or would read or watch us on TV and see the opportunity.

# BALLOONS

The red lights on the back of the boat flashed against a black backdrop. It was raining and nearly midnight. Wind wrapped round the buildings and my body was craving the indoors and sleep.

'One light left,' I shouted as I paced back to the boat.

I rubbed the hull with my sleeve, attempting to dry the rain off before taping the bike lights on; a last-ditch idea, as the trailer lights weren't working.

Mark and I had to be in Bristol tonight. Ideally, we should already be there.

We were in Christchurch to collect our boat but, on arrival at the boatyard, my heart sank as our suspicions became a reality. By the looks of it, no work had been done. It was still just a hull.

'I can't believe this,' said Mark. 'It's August. How on earth are we going to have this boat ready for the ocean and shipping to La Gomera in November?'

'And our qualifying rowing hours?!'

'At least we're switching boat builders after this. Hopefully, a change of location to Scotland will sort this mess out.' said Mark.

'How much time have we got?'

'The guys at the Balloon Fiesta said we need to be there at 07:00 to set up.'

I looked at my phone. Midnight was slipping into the past and we had a four-hour drive ahead of us. We needed the boat to look like a legitimate ocean rowing vessel. If not, then we were just four guys with a dream.

'We have to make this. Hundreds of Bristol businesses will be there. A 100,000 people a day, over three days! We can't miss this opportunity!'

'All done,' I said, as I stepped back to check how visible we were from behind.

Mark nodded. 'I think it's a goer. Let's shift it.'

With the back of the boat visible, I jumped in the car and slammed the door closed, perhaps more forcefully than needed. The car rocked. I was so frustrated. My mind swirled with furious questions.

'What had the boat builder been doing all this time?'

'Would we have a boat ready in time?'

'How would we manage the boat build in Scotland, when we're miles away in Bristol?'

Mark glanced over at me from the passenger seat.

'You alright, buddy?'

I took a deep breath.

'Yeah, I'm fine. It'll be fine. It has to be fine.'

Mark turned the ignition key. The night road trip began. Headlights lit up a white path to pursue against the shadowy black lanes.

The jet-black sky gave way to navy blue poking through the clouds, as the beginnings of a cracking summer's day dawned. With the morning sky now above us, fresh heat was piling down on us as we gingerly pulled into Ashton Court Estate at 06:00. The car and trailer bumped and shook over the grass.

We parked, stationary at last, safe, the boat in one piece. All muscles relaxed and my eyes crumpled under the heavy weight of my closing eyelids. Relieved, proud and exhausted, we'd made it and we even had a spare hour to sleep.

Tap, tap, tap.

It was Steve and Dan at the window.

'Hi guys. It's time to set up. Sounds like you've had quite the night.'

My mind and body were heavy and depleted as we began the short drive to our pitch.

Within the grounds, the organisers had set up a large arena to launch the balloons. Around the outside of the arena were a variety of food and drink stalls, pop-up shops, and companies selling everything from t-shirts to fudge. Close to the arena was our pitch, where we'd established our now familiar thirty-six-hour rowing base. There was one major difference from our usual setup. This time we proudly had our own ocean rowing boat in the background and another huge 'Your Logo Here?' sticker, hoping to catch someone's eye.

The festival opened its gates, and a balloon launch would soon start proceedings. 130 balloons sat deflated in the inner ring. A rainbow of colours filled the foreground as if a giant had dropped their bag of enormous Skittles precisely in the arena. The sound of the burners roared in the background, and the balloons came to life as if waking from a collective sleep.

A few at a time, they launched. The coloured teardrop shapes filled the clear blue skyline as they gradually dispersed into the air. All these balloons had company logos on, I thought to myself. Each company had a marketing budget. All we had to do was meet the right people.

The day began. When not rowing, we handed out leaflets and tried to engage the public. We hoped for that one-in-a-million chance of a potential sponsor coming by and saying they were interested. In between, we went round various stalls attempting to spark up conversations with any company who could be a potential sponsor.

After a long 24 hours, the day's activities came to a close. It was time to enjoy the night glow. The balloons were tied down in the centre of the arena. Their burners fired up, as they bounced off one another in the slight breeze. Music boomed from the speakers and the burners fired a brilliant glowing orange in time to the music, in huge contrast to the evening's darkness.

Morning came, and with one day down, it was time to focus on the event's headline sponsor, Bristol Energy. I didn't want to mess around. Although it was great engaging the public and building a following, we needed a huge cash injection and quickly.

With blood pumping but trying to be casual, I walked over to their much larger pitch, which had several marquees.

'Hi, I'm from the ocean rowing team at the pitch round the corner. Is there anyone from marketing here?'

I'd learned that usually at these events, it was volunteers from the company. It was rare to have someone who owned the budget and could make decisions.

'Yes, actually. He's just there.'

My eyes diverted immediately like a hawk. I couldn't believe it; this was the absolute jackpot.

'Local, Bristol, ocean rowing team……we use solar panels..', I repeated in my head as I strolled over.

I introduced myself to the slender, energetic stranger.

'Hi! I'm from the ocean rowing team round the corner. We're looking to partner with local companies. We use solar panels for power and think we'd be a great fit. There's a lot we can offer. Do you want to see the boat?'

'Yes.'

I couldn't believe it. I was speaking to the right person, and I'd got him interested. We strode round to our pitch. Steve, Dan and Mark looked at me in disbelief as he launched himself onto the deck, striding up and down, imagining the field was the ocean. He poked his head in the cabins whilst asking disbelieving questions that echoed in the confined space.

'And you make your own water?!'

'You go to the toilet where?!'

'And sleep in here?!'

He was in! We agreed to meet a few weeks later to negotiate the details of the deal.

After the adrenaline wore off and the festival came to a close, we came back to the topic of funding. Bristol Energy was a brilliant prospect, but even if they offered a few thousand, we'd still be drastically short of where we needed to be. We currently had an empty hull for a boat and no entry fee.

'Maybe we should host a black-tie event like other teams have. It would be a great charity fund raiser and would also be a chance to earn some funds for ourselves too,' said Steve.

We'd discussed this countless times. The risk was the huge upfront costs with the little money we had. Plus, it was like organising a wedding reception as a small side project to raise money. At this stage in the game, this would be risky. But we had tried pretty much everything else.

As we packed up from the event, the idea settled in our minds. Maybe we could pull it off. With the boat now on the back of the trailer and daylight fading to dusk, we said bye to Mark. He was about to begin his monumental journey to the boatyard in Scotland, to get our boat ready as quickly as possible.

# RACE ENTRY

Raindrops patted the window, gradually running down to form larger drops, which glimmered against the inky black evening. Wallpaper curled off the ceiling round the halogen light in the kitchen, reminding me of the renovations that waited for after the row. As I leant back, the kitchen countertop pressed into my waist. I wrapped my hands round the hot tea in my hand and took a deep, slow intake of breath.

'What are we going to do, then?' I asked Emily.

The September race entry date was round the corner. If we didn't cough up the funds, we wouldn't be going. It was black and white.

She looked at me, words silently exchanged in a knowing glance. We'd talked it over a thousand times. We were both exhausted. She was now as much of this campaign as I was and knew all the ins and outs. Tonight, we needed to decide on finances.

Despite seemingly getting to grips with how sponsorship worked, and our local campaign appearing to take off, we had learnt these lessons all too late. With September two weeks away, we had the hard deadline of the race entry fee, and we had to make immediate payments to the boat builder. Added to this were various logistical expenses to cover. In short, we needed £20,000 immediately and a further £20,000 sooner or later. There would still be costs remaining after the first milestone. However, we needed to solve one financial issue at a time.

'I'm just not sure how this is going to come together. People don't seem to understand the mess we're in,' I reiterated again.

We had worked round the clock for almost two years and found ourselves at this point. The reality was we were skint and exhausted. We knew that some tough conversations were needed to work this out. From the outside, everyone thought we were doing great. I don't think people considered we'd fail to even get to the start line. That somehow, the hard reality of funding the expedition didn't matter, and it would all just work out.

I could see why our campaign was looking good, though. Bristol Sport was helping immensely with promotion. We'd had a fancy launch event at Ashton Gate, the stadium where Bristol City and Bristol Rugby play. Players were involved, we had interviews, our hull was on show – it all looked fantastic. Later we'd had a rowing competition at halftime during a rugby match. It ended up being on Sky Sports. The commentators talked about our campaign and pointed people to our site to get involved. On top of this, we'd had some cracking social media and press from Bristol Harbour Festival and the Balloon Fiesta. It all looked great.

But it was all bluster. Without the cold hard cash sitting in the bank account, there was no hope. We'd failed before we'd even made it to the start line.

My body felt fatigued and hollowed out. I was exhausted. Despite this, I found sleeping difficult. The financial pressures were very real and floated round my mind in the small hours of the morning. The worst thing was that all of this stress, all of this pressure, it was all self-inflicted. We had been the ones who decided to do this expedition. It was on our heads that we weren't able to make it happen.

I drained my mug of tea. The team meeting was in 10 minutes. It would be to discuss how comfortable each of us was with taking out a loan; how committed we were to this expedition. It was a last resort. I had looked at so many methods. Even if we managed to sell the boat at the end of the trip, it still wouldn't cover our expenses. Taking out a loan was our only option.

'You're still sure about this?' I asked Emily again.

Continuing with the campaign would be a long-term decision affecting both of us. We would have to pay the loan back over the next five years. What plans would Emily and I have to put on hold for those five years? How would it affect our relationship?

I also didn't want to delay. This would be now or never. I couldn't take the disruption to my life for another year, putting off social engagements, another year of working round the clock. I'd had to cancel a three-day cycling trip when something ocean-row-related had cropped up last minute. It was rare to see friends now. Socialising was a thing of the past. When I wasn't at work or in the gym, I was at the computer desperately trying to find another way to get the funding.

Emily and I were getting serious, too. We'd already started making plans for the coming years. From where to live to travelling, all sorts were being discussed, and they all required me to have free time. Delaying the row for a year would have a knock-on effect on so many things.

But what was the impact of not continuing? Sure, I'd get my social life back, but what would I be giving up? The team? The boat (which at least part existed)? No, it was far more than that. It was the opportunity. The dream. The unrivalled adventure that lay before us. It was the thought of the challenge, pushing myself far outside of my comfort zone, seeing just what my mind and body could achieve. It was life defining memories out on the open ocean, striving through difficulty as a team, experiencing things that very few have.

We had to find a way to do this.

My phone lit up. My shoulders tensed. It was time for the meeting. I grabbed the phone and walked into the lounge, closing the door behind me.

'Hi guys. How are we all doing?'

The phone call started. But there was already tension in the air. Nobody wanted to start proceedings off. Conversation didn't flow. An ominous silence filled the call. My stomach was heavy, words were hesitant. How had it come to this?

'Well, just to summarise, we need a tonne of money in the next couple of weeks, unless a miracle happens. As we've discussed, our only real option is to each take out a loan.' Mark started things off.

This terrified me. I wasn't someone who got out a loan. I was quite happy not owing anyone any money at all. And yet here I was, about to take out a sizable loan, with all the interest rates, early repayment fees and everything else that went with it. I sat, my shoulders hunched, my one-word monotone answers suggesting acceptance rather than optimism.

'Ok, so £10,000 each to get us through the next couple of weeks and hopefully we get more sponsors on board. And we finish the row, we'll pay some of it back when we sell the boat.'

And just like that, it was done. We'd solved our short term £40,000 cash flow issue. I put the phone down on the table and fell back onto the sofa. My muscles absorbed into the soft cushions.

At least it was done.

Mental fatigue had resulted in physical effects; my entire body felt in need of rest. Every limb was heavy. I'd lost my appetite, and I just needed to be horizontal. However, despite the situation, the overriding feeling was one of relief.

We had one less variable to worry about. The race entry was paid. Whatever else happened, we were going.

# SCOTLAND

The car rocked on the uneven gravel road and the headlights reflected off the window of the house in the early hours of the morning. After a long journey, and feeling like we'd travelled down half of the UK's country lanes at night, we had finally arrived at our destination. We were at our boat's new boatyard in Scotland.

The large wooden country house door swung open. Light streamed out, forming a warm rectangle of light against the dark backdrop of the house. In the middle, a Hagrid-like figure waved enthusiastically and then ran out to greet us. This man was our boat builder. He had several ocean rows under his belt and was as a bit of a legend in the community.

'Come into my workshop and I'll show you your boat.'

The exhaustion of the journey vanished as we briskly walked round the side of the house and up a slight incline to the large garage at the back. Ocean rowing was something he clearly loved, as he babbled about the improvements he'd made to the craft. Excitedly, he opened the door to the workshop.

A halogen light reluctantly flicked on. Dust floated around in the light. Equipment and odds and ends were littered over the floor and in the middle was our boat, covered in a couple of tarpaulins.

Grinning widely, he needed no prodding from us. With one wide sweep, he threw back the dusty green tarps and revealed the sleek black hull, shining in the artificial light.

'Boys, meet *The Nutilus*.'

It now had a deck and cabins, making it look more battle ready. Transformed by the black paint, it resembled a killer whale. It was magnificent.

The ocean row suddenly felt very real. The weight of the campaign lifted completely for a few brief minutes as we marvelled at our vessel. It was changing from the hull we'd bought, into our boat. Our boat! It was finally happening.

I walked round the side, running my hand along the smooth surface, imagining us on the high seas. We'd be standing on this deck soon, with nothing but thousands of miles of ocean surrounding us. I couldn't help but smile.

'When do you think you'll fit the rowing positions and navigational equipment?'

'Oh, we'll get to that!' he said confidently. 'There's still time in La Gomera.'

'Ok, and you received all the equipment we ordered here?'

'Yes, yes, yes, it's all here, in with the other teams' stuff, in the side building.'

'This is nowhere near where it's supposed to be,' muttered Mark. 'We were supposed to be out practising on the water tomorrow!'

The frosty air gave way to heat as we stepped back into the house. Ocean rowing memorabilia decorated parts of his house from years of expeditions. Legs of kitchen chairs scraped the stone tiles as we all sat down round the table. The satisfying sound of a cork went off in the background, and without asking, whisky was being poured.

Tales of ocean rowing ensued. We sat round with open

mouths, listening to the adventures we would have soon. Or rather, adventures we hoped to have soon. The underlying panic about the state of our boat was growing quietly over a polite whisky.

Eventually, we accepted the time and retired to the lounge, where we'd be sleeping. Reality was setting in. We still didn't have a completed boat. The boat builder had had the boat since the Balloon Fiesta. He knew that, due to the amount of work needed, we would miss the shipping date to La Gomera, meaning we'd have to drive the boat to the start line ourselves. He knew the deadline for this, yet our boat wasn't anywhere near finished.

This was it. What wasn't done now would have to be done on the start line… and there was a lot to do. The plan had been to come here and do our qualifying rowing hours on our completed boat out on the water. Then drive the boat to Bristol for our black-tie event, and then on to La Gomera ready to cross the Atlantic. The others were running through the same thought process.

'We don't have a boat. We have no ocean rowing experience. How on earth are we going to pull this off?' asked Steve with uncharacteristic uncertainty.

His exasperated expression said it all. Two year's work, two companies attempting to finish the boat, and it had come to this, with less than a month before the start of the race. The entire campaign was on a knife edge at the last hour.

'It's pretty dire,' said Dan.

I nodded.

'And we've still got to find the rest of the funding.'

Not that any of us needed reminding.

'We have to work this out, guys,' Mark urged.

Since race entry, we again had severe funding issues, needing around £30,000; more than double what was coming in. We needed money to pay for final pieces of equipment, to pay the boat builder on completion of our boat, and for logistics such as shipping the boat from

Antigua back to the UK. Most of it was already overdue or due in the next few weeks. Bristol museum had rightly said if we didn't stump up £9,000 before our black-tie event, they would cancel the entire thing. Although we had managed to pay the museum, we were hampered by locked funds from ticket sales that we could only access in monthly increments. To add to all this, frustratingly, our biggest sponsorship wasn't coming in until January, when we would hopefully be at sea.

I awoke the next morning on an uncomfortable sofa bed with Dan. Mark and Steve were on the sofa. My mouth was dry and a twinge of a headache thumped at the back of my skull. We'd been up later than we should have. I wasn't sure what his family thought of four strangers just crashing out in their living room. Nothing was very clear. It seemed even more bizarre when he told us another person in the race had been staying there for around a month, living on the floor.

I slowly hauled my body into a more upright position, familiarising myself with the environment.

'Let's check all our equipment is in order,' Mark suggested, already up, sounding purposeful.

We had ordered most of our equipment to arrive in Scotland. Combined with the things we'd brought in the car, everything we needed for the expedition should be here. Once we'd gone through it meticulously, we would pack the boat up and drive south, ready for the ocean.

I stepped outside into the fresh morning air. Birds accompanied the winter sunlight that beamed down. I entered another building attached to the main house, the storeroom for all of our equipment.

It was a shambles. The floor was littered with packets and boxes. Shelves were crammed with all sorts. There was stuff everywhere. Which of it was ours? Our gear was mixed in with general house storage and other teams' equipment.

I went to see the boat builder and asked him how the store room was organised.

'Organised? Oh, I don't organise it. Everything just gets put in there somehow. You'll have to sort through what's yours.'

We had to resort to going through our spreadsheet of equipment and hunting each individual piece of kit down in the massive pile of stuff. The problem was exacerbated because the other teams had ordered similar equipment from the same manufacturers.

To add to this, the boat builder didn't start work on our boat until 11:00. I wasn't sure he quite understood the situation. We would row an ocean on this vessel in under a month, and we had no experience whatsoever. We came here expecting a completed boat, ready to tackle the high seas. There was still a tonne to finish, and there was no chance of getting out on the water.

After a few hours, we'd managed to track down all our kit, except for the spare autohelm. Our boat builder assured us he would bring it to La Gomera.

Our equipment, at least, was ready. Everything required to cross an ocean lay in front of us on the wet ground. It looked pretty formidable. With that, we took a rest.

I looked at the boys over a steaming cup of tea.

'Look lads. We're not able to take the boat out on the water. Let's not make this a completely wasted journey. Let's tackle our black-tie event while we're all together. It's in 48 hours and we have so much to sort.'

Their faces were full of disappointment, but they all nodded their agreement.

We clambered back into the lounge. If we couldn't help on the boat, we may as well make progress on our black-tie event. It was edging nearer and was a huge event on its own to organise. With that, we set to work table planning for 200 people, designing the auction brochure, arranging printing, sorting table centre pieces, and on and on.

The last day in Scotland arrived. It was the day we would drive our boat and all equipment south to Bristol and then on to La Gomera, where we would have to complete the boat build. We waited until the eleventh hour, desperately hoping to get in as much last-minute progress on the boat whilst we were still there. Midnight arrived all too soon. We had to be 330 miles away in Bristol that evening to host our event.

The rattling noise of a tractor rose in the background. Its headlights flooded the lane as it slowly approached. The driver, a neighbour, had been called at this late hour to help lift our boat onto our trailer. Straps hugged our precious craft as they hoisted it into the air and gently lowered it onto its new resting place.

Now we began packing. We rammed our carefully organised equipment into the boat, frantically trying to make sure we left nothing behind. Steve and I stood on the deck while the others hauled equipment up to us so we could shove it wherever there was space.

It was 01:00 in the morning before we were finally ready. We departed for the south and into the night. Venturing down the country lane that had led us up to the house a couple of days prior, the weight and length of the boat made itself known. This was precarious; a heavy 30-foot boat in transit that was the culmination of two years' work. Pulling up to the main road, breaking was harder because of the greater momentum we had so easily built. As we approached the junction, we heard a scraping noise.

'What the hell was that?' I said, my imagination painting a thousand different scenarios, most of which involved our boat being destroyed before it had got 10 miles down the road. Had we really come this far only to total our boat at the first obstacle?

Jumping out, it was clear *The Nutilus* was fine. The front end of the trailer was touching the ground. Releasing a sigh of relief, we quickly busied ourselves readjusting the weight distribution of all our kit.

Minutes later, we were back on the road. With the boat, equipment and all four of us now travelling south, it felt like things were coming to a head.

# BRISTOL BLACK-TIE

'Yeah, we're in the HGV area of the services. We're too big for the car bit.'

The slap of fresh air hit my face as I hopped out of the car at Gloucester Services. It was about 15:00, and having driven through the night, none of us had slept much in the last 24 hours. I saw Emily parked on the grass verge. Feeling grubby, and in need of sleep and a shower, I said bye to the guys and got into her car. I had already rented out my flat in Bristol in preparation for the expedition, so I went back to Emily's to freshen up. I would meet up with the team again later that evening at our black-tie event.

I awoke after what seemed like seconds with a dense heaviness that comes from a significant lack of sleep. My eyelids needed every ounce of energy to function. Two hours had gone by in a flash. My body and mind craved respite, but with no time to mess around, we jumped in the car and made our way to Bristol.

'I'll have to do the name cards in the car!' I said.

Everything was so last-minute. We hit the road, the scissors moving in tune with the car's vibration. Swaying between lane changes made accurately cutting name cards tricky. This event was hanging on by a shoestring.

We ran up the stairs to the museum. 17:00. It was only just closing to the public. We walked through the entrance hall and into the main room. Our frantic footsteps echoed as if we were striding to escape them. It was a vast space to fill. Two enormous staircases towards the rear of the room led our eyes down the middle of the huge empty floor. A balcony ran around the first floor, opening up the room straight to the ceiling, the air between us and the roof making us feel insignificant. It gave an intellectual atmosphere as if we were in the museum to learn, not to have a good time.

Friends and family were already here, waiting.

'Hi! We're all here, ready to help,' Mum said enthusiastically. 'What's the plan?'

I hadn't given this a moment's thought until this second. I scanned round. The hall was empty. Tables, chairs and decorations needed to be sorted rapidly for something the size of a large wedding reception.

'Let's start with the chairs. Grab the chairs and covers. Work out some sort of production line and put them all on. I'll check where the tables are,' I said, instantly putting the wider campaign, financial problems and boat worries to bed.

The next issue to solve was how to put this together promptly and host this evening. Thank goodness we had that time in Scotland organising this a bit more. With only an hour before guests arrived, we frantically set to work.

The hall was edging closer to being ready, and guests were appearing. I went to the entrance to check what was happening. I pushed the heavy door open, letting the noise of the city rush in. A queue of dressed-up people was waiting at the foot of the stairs.

*The Nutilus* stood proudly next to the entrance, glinting in the entrance lights. It was doing us proud, giving a formidable ocean expedition presence and showing the queue what we'd been striving towards for the last two years. Little did they know it was half-finished and packed full of equipment, yet to be fitted.

I closed the door. Back in the entrance hall, a string quartet filled the vast room with an incredible sound. It would have been alright arriving here as a guest. It didn't look too bad.

In the main hall, we made the final touches to the dinner settings. Each table looked set for the evening. Guests started flooding in, and before I knew it, all the tables were full. The ambient noise rose as each person added to the background conversation. After a short while, I found I couldn't hear myself talk.

Suddenly, I realised that none of us had given a thought to how we'd start the evening. We'd done a few slides in Scotland, but hadn't considered what we'd say. Now it was time.

Mark grabbed the microphone and went up a couple of steps on the giant staircase. The audience settled and awaited in anticipation.

'Thanks all for coming…' he started.

I didn't hear the rest of his speech. I knew he'd be handing me the microphone any second. The team had decided that, because this whole expedition was my idea, I should say something. I couldn't think of anything worse.

My mind went blank. My stomach overflowed with nerves. I couldn't feel my legs. What on earth would I say?

Before I knew it, Mark stepped towards me and thrust the microphone into my hand. I gripped it as if it had offended me. My hands sweated against the hard plastic as I stepped up and exchanged places with him on the staircase.

Forgetting all advice, I stood right next to the speaker. Ear-shattering feedback filled the room, adding to what felt like eternity. I'd done so many talks recently, it had become like second nature. But tonight, I lost all ability and froze, as if I was trying to learn the English language for the first time whilst trying not to throw up.

Before me, a sea of faces waited. Each face had a story. Everyone had helped us get to where we wanted to be. It was a room full of support. From sponsors to friends and family. Everyone had helped over the last two years; they had their own story and part to this tale.

'Hi everyone…'

It began, unstructured and stuttering. But I got through it.

'Thanks, and let the evening begin!'

I finished and walked down the stairs. Steve looked at me.

'I was up next, mate. You just ended it!'

He was laughing, but I could tell he was slightly annoyed. I think he wanted to say a few things.

The evening was a tremendous success, and people bid on the charity auction. It raced by. After a couple of hours clearing up, we joined everyone in town to continue the party. I hadn't seen my friends in so long, and here they were, all together.

We stumbled back in the early hours of the morning. The campaign hadn't rested for us. In a few hours, we had an ITV interview in Bath, where we had stored the boat overnight. They wanted to do a final interview before the boat left for La Gomera. I dragged myself up after two hours of sleep and hauled myself onwards, every part of my body screaming at me to rest.

Our boat sat on its trailer in a pub car park, looking fresher than I felt. The ITV person was sorting out his camera equipment a few metres away.

'You're not going to believe this,' said Dan. 'He wants to film us packing the boat.'

We'd rammed the boat full of all the things we needed for the long journey to La Gomera and the ocean row ahead. With an offensive hangover, lifting all our equipment off and back onto the boat was the last thing on my mind!

Suddenly, Jonathan Sturley, director of Arc Monitoring, turned up. He was at our event the night before and promised he'd make an appearance. True to his word, here he was.

Interview done, it was time to say bye to Mark and Steve, who had volunteered to drive the boat to La Gomera. The next time I would see them and the boat, would be on the island ready to start the race.

I couldn't believe this was actually happening. Despite all the doubters who said we wouldn't do it, the chaos of the campaign and relentless obstacles, we were here. An outrageous thought in our heads had turned into reality. We still had a vast amount to finish on the boat and massive financial worries, but we were now well and truly on our way to La Gomera. Excited doesn't come close to how I was feeling. This was it.

# PART TWO

# THE START LINE

# LA GOMERA

The door of the plane opened, and a wall of heat struck me. I followed Dan down the wobbly metallic steps towards the tarmac. Baggage trucks were whizzing around like diligent worker ants, collecting luggage and taking it to the terminal.

I looked at Dan and grinned. We were here!

A short while later, we found ourselves on the ferry from Tenerife to La Gomera. We sat on plastic chairs with a coffee-stained table in the middle that vibrated to the tune of the ferry. I looked out of the dusty window at the sea. It was vast. Somewhere over the horizon lay Antigua. How on earth would we row this? Could we row this?

Gradually, La Gomera came into view. I could see the harbour where I'd watched the start of the race countless times on YouTube.

This was it. I could actually see it.

Having dreamt about this island for so long, it had an almost mythical status in my head, and yet here it was, drawing ever closer.

The ferry docked, and I stepped off with Dan amongst a bustling crowd of people, and two faces I instantly recognised. Mark and Steve greeted us.

I could tell by their expressions that things hadn't been plain sailing.

'So, the journey wasn't great?'

'That's an understatement,' muttered Mark. 'For a start, we got stuck in Spanish customs for 24 hours.'

'It's not been the most enjoyable journey, to be fair,' added Steve. 'Sleeping in the car was pretty rough, and I wouldn't recommend towing the boat any great distance.'

Mark sighed.

'Towing two years' work halfway across the planet wasn't good for our nerves.'

Steve and Mark shared a look of mutual hardship. They also informed us about how they'd already been tirelessly working on the boat, trying to get it ship-shape ready for the race-start in a few days.

To be honest, I felt a twinge of guilt about my comfortable four-hour flight. While these two had been sweating away sorting our equipment, Dan and I had been enjoying a cold beer at 30,000 feet. But there was nothing I could do apart from roll up my sleeves and get stuck in.

'Come on,' said Steve. 'Let's show you the boat and the rest of the fleet.'

I could see the Atlantic Campaigns head office down by the marina at the foot of the dramatic cliffs of San Sebastián. On the building hung huge striking posters of Atlantic race winners, as high as the two-storey building itself. The blue and white of the images contrasting with the brilliant red cliffs. I could see the utter relief and triumph stretched across the winners' joyous faces. Holding up flares, arms extended with pride, ecstatic at finally reaching Antigua, and leaving the hard graft at sea behind them. These were the images that had urged and driven me to this point in my life. These were the images that I'd seen a thousand times on my laptop back at home in drizzly Bristol.

But now, here I was under a blistering blue sky with the aquamarine sea lapping the harbour walls. Sea birds circled overhead, diving off the red cliffs, screeching and cawing, hovering and swooping through the warm thermals. The waterfront was busy with ocean rowers, their teams, and the media, as we made our way down to the marina.

The paddock, where the boats were lined up, was on the opposite side of the road to the Atlantic Campaigns head office. As I walked up, I spotted a notice board near the entrance to the paddock. Detailed on it was a list of team names taking part in the race. There it was, our team name 'Nuts Over The Atlantic', under the 'Pure Class team of four' category.

I stood and took it all in. I was proud even to have our name listed. We'd done it. We were in the race.

All we had to do now, was build our boat.

Rowers bustled past into the paddock. On the left, there was a fenced off walkway for the public to explore. To the right, the fleet of ocean rowing boats lined up on the tarmac in perfect formation, all at a 45-degree angle. Flags stating the team name and nation stood by them flapping in the light breeze. The boats looked highly polished, new and full of sponsors' logos. It all looked very professional. It was odd to think that the sight of these majestic boats would be in the next well-oiled marketing video. They'd be sparking the next generation of rowers' imaginations, just like it had mine. The only difference was that our boat would be part of the excitement.

I began the walk to our spot, passing teams I'd been following online for two years, finally putting names to real faces. People's driving motivations for being here reflected in their presence. A few teams had major sponsorship and had clearly spent most of their preparation time in the gym. They were stacked! Other teams were there for the wild adventure and had a more relaxed approach. We all wished we had had more time to train and put on weight.

As we passed, a few rowers nodded their head and said hi. Other teams were too busy with preparations, their eyes and hands focused on making sure their boats were in perfect sea-faring condition.

Damian Browne was one person who gave us a friendly wave.

'Hi chaps,' he said, smiling.

Under the team name of Gulliver's Travels, Damian was a solo rower. An Irish ex-professional rugby player, he stood tall next to his solo ocean rowing boat.

Smiles then beamed from Team O2, who were energetically organising their boat. The Egyptian pair exuded enthusiasm and life.

Next, Team Noble and Team Tenzing, both pairs from the UK, waved as they scurried round their boats. In front of them lay a sea of well-organised expedition food, rope, parachute sea anchor (para-anchor) and various other equipment ready for inspection. With clipboards in hand, the Duty Officers stood ticking off the mandatory items necessary for their safe ocean crossing.

Beyond this, we spotted Ocean Nomads. The Australian pair had had an issue with their food delivery. Other teams had kindly donated their surplus, and they were packing the boat with an odd assortment of food.

A Spanish pair with experience of the ocean stood next to them, Team Remolon.

Next came Atlantic Ladies, a three-person team, who stood next to their well-polished red boat.

Just before we arrived at our boat, Oarstruck, a four-man team from Wales, also in a Pure boat and the same age as us, greeted us with a smile.

Including us, there were 28 teams in total.

After introducing ourselves to Oarstruck, I turned to our boat.

It was the first time I had seen *The Nutilus* with our sponsors' stickers on in daylight. I walked round the perimeter. It looked magnificent.

I stared at the sleek lines, watched as the sun glinted off the forward cabin and gently ran my hand over the hard outer shell. Here, just a few feet away from the ocean, the idea of being far from land had never felt so real. *The Nutilus*, with its thin carbon fibre hull, would be our bedroom, our transport, our washroom, our toilet and our social hang out for the next month and a bit. Would it hold up? Could it last all those miles and everything that the ocean could throw at it? Looking at it now, in the sunshine by the sea, I couldn't have been prouder.

I could almost have ignored the missing parts, the lack of water maker, the seatless runners. Almost.

I looked at Mark and opened my mouth to speak, but he shook his head quickly. He glanced over his shoulder at our boat builder and then back at me.

'Not here,' he whispered. 'Let's get back to our apartment first.'

Now out of sight of our boat builder, our shoulders tensed. Here he was in La Gomera to finish our boat, yet little had been done. We climbed the stairs, dropped our bags, and collapsed on the sofa.

Mark spoke up. 'We have a lot to do. Most teams have a finished boat. We are a mile away from a finished boat. And we haven't even been in the water!'

I looked at Steve for inspiration, but his usual confidence was lost in an accepting nod.

It was incredible that we were even here, but the journey was just beginning. There was work to do.

# UNFINISHED BUSINESS

I awoke to the fierce sun warming up for the day. Light shone through the window, making the room like a sauna and unbearable. I jumped to the window and flung it open. Fresh sea air hit my face. Being several storeys up, we had an excellent view of the bay. I could just about see the boat paddock and Atlantic Campaigns head office from our vantage point. We hardly needed reminding where we were, though. Straight ahead, the sea sparkled, looking innocent and enticing. In the foreground, the town square was directly below us. Locals were slowly waking up, scurrying around, looking for coffee.

With the window open and the stiff sea breeze blowing in, the room was already cooler and more bearable. I turned and walked into the lounge. The floor was laden with our expedition food which we'd carried up to the apartment the previous night in preparation for today. Steve, who was already up, sat admiring the mountain of ocean rowing fuel.

'192 food packs. Can you believe it?!' he said.

Our first task was to pack all the food into ration packs. Each pack would be one person's food for the day. Estimating 48 days at sea, and four of us, it soon added up.

Dan and Mark emerged, and we immediately set to work.

We laid out piles of food on the floor and passed the ration pack between each of us. At each point we'd add to the pack and at the end we'd wrap it in Clingfilm, binding it together. This would, hopefully, act as another barrier if water got into the hatches. Each pack contained two dehydrated meals along with porridge, biltong, dried fruit, nuts, and a chocolate bar. We also had ultra-fuel, a food substitute in powder form. A whopping 6,000 calories. We soon developed a rhythm as music blared out of speakers, and as the midday sun beamed down, the heat increased.

On and off, it took three days to pack the food. With that major task complete, we wanted to take a firmer hold on the boat's progress.

We walked down to the paddock, boats still lined up proudly, basking in the sun. Teams were milling around, zoned out in their own worlds, only tuned into the nuances of their campaign. Our boat came into view. The black hull still looked formidably impressive.

'Hi, how's it going?' asked Dan, his voice sounding light, despite the shadow of worry that swamped all of us.

'Ok. Still a bit to do, but we'll get there, of course,' our boat builder replied with a lack of urgency.

'We'd love to help,' I said. 'We're conscious of time. Anything at all we can do? You've got four lads here eager to lend a hand.'

A protective stare replied.

'No. I'm aware of the time constraints.'

It became clear he wouldn't accept help, despite the job being, evidently, too much for one person.

'I'm ok for now, thanks. Oh, and another thing...'

He looked at us all. I just knew he was about to say something that would throw a massive spanner in the works.

'I can't locate the spare autohelm you bought.'

Mark's eyes tightened. I felt my posture instantly change from relaxed, to rigid. I glanced at Dan and he nodded, suggesting we needed an immediate private team discussion.

'This is a joke!' Mark blurted out to the three of us. 'He told us he would bring it. He knows the autohelm is the component that's most likely to fail. That's why we bought a spare. Without that, we are manually steering for sure!'

Dan sighed.

'Installing the rudder, autohelm, navigational equipment, water maker, and rowing positions are just some of the things we need to sort. There is no way at this pace they will be completed before race start!'

'And we need our qualifying rowing hours on the boat!' I added.

'I can't believe he spends most of the day working on the other two boats he has in the race,' said Steve.

Atlantic Campaigns would soon allow teams to launch their boats into the water to get some additional practice, on top of their qualifying hours. At this rate, we'd be left on shore.

But there was one silver lining. There were strong winds forecast for the coming days. Rumours of a delayed start were spreading like wildfire. If the rumours were true, it might buy us some time.

# INTO THE WATER

'You know that's better with chilli sauce?' Dan joked as we lay on our backs applying anti-foul to the boat.

Tiny loose stones on the tarmac were sticking into my back, and my arm ached as the muscles craved more blood from reaching over my head.

Anti-foul would hopefully deter unwanted barnacles from taking up residence on our boat. Our boat builder, having agreed to let us help, had just given us a top tip that a drop or two of chilli sauce in the solution really does the trick.

'They hate it!' he had exclaimed.

But in the rush, we had struggled to find some on the island. It would have been great if he told us this a couple of months ago!

We stood up to shake out our limbs and enjoy being vertical for five minutes. Steve's head popped up the other side of the boat.

'How's the gimbal position going?' he asked, trying to ease out information from the boat builder.

The gimbal was to be mounted next to the cabin hatch. This was a busy area. Key navigational displays were already in position so that we could see them whilst rowing.

He stared blankly back.

'There's no room for it now…'

I looked at Steve in disbelief. This had not been planned out at all! He'd just put the navigational displays in without thinking about what else needed to go in the area. There was space, but not with the current arrangement. With holes already cut, the damage was done.

Silently seething, we went back under the boat and cracked on applying the anti-foul.

The next day arrived, and Atlantic Campaigns informed us that the paddock needing to be cleared. Our boat was to join the rest of the fleet.

The trailer eased down the slipway. Warm water lapped at my ankles as *The Nutilus* crept into its natural habitat. Steve hopped on and rowed to the pontoon. Work would have to continue whilst moored up tightly alongside other competitors' boats.

The following morning, we came down to start work.

'It's tilted!' Dan exclaimed.

'It does look wonky…' I agreed.

'It looks like it's sprung a leak!' said Mark.

We immediately clambered onto the boat to get a closer inspection. Teams on either side of us looked on nervously. We were late into the water and now our boat had a leak. One hatch had water everywhere.

Our boat was craned high into the air, in direct contrast to our sinking morale. It was placed gently on the side of the harbour next to Team O2, who were also undertaking last-minute preparations.

Scurrying around it, we found the issue. The bilge pump inlet hadn't been secured properly and had simply come loose, leaving a fist-sized hole in our boat. All our concerns about the quality of work were coming true.

I looked at my phone.

'Nearly there!' Mum texted.

I'd completely lost track of time. Mum, Dad, my sister

Charlotte and Emily were arriving today to come to the race launch party and then see the race start.

The large white ferry gradually increased in size as it came into view. Smoke billowed out from the huge exhaust pipes as it docked, just as we had earlier in the week.

'Hello!!' came calls from a few metres away, as they all confidently strode towards us. Eyes glanced around as they soaked up their surroundings. Team flags flapped in the wind next to the row of boats across the water.

'It's warm, isn't it?' said Dad, removing his hat to wipe his sweaty forehead. 'It's snowing at home!'

'That sun!' said Emily, absorbing the rays.

'We've got the things you asked for,' said Mum after a quick embrace.

They all held up bags of last-minute items.

'Oh, this is exciting! Look at all those boats!'

Mum and Charlotte were brimming with enthusiasm, whilst Dad was quietly taking it all in. But Emily was looking at me with concern etched on her face.

'Are you alright?' she said.

I shook my head.

Dad chimed in. 'What's up, son?'

'I'll tell you in a bit,' I said.

I'd just seen the Duty Officer striding purposefully towards us.

'We've got some news,' he said.

By his expression, we knew it wasn't good.

'I'm really sorry, but given the state of your boat, we can't let you start with the rest of the teams in the race. Once your boat is up to scratch, and you have the required qualifying hours, we'll let you make the crossing if you still want to, but I'm afraid you won't be starting with the rest of the fleet.'

'That's not so bad,' said Steve. 'We will just have to dig deep to catch everyone else up.'

'I'm sorry, I don't think you understand. Because of the differing weather conditions you'll experience, I'm afraid you won't be officially in the race. Your race time won't count.'

I was motionless, not knowing where to look or what to do. Two years working towards a single date and we had failed. We'd thrown everything at it and still came up short. The race was over before it had even begun.

We were lost for words, feeling numb all over. We wouldn't be part of the race start ceremony. We could never relive the start of the race with the other teams. We wouldn't appear on any race results. It was as if all our efforts had been for nothing.

I looked into the eyes of my teammates. We all knew that we were out of the race; there was no question about that. But there was no way that we would throw in the towel just yet.

We still had an ocean to cross. We'd still be part of an incredible adventure. We'd still have stories to tell our grandkids about how we'd overcome every obstacle thrown at us, and still rowed the vast ocean despite everything.

'There's one more thing,' said the Duty Officer. 'We need all teams at the launch party tonight. Even though you'll not officially be in the race, you need to be there.'

Given the amount of work left, we had intended skipping the launch party. We hadn't had time to socialise with any teams yet and desperately needed to finish the boat. Why should this evening be any different?

'Good luck,' said the Duty Officer.

It sounded like he really meant it, too. With nothing further to say, he turned around and walked back to the head office.

'What are you going to do?' asked Emily.

'I can't defer for another year,' I replied. 'We get to work.'

I looked at the guys. A few days didn't matter. We had to row this ocean!

# RACE START DAY

December 11th, one day to the start of the race. They summoned all crew to the Atlantic Campaigns office for a briefing. Heads low and dragging our feet, we followed the droves of enthusiastic rowers to the building. Before us, rows of white plastic chairs awaited and the Atlantic Campaigns team stood in front, ready to deliver fresh information.

'Regretfully,' the Safety Officer started, 'we're going to have to delay the start of the race. The winds are simply too high. Although great for the open seas, we need a weather window to ensure that you make it out there safely. I know you're all eager to get out there, and you will. One thing's for sure, it will be an exciting start to the race with the big seas.'

The rumours about a delayed start were true! The wind was pretty full on. Last night, the wind had taken down a stage in the main square. If we needed evidence of strong winds, that was surely it.

We headed back to our boat; heads held slightly higher. The faster we could work to finish the boat, the less time there would be between us and the rest of the fleet. Despite not being in the race, we were keen to prove a point.

When we got there, our boat builder had now refused to finish the job, scuttling away to try to salvage the other two boats instead!

Mum and Charlotte were cutting the foam seats to size and putting foam on as many nuts and bolts standing proud of a surface as possible. Dan was sanding and then anti-fouling the daggerboard, the removable vertical keel. Mark was sorting the storage nets in the cabins. Emily was organising the spares (of which there were loads), each box meticulously labelled so we could easily sort through in a hurry. Dad was making extra brackets for the jackstays (the safety lines running the length of the boat for clipping our harnesses to). Steve and I were removing the bearings from the seat wheels and repacking them with the special grease we had bought. Supposedly, this would help resist the corroding sea water for longer.

After this, I set to work on the reflective panels for the hatches, scavenging around, and sourcing from shops on the island. I returned with a car windscreen reflector, cutting it to shape and using Velcro to apply it, so we could remove it when we wanted. With every job, we needed something from town to help it along. Each of us running back and forth through the heat of the day.

'So how do we sort the autohelm and rudder out, then?' Dad asked.

It was the major part of the boat we hadn't yet attended to.

'I'll stick my head in other people's boats,' I said, 'and see how it's connected.'

I then ran off to ask other teams if they'd be kind enough to let me into their cabins and take photos of their setups.

'I think I've got it,' I said to Dad, slightly out of breath, pointing to pictures on my phone. 'The drive unit operates the cable and push rod to move the tiller arm.'

But Dad already knew. Charlie Pitcher, owner of Rannoch Adventures, who make the popular Concept boats, had kindly explained to Dad how the autohelm worked.

After talking things through, we agreed on a rough

layout. Dad, anxious about rough seas, went to source some box section to beef up the tiller arm, and bought locking nuts to attach the tiller to the push rod. We then rushed back into town to get our hands on a protractor and measured the angles for calibration. Next, we decided on the location of the autohelm drive unit, drilled holes through the side wall of the hull and got to work. The last piece was the rudder, requiring the boat to either be in the air or in water. The latter being harder, as someone would need to be underwater to fit it.

Dad hopped into the boat, drill in hand. Straps hugged the boat once more as the crane lifted it from the water. *The Nutilus* slowly rose into the air as if the crane had been fishing and caught a sleek, black killer whale. The hull shone proudly in the sun as it swayed in the breeze.

'OK, ready when you are,' said Dad, muffled from inside the cabin.

We lifted the rudder and heaved the shaft up through the base of the hull, into the aft cabin. Dad then drilled a hole through the shaft to connect it to the tiller arm.

The crane then lowered the boat back into the water. Now more confident of its water tightness and with the rudder and autohelm in place, I felt my shoulders relax. We'd just taken a major step forward.

Moored up slightly away from the rest of the fleet, we continued finishing odds and ends. A rather hefty to do list remained.

December 14th dawned and conditions were ideal. The day had finally arrived. The Atlantic Challenge was on… for the rest of the teams, anyway.

The atmosphere had transformed. A frantic, electric rapidity accompanied each team. I watched them from the other side of the dock. We'd been instructed to move our boat further from the starting line-up and now sat all alone, away from the action. The physical separation was clear. We weren't in this race, and that was final.

To make things worse, we could feel the emotion and hype only metres away from where we were working. We would have to watch every other team row out to sea to start their challenge while we waited to begin ours.

For two years, we'd been working towards this dream. The dream of leaving the harbour with the rest of the fleet, setting out with other boats beside us, taking on the challenge of our lives. It was a dream that would never be realised.

Along the dockside mingled hundreds of excited people, clambering to see each team row to the start line. The first team rowed nervously out into the harbour. Spectators cheered, wishing them luck, clapping loudly. The boat edged out of the harbour and, as they straightened up……..

EEEEERRRRRR! went the air horn.

Oar blades slapped the choppy waves. Their crossing had begun. In front of them lay 3,000 miles of open ocean.

I ducked back into the cabin and busied myself. The heat of the sun made the cabin like a greenhouse, the air close and still. But I'd rather be here making a difference to our chances of joining the crossing than out on the docks, wasting time seeing other rowers' dreams come true. Sweat ran down my nose as I irritably screwed storage netting into the cabin.

EEEEERRRRRR! The air horn sounded again.

Another team had begun their expedition. The sound ripped through me, mocking me, reminding me that we had come so close, and yet, we were still so far from being ready. More than ever now, we were in a race against time. Every second working on the boat was crucial. The quicker we could get out to sea, the quicker we could start chasing the other teams down.

After the last boat crossed the start line, the crowd dispersed and the excitement and atmosphere evaporated.

The harbour was still and silent.

This was a blessing. The added pressure of witnessing the start of the race seemed to go. Now it was just us, our boat, a heap of jobs, and our rowing qualifying hours to rack up before we headed out to sea. We knew Atlantic Campaigns would not wait much longer for us to be ready.

The clock was ticking.

# SEA RESCUE

The oars made a gentle splashing sound as they caught the water. The wheels beneath the seat made a therapeutic hum as they ran back and forth. Salt spray filled the air, falling on our faces as we pulled the stroke.

'Looking good, guys,' said Steve from near the forward cabin.

I grinned. Despite the difficulty of getting the boat ready, we were finally out on the water, putting in the qualifying hours so that we could properly start the Atlantic crossing. My family and Emily had come to watch from the docks as we headed out for our debut sea row.

'Anyone else get the feeling that these waves are getting bigger?' asked Dan from the other rowing position.

Dan was right. The waves had slowly rolled into larger formations, barrelling down on us from the open ocean. The sea air was feeling breezier, whipping past *The Nutilus* as she battled the waves.

I glanced back to shore.

'We've gone quite far now guys!'

Vegetation on land had become very distant. With the current on our side and getting some good, well-timed, strong oar strokes in, we had gone much further out than planned. Time had passed rapidly. The current was strong, and we were now at risk of getting funnelled into the open ocean. We needed to turn the boat, but rowing against the increasing waves was futile. They were jagged, aggressive, lapping over the side of the boat. Even trying to row against them felt like we were getting pushed out to sea.

It was difficult to keep our balance. None of us were used to this situation, all frantically struggling to haul the boat back. Even an inch would have been nice. The boat lolloped about as we got pushed further out. The burnt orange sun was now setting and land was becoming a dark smudge on the horizon. Street lights were a row of sparkling dots. The evening sea wind felt cooler and more assertive, and with the light fading fast, a menacing character occupied the sea.

My body was tense, fuelled by adrenaline. I put everything I had into the oars. The more time we spent trying to rectify this situation, the further we drifted out and succumbed to the ocean's current. The boat was rolling side-on to the waves, as we battled, trying to turn.

'Let's call it,' said Steve. 'Grab the radio. We need help. There's no way we're rowing back against this.'

Water crashed against the hull, the boat rocked back and forth. We were rapidly learning that the boat was more capable than we were as the side came level with the water.

'Mark, grab the radio and call Atlantic Campaigns,' I yelled. 'We can't row back from this.'

But he couldn't hear from inside the cabin. Unaware of the situation, he'd been fiddling with the navigation software, something that, suddenly, didn't seem a priority. Broken dialogue persisted as we were swept further out with each minute that passed.

Eventually, Steve got Mark's attention, who dutifully grabbed the radio.

'Hello. This is *The Nutilus*. We're too far out and we're struggling to get back.'

The call had been made.

Luckily for us, the support yacht for the race wasn't too far out and came back to give us a tow. As its white sail appeared on the horizon, I stopped pulling on the oars.

None of us said anything. Only the sound of the waves slapping the hull accompanied us as we sat quietly waiting. What would they think? We had no experience, and on our first time out, we had had to call for help. What a disaster!

Thor, the race doctor, sailed towards us on the support boat, Suntiki. He waved at us from the foredeck, his bright smile beaming across the waves.

In his hand was the radio.

'Hey gentlemen, did someone order a taxi?'

None of us was in the mood for jokes.

He threw out a rope attached to a small buoy for us to grab. Their boat circled ours so that the rope came alongside our boat.

'Right,' said Thor over the radio. 'Whatever you do, don't let the rope go under the boat. It'll catch the rudder, and then as the yacht goes further round, it'll pull and tip your boat.'

I grabbed the wet rope out of the sea and tried to flip it over the aft cabin as the yacht went behind our boat. As I flung the rope over the cabin, it caught the aerial, dropped and rested on the roof.

I pulled it back and attempted the manoeuvre again. The rope caught a second time.

Now the yacht was on the opposite side of our boat and with it, the rope had looped round the boat like a snake assessing its prey. The rope got dragged round further, and within seconds, it was stuck on our rudder, just as Thor had told us not to do. It began dragging *The Nutilus* through the water at an angle, almost throwing us all into the water.

We looked blankly at Thor.

He instructed us over the radio.

'You'll have to cut the rope and retie the knot.'

A lot easier said than done when under pressure, a boat bouncing around and feeling extremely embarrassed. I had now made the situation worse. Grabbing the knife next to the cabin, Mark cut the rope, retied a knot, tied it to our bow line, and gave the signal on the radio to Thor. We were finally ready for the tow back.

At least we were now in safe hands. Darkness filled the sky and rain began to fall. I grabbed the oars and started rowing. Even the yacht needed a helping hand against the current.

The hazy orange lights of the town became clearer and buildings became more defined as we drew closer to the harbour.

My legs like jelly, shaking and exhausted from the toll of the adrenaline, I stepped onto solid ground. I looked into the eyes of my relieved family. They had been desperately staring out at sea looking for us for six hours, and with no call until an hour ago, they had no idea of the situation.

An air of relief but overriding embarrassment loomed over us. The now dark, tormenting ocean behind us, we made our way to the Duty Officer to explain ourselves. There was surely no way they would let us row the Atlantic after they'd had to rescue us after our first few hours at sea.

'What happened, lads?' asked the Duty Officer.

We mumbled our explanation of the events.

'We thought you'd had enough and had decided to go for the entire crossing,' he said. 'But then, when we got the distress call, we assumed you'd bottled it and asked for a tow back!'

He sucked his teeth in. Our ocean rowing future hung on what he said next.

'Don't worry, lads. What's done is done, just….. don't do it again, alright?'

Like a group of school miscreants, we left the office with our tails well and truly between our legs.

# THE FINAL HURDLE

It was the night before my family had to catch their flights back to the UK. They had hoped to have waved me off by now, but instead they had to leave me still stuck on the island. We stood outside the restaurant after our final meal. The chilly night air howled around us and the street twinkled with Christmas lights.

'Good luck son,' said Dad. 'Let's hope that rudder holds up!'

'Take care of yourself,' said Mum, holding me firmer than usual.

Charlotte hugged me reassuringly.

They gave me a few small presents wrapped in Christmas paper, an A4 book of plastic pockets with photos and messages. I was under strict instructions not to look at any of it until out at sea. I didn't want the Christmas presents as space and weight were precious commodities on the boat, but I smiled and promised I'd find a space for them.

Gradually, everyone connected to the race left La Gomera. Just the six people remained; the four of us, Emily and the Duty Officer. The hype of the race had vanished from the island, and it was just us.

We rowed out into the harbour every couple of hours to

get our training time up, making any adjustments when needed. This went on for ages. We were itching to go. Rowing round a safe harbour on flat water, just eating up time, was exasperating and didn't seem to add much. We were ready.

Eventually, the call came one evening to have a chat with the Duty Officer. We ascended the stairs of what, only a few days ago, had been a bustling office. Now the desks were empty. The walls, which had once housed advertising posters and race photography, were blank.

We found the Duty Officer sitting behind his desk, scouring over paperwork. A fan spun lazily in the corner, languidly moving the warm air around the room.

'Well, lads,' he said. 'How have you been getting on with your qualifying hours?'

Avoiding eye contact, I hesitated to speak.

'Hmmm,' he continued slowly. 'Well, you did three hours today and four hours yesterday and another four then… Yep, I would say that's about 20 which is near enough 24 so… yeah, I think you're ready to go.'

I couldn't believe it. He'd rounded up all our hours. But I wasn't going to argue.

We didn't have the required minimum of 72 hours qualifying time. We didn't even have our revised target of 24 hours, which, given the circumstances, Atlantic Campaigns had kindly agreed with us.

The team all looked at each other, our lips tightly sealed, hoping against hope that the bubble wouldn't burst.

My chest was almost exploding with excitement.

We had just been given the green light.

Tomorrow we would row the Atlantic.

PART THREE

ROWING THE ATLANTIC

# THE LAUNCH

## December 17th

I awoke in my hotel room. The bed felt familiar, but this time, my entire body felt different.

I hadn't slept well, which added to the feeling in the pit of my stomach. Everything was tense and the background urge to vomit lingered. It was like I'd woken up on the day of an exam, but on a whole new level. I couldn't fathom what was going to happen today; it was too vast to get my head around and my body reflected this all-encompassing dread.

We had actually got the all clear. The boat was ready and there was nothing to prevent us from going.

Today I would step onto a boat and row across the Atlantic Ocean!

What a ridiculous, yet incredible, notion. Imposter syndrome had been ever present on this campaign, but now, with my final hours on La Gomera looming, it was all-consuming.

Surely this can't actually be happening? At some point, someone will step in and say that we can't go. It's utter madness.

But, of course, that wasn't going to happen, and the clock was now running down until we were due to leave.

Finally, this huge expedition was real. We were ready. I couldn't wait, and yet, I could have waited forever.

I brushed my teeth, chucked on the clothes I would begin the expedition in, and headed outside with Emily. The sleepy town looked like its usual self; the white-walled buildings reflecting the early morning sunlight; locals going about their usual morning errands. Emily's ferry was due to leave. With the sea breeze brushing my face, we walked to the harbour for the last time.

This was it then. No more delaying tactics. I had to say goodbye.

Our smiles felt false, as if the muscles knew this wasn't the emotion we really wanted to convey. Although we were as ready as we'd ever be, a safe crossing wasn't guaranteed.

Subdued and unsure, I looked at her. A firm, 'you've got this' gaze met my eyes, instilling a confidence I desperately needed.

And with that, she walked to catch her ferry, beginning her journey home, waiting to be reunited after, what could be, a couple of months at sea. With one last wave in the fresh early morning light, she was gone.

I turned back to the boat where the rest of the team were doing some last-minute preparations.

It was a tranquil scene on the waterside. The crowds had long gone. The water was calm, and the sun was shining as the morning settled in. It was a huge contrast to the mayhem within my mind and stomach.

Final checks done; our departure time loomed. Emily would now be in Tenerife, waiting for her evening flight. It seemed strange that she would be on an island nearby, waiting to leave, while we were also waiting for our own departure here on La Gomera. It was difficult knowing we were so close to each other geographically but unable to say farewell as I'd imagined, waving from the boat as we slipped further and further out to sea.

I stepped onto the boat. My legs quivered as I realised that the next time I would step on land, it would be on another continent and with only ourselves, prevailing winds, and the current, to get us there. I strapped my feet into the Velcro, undoing and re-strapping them over and over again, searching for some reassurance in each micro-adjustment. Readying the heavy carbon oars, like a clumsy knight preparing for a joust, I cast my mind back to the try-out session for Bristol Rowing Club.

We were in our positions. It was time.

We pushed away from the pontoon. Although land was only a few feet away and we could still speak to people, it represented something of huge significance. We were now bound to this vessel for what could be around two months. Confined to a few metres of deck and exposed to the elements.

Nervous energy was now being put to use, instead of being wasted on anticipation. We were, all four of us, on the boat, and we were ready. After working for two years to reach this one moment, it felt completely unreal that it was finally happening.

My muscles eased a tiny amount as we were locked in, ready to go. Smiles, laughter, and disbelief flooded the boat, accompanied by an overwhelming feeling of dread from the depths of my stomach.

We rowed around the corner of the dock for the last time. Three or four strangers stood by, coincidentally witnessing the start of an ocean rowing crossing. The calm, safe dockside water glinted in the sun.

As we straightened up out of the corner, the air horn sounded.

EEEEERRRRRR!

The sound that had mocked me so harshly a few days before, now signalled the start of our very own adventure.

The clock had started.

14:45

It had begun.

We were seconds into the biggest expedition of our lives. I thought of my family. Now they'd have to sit and wait for updates every four hours on a screen to check we were safe. But, in reality, the update would only give our location. We hoped to send a few photos from our boat to go on social media, but these photos would only show a moment in time. My family wouldn't know how we were or what was happening. We were doing this on our own.

We settled in as we rowed out of the harbour. The sun beamed down and there was such a sense of excitement and optimism, we had started our race. Despite the odds stacked against us, we were actually rowing an ocean. This was our moment. We were embarking on the journey of our lifetime. We didn't know what to expect, both externally from the environment and internally within ourselves. There was an entire ocean between us and the finish line. None of us knew what was coming next.

The waves became choppier as we went further out and became less protected from the island. The sun pounded its rays down, making both heat and visibility difficult as it reflected off the surface of the water. In front of us, a vast abyss to the horizon, a sight we would see every day until we reached the other side of the ocean.

We were about to have an experience few people have had; we were going to row across the Atlantic Ocean. With every oar stroke, we edged further from land, further from the known and into our own world, on this little deck in the enormous sea.

After the initial burst of excitement, with spirits high and adrenaline running, reality slowing sunk in. Progress was extremely slow. It had taken a while just to get out of the harbour, and now further out, land still seemed huge, looming in the background.

This challenge was vast. After knowing all the statistics about the crossing for so long, I had no idea what facing the challenge would be like. It was enormous.

I was already struggling with the waves. Unable to

anticipate them, I just succumbed to a battering. Short, sharp jabs; long, swaying movements. The waves were so unpredictable.

The boat was moving in all directions, all the time. I could barely stand even when holding onto something. With no experience and learning on the job, I surrendered to crawling around on all fours.

There was no relief in the cabin, either. My senses and body were under assault. Everything I'd learned about how to move around for the last three decades was now out of the window. The world swayed, then shunted erratically and unrelentingly. It was a shock to the system. This was our new reality.

But a reality I had to overcome. With the bucket at the other end of the boat, I had to make my way past Mark and Dan, who were rowing, to get there. Asking them to stop, I grabbed the jackstay to keep balance. Slowly, I progressed down the deck, inch by inch. Landing my hand on Mark's shoulder and stepping over Dan's oar, I made another step until I eventually traversed the entire deck. I had already fallen into them countless times. If I needed to get somewhere, it was always a lesson in patience for me, and for whoever was rowing.

The sun slowly descended as the night drew in, and a chilly wind picked up. The black of the night added to the unpredictability of the waves. The sea had already changed character as if a set change in a play had occurred. A dark, oily black surrounded the boat, with moonlight glistening off the crests. Each wave had its own unique, rippling movement and looked like dark cornflour bouncing around on a speaker.

The night sky was a thick blanket overhead. Bio-luminescence decorated each crash of a wave, glowing in contrast to the dark sea, and made even clearer when our navigation light momentarily turned off.

What an experience we had had already, and we were only a few hours in.

## Chasing Horizons

22:30 Mum:
Hi there :) great to hear from you. You're looking good on the tracker. Fab straight line ploughing towards the other boats.

22:35 Jon:
Yeah, we didn't realise we were doing well! How's home?? I haven't got my sea legs yet. Can't wait for Antigua.

# IT'S BRUTAL

## Day 1: December 18th

The glow of the early morning sun shimmered on the horizon, marking an end to the first long night. For the first time, I could see our surroundings clearly after the hours of darkness. Blue encircled us in every direction. However, on closer inspection, I realised that there was a myriad of shades from bright aquamarine to the deepest, darkest blue. And every wave had its own shape as it rolled and churned past the boat. I'd expected to see a monotonous landscape, but the one that presented itself to me that morning was thrilling, dynamic and constantly changing.

The boat seemed to shunt itself around erratically, but it was more likely that I wasn't used to it yet. The more the sun rose, the more I felt relief sink in, and with it, my morale increased bit by bit.

Our first experience of the night was an eye opener. What on earth had we let ourselves in for? It felt like pure survival. Still getting used to the layout of the boat, we were manoeuvring over each other on the tiny deck when changing shifts. I was not coping well with the random instability of our new world. Still unable to master the basic movements expected of a toddler, I grabbed whatever was within reach to help drag myself around. On top of this, the darkness brought unease and disorientation. I couldn't anticipate the harassment of the waves and was constantly jolted around on and off shift.

The biggest shock, however, was the immediate hardship of the two hours on, two hours off. Despite our thirty-six-hour rowing tour, I found that repeating the sleep pattern at sea was on a whole new level.

I was a psychological mess. A battle of wills had begun. My brain screamed at me to stop, to seek dry land, to lie stationary for five minutes. And it was only the first night! On top of all this, it was surprisingly cold; I had worn full wet weather gear.

Now a bright yellow circle appeared as the sun rose above the horizon. The heat felt like it was directed exclusively at our boat. I was immediately roasting. As if walking into a shop at Christmas, I threw off my jacket. The warmth on my skin was glorious.

Before leaving, the Duty Officer had given us some advice to make it through the first week.

'Just complete one day. After that you know you can do 24 hours. Next, aim for two days. It's just repeating what you can already do. After that, repeat for four days. Once you know you can do four days, you know you can do another four because you already have. Once you have made it through a week, the seasickness will disappear, you will have settled into the routine and you'll have got it. By then, you'll just be living at sea. Easy!'

It was logical, but easier said than done. Thinking of another night shift didn't exactly fill me with joy. I had to summon everything in me to believe those words. I mustn't think about the greater task, just live in two-hour segments. Just make it through the next two hours until my mind adjusted.

The first sunrise shift ended. Time for another change

over. The thought of instant relief from being horizontal was all-encompassing.

The cabin hatch opened, and Mark popped his head out. I clipped both harnesses onto one jackstay so that we could manoeuvre round each other. With both hands on the jackstays, I pushed myself up, then grabbed the cabin roof and clung on while the boat rocked. I waited as Mark precariously manoeuvred himself into position. I plunged one foot into the cabin, and as I rotated in, I instantly felt more secure. I sat down, closed the hatch and lay back, feeling cocooned and protected from the elements.

Instead of hearing the waves crashing on the surface, I heard them thumping against the hull instead. But it was drier at least and warmer than being out in the fresh air. I wasn't being constantly battered by the sea spray, which was a welcome relief.

I looked at my legs. I already had bruises forming. The first few shifts had been like a normal gym session on the rowing machine, except that someone was constantly pushing you over or kicking you in the shin. There was no point in complaining. Everyone was going through the same experience. And this would pass. My brain just needed to adjust.

A faint dull headache accompanied a burning acidic sensation in the back of my throat – the early signs of seasickness. But with the boat never stationary, there was no escape. An ambient acidic tone rested in my stomach, and I constantly felt like I was going to vomit. I hoped they were right about it only lasting a week.

I turned to the netting I'd screwed in at the last minute during the official race start and grabbed my phone.

```
11:07 Jon:
Still alive! How are you?

11:12 Emily:
Hurrah! How's the seasickness? You're going so
quickly on the tracker! Over twice the distance
```

```
of Oarstruck in the last 12 hours. You'll catch
them in no time!

11:23 Jon:
Haha, are you making this up? We think we're
slow!

11:25 Jon:
Sickness is horrible. Most things are. Can't
wait for land!
```

It wasn't just that we were finding things difficult; the race had been delayed for a reason. With huge weather conditions, things were tough. Two of the solos had unfortunately given up because of the extreme weather.

In the last eight hours of rowing, one solo had made less than one nautical mile. Despite deploying the para-anchor, the raging ocean had pushed him to a point further back than where he had started. After a capsize and the knowledge that a weather front was moving in which would push him further north, his ability to continue became untenable.

The exit of the two solos highlighted that, despite their well-prepared boats, mental preparation and physical fitness, Mother Nature will always win. They were incredibly unlucky. Even though we were finding it hugely difficult, at least there were four of us. Being in a four meant we had more power to put down and a better chance of making it through the rough conditions and out into the open sea.

Being in a four also meant that we could be there for each other, mentally. If one of us was having a low moment, his teammates could support him. If he needed a break to grab a drink or whatever, his rowing partner could carry on pulling on the oars. We were there for each other, something that the solo rowers didn't have.

Midday arrived, and I flung myself into the cabin for another rest. The heat had built significantly, and all I wanted was to be out of direct sunlight. As I gently swayed in the cabin, I could hear Mark and Steve debating the navigation.

'We're going round in circles!' said Steve.

'Agreed, we keep looping round and then parallel with the waves and then back round again!' said Mark.

I cracked the cabin hatch open, fresh air rushed in. I looked out at the guys on shift, with the bright sky and ocean surrounding them. They were both right. I could clearly see that we were going round in circles, about 30 metres in diameter. One minute the boat was facing the waves and then the next, we weren't. When side-on, the boat rocked immensely.

'Lads, I think there's something wrong with the navigation. I'll see if I can fix it.'

Thinking the autohelm needed recalibrating, for some reason I started undoing the two locking nuts on the tiller. Sweat instantly streamed off my nose whilst I got thrown around. The boat only had to rock slightly, and it threw the spanner right off. I'd have to start again, furious with myself and worried I'd round off the nuts.

This process seemed to take forever, maybe an hour. The heat of the cabin and ceaseless rocking made my already seasick brain feel even worse. Mark and Steve waited patiently on deck for me to finish, glancing back through the cabin hatch every now and again to see how I was doing.

After an hour of sweat, frustration and one or two choice swear words, I'd got the autohelm working correctly. The entire episode took place within a four-hour window on the tracker. As far as everyone at home was concerned, it looked like everything was fine. The reality, however, was that I was already exhausted, and we had barely even begun our journey.

```
15:56 Emily:
No, you're smashing it, honestly! The tracker
says you're doing 2.3 knots, Oarstruck are doing
1.4 knots. Sickness shouldn't last much longer,
but keep hydrated. I'm so proud of you. You're
doing amazingly well!

16:18 Jon:
Well, I didn't expect that! The part where we
```

```
went round in circles was us trying to fix our
autohelm!

16:23 Emily:
Haha, it only plots the location every four
hours so can't see circles! Is it fixed now?
```

It was fixed, and we were back on track toward our next waypoint. Having left later than the rest of the teams, we were experiencing different weather. Other teams had chosen a route further south, trying to take advantage of the winds. Team Antigua were forging ahead despite power issues. Mark Slats, a solo, was rowing a mind-blowing 20 hours a day and loving it, apparently. We, however, thought we'd missed this opportunity, and were opting for a straight line, pointing directly to Antigua.

Our boat straightened up on the navigation screen, and with the news that we were doing better than we thought, we cracked on.

# VOMIT AND ROUTINE

## Day 2: December 19th

I stared at the orange navigation displays, already obsessing over our speed and heading, as if I could think the boat into the best position with the waves. Our speed varied slightly, but the clock never seemed to move. It was another night shift with Steve, and the monotony of rowing was already taking effect. Conversation drifted in and out, waves rocked the boat and the darkness enveloped us.

We couldn't see the waves, only feel their aftermath. Waves crashed around us, sometimes missing *The Nutilus*, leaving the sound of rushing water in the darkness. Other times they'd plough straight into us smashing our little boat, rocking us up and over, or side-to-side.

I continued rowing in silence, staring back occasionally at the navigation display to see if we'd made any progress. I was feeling increasingly seasick. My head was pounding.

Suddenly, I felt acidic pressure becoming overpowering. The acid taste in the back of my throat became unbearable. Without warning, I felt the bile coming. I lurched my head to the side, oars still in hand, and with a failed attempt at aiming over the side, I launched vomit all over my right arm and onto the deck.

Steve burst out laughing.

'That was disgusting!'

I grabbed my water bottle and attempted to clean the mess. I felt horrific. Before I could even pick the oars back up and collect myself, the boat rose up the hill of a wave. The crest came smashing down and covered us in dark water. The crash roared in our ears.

Welcome to the night shift, I thought.

An accepting laugh overwhelmed us. This was ridiculous! What on earth were we doing? With the vomiting came immense relief though - I felt better. I was moving through the process of the first week. Ticking off the symptoms and the progress, as if it was a to-do list, just as we had been advised.

Nearly two days completed - just repeat and I'll have managed four.

Seasickness is progressing - it will probably go after the first week.

Just get through the first week... I'll acclimatise...

We were nudging through our first week, and my brain had already started to adjust to the conditions, aligning itself to our undulating home. We'll get there, I thought.

Resigned to our never-ending task, we grabbed the oars and continued to row. The thought of being back in the warm, dry cabin filled my mind as I looked back at the glowing orange time on the digital display.

```
00:02 Jon:
Was sick over the deck a lot and then got smashed
by a wave. So, I dipped into the book of messages
and photos that Mum gave me. It's immense!
Thanks so much! I'm saving your message though.

04:15 Emily:
Sounds brutal. Glad the messages are helping to
lift your spirits. Hope you're ok with the shift
patterns and are getting some sleep.
```

After what seemed like an eternity, the shift changed. I stepped into the cabin, shut the hatch, and sighed. In full wet weather gear and just wanting to collapse, I had no enthusiasm to get out of my clothes, clean, or eat in this bath tub sized makeshift bed.

Everything was more difficult at sea on a small boat. There's not much space, and the world is constantly moving. On top of this, we were contending with a maximum of 90 minutes of sleep for any one period. Even basic things were taking a tremendous amount of time, and discipline was now crucial.

The race against time had begun. As soon as I stepped into the cabin, the clock was ticking for our next shift on the oars and I wanted to make the most of every second in the sealed haven. We aimed for 90 minutes of sleep, leaving 30 minutes to undertake all admin.

I sat in the cabin, my legs hanging down into the footwell, staring at the hatch and the foil I'd cut to reflect the sun only a few days earlier. My body rocked to the motion of the sea and the autohelm made its whirring noise as it corrected our heading.

I couldn't lie back until my wet weather gear was off. Since a wave had just soaked me before coming in, I didn't want to get the mattress wet. Removing wet weather gear was an ordeal. With no room to move, it was the ultimate faff. Wriggling around, shaking limbs, boat rocking, not able to fully move my body in the cramped conditions, it seemed to take forever. I'd even fallen asleep whilst attempting to get them off, only realising when I got called on for my next shift that I was still dressed. Eventually I managed it, and stuffed them in the corner, ready for the next time I'd need them.

I grabbed my bag and took out the cleaning products. The cabin light shone in my eyes as I could now lie back. Cleaning was vital. Discipline in this area couldn't be underestimated, as infections and sores are hard to fix at sea. Prevention rather than cure was the philosophy. We used antibacterial gel, biodegradable wet wipes and Sudocrem (crucial for areas of potential friction). In a world of relentless, unpredictable movement, nothing was easy. Whilst on my back, I pressed my feet into the cabin roof for stability, into a weird cleaning tripod, leaving my hands free to administer Sudocrem where needed.

I sat back up and glanced at the clock. I was doing well for time. I reached for my food box where my cold rehydrated meal awaited. Although we could use the Jetboil without the gimbal, it required more faffing around with setup time and waiting for water to boil. With no gimbal, the Jetboil would be on the deck by the rower's feet, which is not at all safe in choppy weather as boiling water could spill everywhere. With only about 30 minutes for admin, and with the mounting exhaustion, eating hot food was a luxury that nobody had time for. Getting calories down our neck was the priority. Cold food, it was. We reserved the Jetboil for group coffee when other tasks needed doing, such as cleaning the boat, when rowing was on hold.

I grabbed the metal spoon and tried to pile the food in my mouth. I rammed as much in with each mouthful as I could, attempting to get through an entire meal as quickly as possible. Chewing was already laborious. I wanted the calories, but my want for sleep was greater. And because of the seasickness, I wasn't even hungry. We'd all lost our appetites and weren't getting through enough of the 6,000 calories we were supposed to eat. I didn't particularly want to eat, but I had to.

Now for water. Having used the last of my bottle to squirt sick off my arm, I needed a refill. I grabbed the hose, put it in my bottle, and flicked the switch. A buzzing noise rang through the cabin as water pumped through the filter. Forgetting the time taken to purify, salty water flowed into the bottle. I opened the hatch and put the hose out on deck and waited a few more seconds.

I glanced at our battery power display, not knowing this would be something we'd have to do at sea so often. Making water took quite a while. As it ran, I watched the battery drain 1% at a time. Getting below 50% was bad and meant we would have to run the fuel cell.

With the pipe out on deck, it was public knowledge I was making water. The whole team requested top ups. My stomach sank slightly. Although essential, this could take up to 20 minutes. It was valuable sleep time that I'd be giving up. The problem was, this was happening regularly and was even more unpleasant at night.

With the water maker running, I stared obsessively at the navigation screen, zooming in and out, trying to absorb the scale of this expedition. It still looked as if we were right next to La Gomera. I could only think about the next day, or the next two hours. I couldn't contemplate an entire ocean.

With the team hydrated, it was finally time to rest.

The cabin was so small, my feet fell into the footwell. My head was only centimetres away from the tiller arm which was at the back of the cabin in the centre. I didn't want to roll into it in case I damaged it, and there was no protection from its wide sweeping radius and sharp edges. The drive unit buzzed constantly as it fought the waves, trying to keep us on track. Despite the noise, I lay back on the mattress and instantly plummeted into a deep sleep.

Bang, bang, bang.

A fist on the cabin hatch woke me.

'You're up in 10 minutes, mate.'

Surely this was too early? I checked the display. It was right, 10 minutes and I had to be on deck. My off-shift had vanished into thin air.

The cabin hatch opened.

'Five minutes, Jon. Get your wet weather gear back on. It's pretty choppy out here.'

I'd fallen back to sleep without realising. In a haze, I forced myself to sit up. Five minutes to get ready. I'd been known to fall asleep whilst getting dressed. I scrabbled around for my wet weather gear that I'd stuffed down the side earlier, and shuffled my way into the wet clothes. Then

I dragged my harness up around my waist. Wet weather gear not only kept you dry but also warm during the night.

Air hit my face as I opened the hatch; quite a relief from the hot, humid cabin I'd been in for two hours. I stepped on deck and clipped in. The dark night sky felt like it surrounded me. My weight fell into the jackstay and a cold, choppy wave lashed at my hand.

I glanced at Steve, crawled into position and readied myself for the next two hours, taking no time at all with the Velcro straps around my feet. Such a stark contrast to the readjustments I kept making at the start of the race. I just hoped for minimal knockdowns in this weather.

Knockdowns were a frequent assault by the sea, something we were already getting accustomed to. Waves would slam into the boat at any angle. We'd have half a second to grab hold of the jackstays and try to prepare. Other times not. Waves would come out of nowhere, hitting the boat unexpectedly. With an almighty crash, we would be instantaneously launched from our seats and thrown somewhere else on deck. In the day we could see the waves and may have time to brace. At night, this was a different game altogether.

At least this was the sunrise shift, I thought to myself. Yesterday's sunrise filled me with warmth and boosted me; it would come again.

Before we could even get going, I had to succumb to the inevitable. I needed the toilet. Tied on with netting, the bucket was secure from the ebbs and flows of the sea at the forward end of the boat. I'd have to crawl past Steve to set up. Steve remained stationary as I wobbled past. He'd have to stop rowing whilst I was on the bucket, as there was no room for his seat to roll back while the bucket was in use.

I removed the netting, leant through the jackstay and scooped up about 10 centimetres of sea water, placed the bucket in the middle of the deck and began. Luckily, the rowing positions were facing the other way, so Steve couldn't see anything. Even better was the sea, which was crashing and thrashing noisily while I did my business, so it really wasn't that bad.

Difficulty came when an unexpected need for the bucket arose whilst in the cabin. Strapping on my harness in a rush, at night, in choppy seas, was hard enough. But having to tell the guys to stop rowing so I could open the hatch and get out, clip on, clamber along the boat and set up the bucket, was a challenge.

Finally, the shift passed, the sun rose, and before I knew it, I found myself in the cabin.

```
12:33 Jon:
Hey, sorry I haven't texted in a while. It's
been busy trying to fit sleep and eating in, let
alone charging a phone! The seasickness has been
a bit rough, but hopefully that will be it.
Can't quite see how we're going to make Antigua.
Would happily get off now!

17:40 Emily:
You're making such good progress. You should
overtake Atlantic Ladies and some of the pairs
towards the end of the week. You will definitely
make it to Antigua! How's the food? Did you find
a solution for the Jetboil?

18:32 Emily:
At your current pace you could overtake all the
other Pure boats except Row 4 Cancer, who is a
Pure solo - he must be a machine! Oarstruck are
due to arrive in Antigua 11 days after you, but
obviously that could all change in the next 6
weeks. You're doing so well, keep it up!

19:48 Jon:
That's immense! Yeah, we don't really know where
we are, so just doing the best we can. How's
home?
```

It didn't feel like we were overtaking people. We were just doing the best we could, and the best we could do felt brutal. An unforgiving environment and sleep regime meant it didn't feel like we were doing as well as it seemed on the tracker.

Without a defined start and end to the day, it all became one long blur. I would come in from a shift so exhausted, clean, eat and then collapse, thinking I'd text on the next off-shift, but I just kept repeating this routine and so didn't text. It was odd because, without a clear break between day and night, there were just two-hour increments that rolled into one.

The shock to the system was like no other. This was an onslaught to every sense, and I felt like I'd only just survived the last two days. This was it. It could only get better from this point on.

# MONSTROUS WAVES

## Day 3: December 20th

I stepped out of the cabin and glanced at Steve as we silently readied ourselves for the next two hours. The night's dark veil surrounded us and an aggressive sea awaited. In the day, it was terrifying and awe-inspiring, but at night, this balance led more to terror. Hearing waves crash and reverberate from inside the cabin, as it rocked violently around, was horrific. I had a deep-seated dread of stepping out of the safety, into the darkness and clipping in.

In wet weather gear, I made my way to my seat and sat down. Without communicating, we both knew this would be a silent shift. Steve grabbed the iPad, and we continued with Harry Potter on audiobook. Listening to Stephen Fry in the dead of night, booming out from our boat had become a staple of our shift.

We had been told to expect the wind in an easterly, and maybe southerly, direction in the next few days. The wave direction was also due to come around and run east to west. If the wind and waves aligned, the conditions would get ever faster. This meant enormous seas, vast mountains of waves, and a bumpy but quick ride. Hopefully, this would be the case – scary, but quick.

But it already felt scary and quick. *The Nutilus* felt more precarious than ever, its crew being tested to the extreme. I didn't want to be the first to admit it, but I was terrified.

My hands shook as I checked for the hundredth time that I was clipped in. My life depended on it. If I wasn't tied onto the jackstays by my harness clips, I could be dragged overboard and lost to the dark, freezing ocean in seconds.

A message came in from our weather router.

'Tonight will be a huge night. There's no shame in admitting you're scared and getting into the cabin.'

We looked into each other's eyes. Trepidation was felt by everyone.

We pushed on, the waves getting increasingly larger. They were monsters that towered up, arched over and looked down on you, ready to devour you. Wave patterns would combine; waves built on top of each other. Other times we would have odd currents. Every fourth or fifth wave would come from a completely different direction and hit the boat side-on.

Atlantic Campaigns warned us that this year would be the biggest weather since the race began. Although we had no reference point for what that would look or feel like, it certainly felt as if we were in significantly sized waves. Waves would build slowly into what looked like a couple of houses stacked on top of one other.

The angle of the wave was not as you see in surfing videos, where there is a beautiful curving tunnel of water. These waves were enormous but only had an angle of about 45 degrees. Although a daunting mass of water, *The Nutilus* rose with ease.

At the top, we could see a panoramic view. Crests of waves surrounded us like a mountain range. It was as if we were in an alien world of liquid mountains and valleys. Below us, a vast aquatic chasm, looking fantastically deep, and we had no choice but to go down. At the bottom of a gigantic wave, it was like being swallowed into a valley, surrounded by vast, moving mountains that loomed over us. I stared upward with no choice but to begin our next ascent. The crest of the wave would unfold, curling over, taking on an even more menacing character, hitting the boat and thrusting us across the deck.

The aggressive waves attacked multiple times on a shift, so often, in fact, that it became the norm. We would shout out, grab onto the jackstays and hold on with white knuckles. The wave would batter us from our seats and we'd end up flung across the deck.

The ocean had changed temperament this evening. The vast mountains that we were ascending and descending suddenly felt even more violent. The tremendous sound of the aggressive crashing waves filled our ears, as dark avalanches plummeted all around us.

With each wave and knockdown, I felt another attack survived. It was relentless.

The unpredictability and darkness meant Steve and I never relaxed, and with the volatility of the waves, we struggled to find a rhythm. For the entire shift, we'd be fighting the sea, trying to turn the boat perpendicular to the waves. We grabbed one oar only, dug it into the water and pulled it with everything we had. The boat rose violently out of the water and the oar would fling into the air, rendering it useless. Still side-on, we timed the next oar stroke at the bottom of the wave again and restarted the movement. Whenever we got close to straight, another wave would knock us side-on again and, in an instant, we lost any progress we had made.

I looked up to our port side, a vertical tower of water now poised above us. If we were side-on, we'd be more likely to capsize. This was a precarious position. We were sitting on a knife's edge.

The white crest of the wave glistened in the moonlight like the whites of someone's eyes, hesitating, curling, ready to crash.

The ocean was about to plunge on top of us.

The roar of the wave made a whooshing sound just before impact. It shunted the entire boat with a tremendous force as if it was playing with us.

Without time to think, the weight and force of the wave obliterated us. It slammed me across the deck with its almighty hit. Water rushed over my face and eyes, pouring into my ears, draining me of my senses. I was totally disorientated. I couldn't work out where I was or what had happened until the wave had moved on.

We were both on the edge of the boat. We stared at each other; no words needed. That was the biggest impact we'd had. But we'd taken it, and we'd survived.

Shift over, I was just thankful I didn't get smashed by another wave as I clambered back into the relative safety of the cabin. There had already been a few times that changeover was late, only by a couple of minutes, but enough to get soaked by a wave on what was technically not my shift. It was difficult not to think negatively, that I shouldn't have had to get hit by that wave; that I was soaked through and about to try to get some rest.

Luckily, this was not one of those times and, for the first time, I crawled into the forward cabin.

Mark was seasick in the aft cabin so I'd temporarily switched to the forward cabin. I heaved myself in, shut the hatch and collapsed. Limbs exhausted from adrenaline; clothes soaked with salt water. The relief was instant, and this cabin was huge in comparison. Not only was it more stable, but with no autohelm, it was spacious, cooler and quieter. The aft cabin took the hits from the sea as waves crashed on top; this was a completely different experience all together. With that thought, I reached for my phone.

```
08:13 Jon:
Think sickness has passed, fingers crossed! We
are all smashing out the Potter!
```

## Chasing Horizons

09:14 Emily:
Phew! Got to love the Potter! How are you finding the shift patterns?

17:08 Jon:
Getting better, but the nights are tough. We've hit some awesome waves so should overtake some teams soon! How's the tracker looking?

17:34 Emily:
Glad it's getting better. Tracker is looking awesome. You're only 3nm behind Oceanomads and going twice the speed!

22:36 Emily:
Overtaken Oceanomads! Atlantic Ladies are next, only 2nm ahead of you!

# THE DROGUE

## Day 4: December 21st

Drip.
Drip.
Drip.

Lying on my back, swaying with the rhythm of the boat, I gazed up at the vacant hole I'd become acquainted with over the last few days. With every wave, fresh sea water would drip through the tiny hole and into the cabin. Annoyingly, the hole was right above where we rested. It wasn't enough water to be dangerous, but enough to be a constant drip while sleeping.

The rush of getting to the start line was now being paid for. Even though we'd had the all-clear to take the boat out to sea, there were still things that needed adjusting or fixing. Vacant holes littered the boat's hull where equipment was supposed to be screwed in but, for whatever reason, was elsewhere. I averted my eyes slightly left of the drip. Water slowly crept down a tangle of wires connecting the solar panels on the outside of the cabin, to the inside of the boat. I didn't even think the solar panels were working, and wondered if we were relying solely on our fuel cell. My mind drifted to the enthusiastic Bristol Energy meeting; their money used on these panels. I hadn't imagined the reality to be like this.

Hands covered in sealant, beside me rested the sealant gun. A few days in and we'd nearly used all our sealant. I couldn't believe it. Before I slept on this shift, I'd been trying to sort a leak in the cabin deck hatch. There was quite a lot of water in this hatch and we couldn't find where it had come from, so I'd chucked a load of sealant in the hatch, hoping to isolate the issue.

I gazed at the clock; I would be on deck soon. I was exhausted. This week was an absolute onslaught. On top of the already monumental challenge, we were trying to make minor fixes to our boat. I looked again at the tangle of wires which resembled a snake's wedding, and taped them together so they proudly led to the solar panels. Happy that I'd sorted a few of the issues, my head fell back as I waited for the first warning call at 10 minutes to go. Every second of rest counted. I was annoyed I'd woken up before my call.

Out on deck, I was greeted with an immediate side-on situation that had clearly been relentless for Mark and Dan. The gloomy seascape taunted us. Towering grey waves and an overcast sky awaited. Steve and I changed over swiftly and readied ourselves. Daytime had struck, and with it, the light aided us, helping us to see the frantic waves once again.

The draining and futile battle against nature began. Rowing with one oar, we instantly wrestled to turn the boat around against the side waves. The oar felt stuck in a sea of concrete as we battled against the wave direction. Every stroke of the oar counted. Every ounce of energy vital. As we rocked down into the trough of the wave, it felt like we would capsize at any moment. The boat rocked dramatically as every wave rose to a peak and then slammed down in the opposite direction. With every smash, we were flung against the jackstays. All technique we'd learnt at the rowing club went out of the window; this was pure attrition.

Slowly the boat edged round and, just before it straightened up…...

'Two oar rowing,' shouted Mark, holding the tiller straight.

We searched for more energy, hands in pain and thighs screaming as we put power down, heaving the boat straight before the sea caught it.

If we timed it right, we would be back on target, head-on to the waves. But if the sea had its way, which happened countless times, it would catch the turn, sending us round 180 degrees and side-on in the opposite position to where we'd started. It was a delicate balance of shear effort and crucial timing.

Another shift passed. We'd made little ground and handed over the oars to the guys in the same situation that had welcomed us. Another side-on battle awaited them. It was relentless, taking several exhausting shifts to get the boat straight.

I crumpled in the cabin and picked up my phone. This experience was hard to articulate home. It felt abstract and anything I wrote felt somewhat muted. The sea was intense, like a wild creature, monstrous, aggressive, battering us around.

```
08:52 Emily:
Passed Atlantic Ladies in the night! Next up are
Team Noble, who are 35nm ahead and travelling
1.3 knots. You're doing amazing! So many likes
and  messages  of  support  on  Facebook  and
Instagram!

10:27 Jon:
Feels a little different here! Surprised we did
that, last night was a bit sketchy and we're all
exhausted today. Let's get hunting Noble then.

11:38 Emily:
You've been consistently fastest in your class.
```

## Chasing Horizons

```
Everyone is struggling with the weather, but
apparently it should be faster next week. Try
to learn to surf the waves. I've heard that's
the key, but most teams don't master it until
halfway across. Why was it sketchy? Big waves?
Any blisters yet?
```

Our game plan was to get down south with the other boats. Having left three days later, this seemed impossible. The winds had changed, which meant we had to take a more direct path. Although this looked great on the map, as we were making more distance early on and appeared to be catching up with the other teams, we all knew the consequence. The reason people head south is to catch the stronger trade winds. If we couldn't get south, we would miss them.

Darkness fell, and with it, the weather had built once again. Capsize felt imminent. After hours of battling the side-on waves, we decided it was time for the drogue. A funnel shaped device with open ends, towed behind the boat to prevent us from being side-on. The aim was to straighten us up and slow us down, getting us back on track.

We tied the oars and bucket down, and I opened the hatch to retrieve the drogue and rope. But what I found was a wet mess. We had used it the previous night, and put it away neatly, but somehow this had ended badly. I was met with the equivalent of inevitably tangled headphones, but this was 50 metres of thick rope. It was night, and with the boat all over the shop, the pressure was on.

Every wave that struck jolted me over, knocking and launching me around. Sea spray was everywhere. Cold, wet and adrenaline had sapped the nimbleness from my hands. Head torch lights beamed down on the deck to help me see. I hurried to untangle the mess. Getting the drogue out would prevent a potential capsize.

Finally, I reached the end and handed it to Steve, who tied it the bow. I hoped the knot was decent and it wouldn't get swept away.

The drogue filled up and drifted into the oil black water. The weight of the water in the drogue adding an instant tension to the rope. I hoped that this would be it, that all our instability and fear of capsize would be over.

Then we noticed our mistake. The ropes had both gone out the same side of the boat. It wouldn't be able to straighten.

We instantly began flinging the heavy rope over the aerial. *The Nutilus* rocked violently beneath us. Our bodies stretched over the cabin.

I then noticed a length of rope had snaked around Steve's leg like a thick python, getting ever tighter as the drogue made its way out. With only a few metres left, we scrambled back to deck and began frantically untying another mess of rope.

Finally, we had done it. We dived into our separate cabins and locked ourselves in.

With no room in the cabin, Mark and I were lying on top of each other. It was stifling hot. We desperately wanted to crack the cabin hatch open for some fresh air, but we knew that if we did in these waves, we'd only get drenched for our efforts.

Being on the drogue was not a pleasant experience. Each wave that crashed onto the cabin sounded like a shotgun firing with the resultant lurch, flinging us around the tiny cabin. Every time the boat was hit, it pulled the rope from slack to tight, like a car being pulled on a tow rope. The resulting slam reverberated around the boat. The rope would pull so taut, it felt like being connected to a steel rod. All this time, water cascaded over the cabin roof. Each impact from on top, the side or behind, shook the little cabin.

We lay in the humid, loud cabin, in silence, waiting for the attack to end. I could feel each one of the 10 millimetres of carbon fibre between me and the entire ocean as it raged angrily against us.

# TEAM O2 RECOVERY

## Day 5: December 22nd

We awoke to find one of our precious buckets had gone missing in the storm. Less than a week in and we were down to two buckets for the toilet!

14:26 Jon:
Hey, hey. We were caught in a storm last night so hunkered down. Had the drogue out. Found a few leaks, so had to fix them. Yeah, we are surfing the waves. Where are you getting your insider info from? How's home?

14:37 Emily:
Hey! I spotted you were slower than normal, so guessed it must have been a bad night. Everything ok now? I saw the picture of you with sealant stuff all over your hands! I watched a Facebook live from the boat builder and he said about the surfing. How are you finding it all now you're five days in? Home is ok, last day at work before Christmas!

17:53 Emily:
I've just seen the picture of you rowing.

```
You're incredible!

19:58 Emily:
This was a post from Carbon Zerow that might be
useful: 'Yesterday was harrowing. Finally have
a solution to increase stability in the boat by
towing a 70m line with knots in it.' Hope you're
ok, sounds brutal out there.
```

The word harrowing resonated. It had been a brutal first week. Any start to an ocean row is tough, but with the biggest weather in race history, this was next level and last night had proved it. With no update to Team O2's tracker since 04:00, Atlantic Campaigns released the following statement:

```
    'At 09:35 Atlantic Campaigns received a
signal that the Emergency Position Indicating
Radio Beacon (EPIRB) was activated on 'JAN' Team
O2's ocean rowing boat.
    'At the time of writing, our Duty Officers
have been unable to make contact with Team O2.
Atlantic Campaigns are working closely with MRCC
Falmouth; a commercial vessel has been diverted
to the area and both Atlantic Campaigns Support
Yachts have been tasked to the team also.
    'We will update you as soon as we have new
information.
    'Atlantic Campaigns.'
```

I froze and looked up at the guys in disbelief as the boat rose up and down the enormous waves. With no knowledge of what was going on with Team O2, other than the update, we could only imagine what had happened to them last night. Team O2 were relatively close by and had experienced the same conditions that we had. We thought it was rough, but with no previous experience, we had nothing to compare it to. We had just done the best we could. We hoped they were okay and that rescue would come quickly. I could only guess what our families were going through; knowing we were in the same area; seeing our speed reduce drastically and resigned to four-hourly updates on the tracker.

I came out of the cabin for my shift. The sea air struck me and woke me up from the groggy daze I found myself in. Mark, Steve and Dan were discussing what to do with the jackstays. With each relentless knockdown, getting launched from our seats and across the deck, we'd put an incredible strain through them. The jackstays were now slack and rubbed our hands while rowing. With the sea a little less violent, they'd already untied one and were about to retie it. With no barrier between us and the sea, I felt a sudden vulnerability. I still couldn't move around without holding on to the jackstays. We now had to continue rowing, knowing that we'd retied the knots that kept us safely attached to the boat in this huge weather. If the knots gave way, we'd have no one but ourselves to blame.

Another message came through:

'Team O2 Update: At 21.25 GMT Atlantic Campaigns received the news that Omar Samra and Omar Nour from Team O2 have been safely rescued and are on board a bulk carrier. More updates coming soon.'

The air had cooled, the blue sea changed to black, and the night took hold once more. It would be another night of battling the enormous, soaring waves and desperately trying to snatch some sleep while the water boomed across the roof.

On the drogue once more, we felt the boat was stuck against the waves. They slammed into *The Nutilus* from every direction. The drogue didn't seem to have straightened the boat at all.

I stepped out onto the dark, treacherous deck, spray instantly pelting me. The only light was the small beam from my head torch. Rain lashed horizontally through the beam, looking like little sparkling stars in the noisy darkness. The sound of the waves roared around me. I was a minute early for our shift and wanted to alert Steve of the situation. I banged on the forward cabin. A hand wiped the condensation from the window, understandably reluctant to open the cabin hatch.

'We've got to turn the boat, otherwise we've got another night of getting slammed!' I shouted over the crashing waves.

Steve nodded, and ducked back to put on his wet weather gear.

Soon, we were both strapped in, grabbing the oars and continuing to wrestle in the dark, relentless storm.

# TEAM TENZING RECOVERY

## Day 6: December 23rd

The torment of last night lifted somewhat, and the sea took on a new character. Jagged, sheer, mountainous waves were replaced with choppy, rolling, bluey-grey hills. Knockdowns and crashing waves on the boat were still frequent as we got battered across the sea, but the overall temperament seemed different. I could now see far and wide. Rolling waves went on for forever. The white peaks of waves were in every direction I looked. I had time to soak it up. The sea scape had changed so dramatically, I felt we were on a different ocean.

Although it was morning, my body was cold. My muscles ached from the previous day's onslaught and took a while to limber up. My first week of sea life had left its mark.

```
11:42 Jon:
Hey, had another night on the drogue, but
hopefully back on track today. We fixed the
jackstays too. What have you been up to?

12:32 Emily:
Hello! Fingers crossed for improved weather
soon. You're smashing it, though. Good work on
```

the jackstays! How is all the equipment holding
up? Saturday today, so it's a dog walk up the
hill and I'm now writing Christmas cards.

The storm had taken its toll on my mind, and I feared another night on the drogue. Listening to the shotgun-like sound in the cabin as we got pounded, would drive me insane.

Atlantic Campaigns sent through another message:

'During the search and rescue operation for
Team 02, the Duty Officers received a call that
the EPIRB was activated for Team Tenzing. A call
was quickly made to Tenzing, who informed the
Duty Officers of their current situation. Gusts
of 45 knots and six metre waves in the area
caused the team to suffer a capsize, resulting
in an on-board battery fire and total loss of
power for the team.
  'All crew were safe and unharmed and
assessing their situation, but after a lengthy
discussion with the Duty Officers, who advised
Tenzing on their lack of options with total loss
of power and fire damage, they began preparing
for an abandonment and rescue.
  'At 04:00 the rescue vessel arrived at the
area and we are thankful to announce all crew
members are safe and on-board the cargo ship.'

I sat in the aft rowing position, now behind Dan for a change. We'd swapped rowing partners, deciding that a week's rotation would enable each pair to get into a rhythm together but would also allow for some variety. The last couple of days had been monumental, and it seemed like we were lucky to still be on the expedition. Fortunately, we had nothing like a battery fire, but our boat was starting to creak under the bombardment of the first week.

To my right, the oar wobbled increasingly with every stroke. The oar gate was on its way out from the force being put through the oar. Finally, it snapped. I'd have to replace the gate. We only had five spares, and we were already on the first.

We reluctantly drew the oars in and rested them across the deck. I opened the deck hatch and stuck my head in, searching for the tool bag and spares as efficiently as possible. I wanted to avoid water charging its way in from the edge of our fortress-like boat.

I lugged my head and shoulders out of the hatch and laid everything required on deck, keeping an eye on anything that wanted to break free into the choppy sea. We didn't have spare tools.

The gate hung off the side of the boat. With Dan acting as a counterbalance hanging over the opposite side of the boat, I grabbed the spanner, nuts, washers and new gate, and began.

The world was in constant motion. The waves lapped at my face, and beneath the gate was the vast ocean. Locating the spanner on the nut took a few attempts with the rocking environment. I daren't drop the spanner. Why hadn't we put lanyards on the tools in La Gomera? With no spares, I couldn't have been more aware of the ocean only a few centimetres away.

Gate off, I grabbed its replacement along with the nut and washer. My hands shook with the sea, making aligning the threads tricky. I tried to work quickly but carefully. I didn't want to lose my tools to the murky depths of the Atlantic Ocean.

A short while later, it was fixed. I put the tools in the deck hatch, shoved the oars out and we got back to it.

But the oar still had play in it. I was sure I tightened everything up. I leant in closer. It was the rigger, the support for the gate, that was moving and lifting out of the deck. I checked in the hatch under the rigger to tighten the nut but found there wasn't one.

I looked at Dan, who instinctively checked his two riggers. None of them had nuts. None of them had been secured to the deck! Why on earth had this not been done by the boat builder in La Gomera? It was infuriating. We had no way to fix them. They wouldn't go anywhere as they were wedged into the deck, but the energy loss on every oar stroke played on my mind.

On top of this, we'd also noticed that the foot plates weren't in line with the seats. This meant that our bodies and legs were at a very slight angle. It was fine for a short time, but not with the prospect of weeks at sea. In addition, the forward port oar wouldn't sit square despite our fancy rowing gates, meaning we had to hold it square. If not, the blade would tilt and then get pulled under the water, rocking the whole boat.

Mind rattled, we continued. The plunging waves accompanied our grumblings. The only thing to interrupt our introspection was an oar being accidentally flung into the air, untimed with the waves, throwing us off for a second.

Something about the rowing action just felt wrong. We weren't facing the waves like we had been that morning. We were now rowing parallel to them. Our world had moved orientation. Huge waves cut across us like a production line of helping hands, but not only were we missing every single one, we were actively fighting them.

As we rose to the peak of a wave, we could see the vast body of water moving diagonally across from our heading. With the boat swinging from side to side, our oars spent half the day in the air. Timing our oar strokes and maintaining any momentum felt impossible. We could get no rhythm whatsoever. Exhaustion overwhelmed us, and to make matters worse, our minds were aggravated.

We were sure the wave and wind direction were southwest, the direction we wanted to go. We double and triple-checked the navigation screen, and begrudgingly battled against the waves, against the force of nature.

Our fears were later confirmed. We had been heading in a westerly direction all day. Not only was it mentally draining to know that we had made little progress at a tremendous expense of energy, but we knew we could have made use of the big waves. Instead of fighting them, we could have been rowing with them and using them to propel us forward. This was a massive missed opportunity. The bigger weather wouldn't last forever and we wanted to make the most of it.

Without understanding what was wrong, I grabbed the adjustable spanner from our already rusting set of tools and moved towards the locking nuts on the tiller. A wave hit just as I had got the spanner in position, rounding one of the nuts slightly. If we needed to do this multiple times, it could easily become a problem. We reset the entire steering system and recalibrated the autohelm.

```
21:07 Jon:
Not sure we're smashing it! We recalibrated our
steering today as we were going the wrong way,
so will smash it now.

22:20 Emily:
You're still going west though, so all good!
Most boats are zig zagging around.
```

# NAVIGATION PROBLEMS

## Day 7: December 24th

I scrabbled in the back of the aft cabin for the charts I thought we'd never have to use. Finally, I prised them from the netting in their water tight sleeves. Along with them, I retrieved the compass. How had our navigation gone wrong again?

I opened the cabin hatch to find Steve and Mark on the deck, rowing as always. The sea undulated around us. The boat rocked gently for once. I couldn't remember how to use this equipment. I grabbed the compass, held it up to my eye and looked at the horizon for inspiration, hoping that the lesson on how to take a bearing would be found in the distance.

It didn't. I passed it to Dan, who had a similar experience and passed it back. It was time to ring our weather router. Maybe he'd have some words of wisdom.

Each day, we called Stokey, who was thousands of miles away on the Isle of Wight, to learn our new heading. An experienced man of the ocean, he studied the localised weather surrounding us and plotted our course. The difference in weather, even a few miles apart, could be astounding and make a huge difference to our experience, morale, speed and progress. Every day, he tried to position us in a strong wind and wave direction to edge us bit by bit towards Antigua.

Steve opened the deck hatch and retrieved the satellite phone, quickly shutting it to avoid water invading. To get the best signal, we needed to use the sat-phone on deck. But this was risky. There was always a nervousness around trying not to drop the phone when the boat was hit by a wave. Activity lessened on the boat as the three of us readied ourselves to read Steve's expression, trying to gauge the information on the other side of the phone. The boat rocked. Steve gripped the sat-phone with two hands. He shielded the microphone from the wind, so his voice made it through, whilst taking notes in between instructions.

I sat in the aft cabin, hatch open, looking down the deck at Steve. Steve repeated the coordinates and information back to our weather router to ensure he'd heard him correctly. Waypoints were sometimes hundreds of miles away, sometimes closer. The call ended and Steve shouted out the new coordinates to me. I typed it into the navigation screen and stored our new heading for when we worked out what the issue was this time.

I lay down in the cabin and stared at the light in the ceiling. My body swayed with the motion of the boat. The cabin had a damp, salty musk as the sea's character had absorbed into the mattress. Every so often, a wave would hit the cabin and make the sound of someone chucking a bucket of water at a window.

It was now day seven. The first week of the expedition had passed, and what an experience it had been! I couldn't fathom how we'd make it to Antigua and tried to recall the advice of the Duty Officer. We'd made it through one day, then two days, then four days, then a week.

We'd now done a week! He was right; the seasickness

had dissipated; I felt more at one with the ocean after a treacherous start. Now we just had to repeat weeks, one shift at a time. We were doing it! We were living at sea.

The first week was done. At least the environment and daily routines were becoming more normalised. With more of a hold on those, there were fewer variables to worry about. But the first week had been incredibly tough. It was not only because of the menacing conditions and repairs, it was a general shock to the system. I had found it tough mentally. I'm sure we were all struggling.

Not wanting to get everyone down, I kept it to myself. I just had to get through each two hours on, two hours off shift, just robotically going through the motions. I had general conversations with Steve and Dan as I was rowing with them, but it was difficult with Mark as we were sharing the same cabin, so I only saw him on change overs.

Living so closely on the same boat, on top of each other, it's odd how distant I sometimes felt in this week. With nothing else to think of, I was consumed. I was desperately in need of someone to offload to.

I wanted to explain all this to Emily, but I was all too aware that the app we were using used a shared inbox. There was a lot I didn't want everyone else to read. I knew Steve could contact Becky privately. He was sending private emails home. The rest of us couldn't get this working. If only I could use his phone to email Emily and then delete the evidence. The issue was that Steve's phone was in the forward cabin, and with the shift patterns, I would need a reason to venture up that end of the boat. It was obsessing me.

I didn't want to tell anyone I was having issues, as I didn't want to create conflict. My mind was hell, and I decided to just get on with it. I eventually sent a vague message to Emily, hoping she would read into that.

```
17:15 Jon:
We need to be heading south to get good wind,
not good if we continue west and don't go south
enough! There's a lot I want to say to you but
```

```
don't want to do it in the common inbox!
Basically, I miss you. We forgot it is Christmas
Eve this morning. Feeling festive?

17:23 Emily:
You are the furthest north out of all the boats,
but not by much, and you're south of the line
that shows the most direct route. Are you
getting advice from this weather guy? Let me
know if there's anything I can do to help. I
know what you mean; I miss you too. I opened
your Christmas card, thank you! Just got back
from your parents' house to get the Christmas
presents! Can't wait to open them tomorrow.
```

I got back up, looked at the navigation screen again, and decided to reset the entire thing. It worked! Why hadn't this worked before? I opened the cabin hatch and found a corresponding nod as they both saw the display register correctly.

With an exhaustion that reached deep into my heart, I crashed out in the cabin. I needed to grab some sleep before I was up for the next shift. At least, I thought grimly, we had our navigation sorted.

# CHRISTMAS DAY

## Day 8: December 25th

The square cabin hatch framed my view as I looked down at the guys on deck. Rowing had stopped for a while. The oars were in as my teammates rested against the jackstays on either side of the boat and chatted. It was Christmas day, an odd feeling on a rowing boat in the vast ocean. The sea was calm, and the boat wobbled every so often, adding half a second midway through a sentence as people readjusted themselves from the sway.

I sat in the aft cabin, happily looking out of the hatch; feeling involved in the conversation, but shielded from the elements; cocooned from the slight breeze. Spending so much time exhausted on deck, I took solace in any time in the cabin. I didn't want to stop rowing for long today, but we should acknowledge Christmas for a few hours.

'Come out and join us, Jon,' they all said.

I felt I probably should go out and join in. Lifting my body up and out of the cabin hatch, I rested two hands on the jackstays. I still needed support even in calm seas, especially when walking further than the usual metre to my rowing position. My full weight now through the jackstays, I thought back to the hastily re-tied knots. They'd proved themselves through endless knockdowns and now bore the weight of everyone leaning back on them.

I rested on the drizzly deck, moisture seeping through my shorts, and leant back into the jackstay that dug into my back. A gentle breeze fanned round me as I constantly tried to find a comfortable position in a place that wasn't designed for luxury.

A tiny bottle of whisky was thrust into my hand and we toasted Christmas. The dark liquid stung the back of my throat. I leant forwards to open the deck hatch in the centre of the boat to retrieve our presents.

My weathered hands fought with the knot in the plastic bag, eventually opening it to unveil loads of chocolate. Yes! This could not have been better. Without needing to be asked, we ploughed through them.

Back in La Gomera, I had been reluctant to take the presents on board as they took up weight and space. I argued that, if we took a present, it should be useful and if it was useful, it shouldn't wait for Christmas. Now in the moment, guzzling my tenth Cadbury's Hero, this was superb. The chocolatey sugar binge broke the monotony of eating the same cold meals day in, day out and brought a smile to every team mate's face.

The next present was from my family. Again, my hands wrestled with the plastic bag to reveal a new shirt. I'd already forgotten what fresh fabric felt like. My current tops were salt laden, heavy, smelt of the sea and grated on my skin. This felt smooth, clean, and light.

Excellent.

With presents done, we took it in turns to ring our families. I clambered back into the cabin. Although the sat-phone didn't work unless pointing at the sky, I thought I'd risk it for the privacy. I removed the reflective foil from the top hatch window, so there was an unobstructed view to the sky for the satellite signal. Although the window was foggy, it felt wonderful to have the natural light streaming into the cabin. It reminded me we were all under the same sky, us four on the ocean and all my friends and family back home.

The hatch was above the tiller, right in the centre of the cabin at the back, meaning I couldn't sit directly below it. I would have to manage a weird half-squat for the duration of the call. I jammed my leg against one side of the cabin, allowing the tiller arm to move beneath me, and leant my back against the opposite cabin wall. My head and other arm wobbled with the boat as I tried to keep the sat-phone pointed at the hatch window.

Emily picked up. It was the first time I'd heard her voice since we'd left. She was at home with her parents, enjoying the usual Christmas traditions. It felt like the other side of the universe. My legs ached as I desperately tried to keep the sat-phone in position. Signal was intermittent, words half received. I was only grasping the odd word or sound, nowhere near a conversation, but it didn't matter. It had transformed my state of being instantly. I texted her.

```
13:22 Jon:
We had the morning off, which was ace. What's
the plan today, then?

18:10 Emily:
So nice to hear your voice. I couldn't hear much
of what you were saying, but enjoy the rest of
Christmas day.

18:12 Jon:
Signal was terrible :( Love you and hope you're
having a good day.

18:26 Jon:
Really hard to hear you, unfortunately. I miss
you loads. I can ring another time when you're
not at your parents' so we can talk properly.

18:28 Emily:
Yeah, I struggled to hear you too; the signal
```

is bad at my parents', which doesn't help so I was standing outside in the rain! I miss you too. I will be at home tomorrow evening if you're able to call again.

22:32 Jon:
You should have said you were in the rain!! I can call tomorrow :)

23:41 Emily:
Amazing, speak to you then :) Has the seasickness gone now? Hope you were able to enjoy some Christmas chocolates! You're still looking good on the tracker!

# IMPACT

## Day 9: December 26th

The day was overcast. Gun metal clouds stretched from horizon to horizon like a thick, dark blanket. Complementing this, a volatile ocean accompanied me and Dan as we battled the waves.

Nothing was going easily. The ocean was deciding our fate today. The boat got endlessly pushed around by larger waves, getting stuck against them. We resorted to rowing with one oar to try to turn the boat. Smaller choppy waves came from all angles and slapped up against the hull or on the cabin, relentlessly showering us with spray. These cut into what little rhythm we had, shunting the boat and us laterally across our seats. Wind picked up water from the surface of the ocean and dumped cold fountains of it all over the boat. It was an energy sapping struggle against the will of the ocean.

Too many waves were crashing as we met the crest. We'd stare up at the top of the wave and, as if it was glaring back, making a decision, it would turn in character. A white peak would form, curling over and then falling under its own weight. It would angrily smash into us, sending us all a kilter.

I looked up. An angry wave looked down at us, poised to attack. *The Nutilus* slid up the wave's sloped flank, cutting across it at a slight angle. In this position, we would roll for sure.

The familiar signs were there. The crest of the wave turned white. The lip curled over. It snarled at us. Then it towered over us, 40 foot high and menacing as hell. It smashed down on us like a tonne of bricks, crashing over the entire boat. The water roared in my ears. Freezing water pulverised me, seeping into my wet weather gear where it could.

Unable to do anything but ride it out, I grabbed the jackstays with icy fingers. Holding tight, I hoped it would be enough to stop me from being flung across the deck again. The boat pitched at an angle and travelled a few metres off kilter. But thankfully, I stayed on my seat.

Just as suddenly as it had arrived, the force of the wave dissipated and the sea settled. White water streamed off deck and the roar of the ocean gave way to comparative peace.

I turned around to check on Dan. He lay sprawled on the deck. Next to him lay the bucket, badly cracked. The wave had launched him straight into it, rendering it completely useless. We were now down to one bucket!

Dan had been hit worse than me. I signalled to see if he was ok, but he delayed in giving me a sign that he was alright. Getting slammed off his seat and into the forward cabin, he'd caught several edges on his way to the deck. I could tell this knockdown had hurt a lot.

I turned to the aft of the boat, towards the wave direction. Without warning, we were now staring directly into another vast wall of water. With Dan on the deck in a precarious position, the sea prepared for another attack.

I grabbed the jackstays once more. The wave pummelled into us. My grip got instantaneously overridden, and submitting to the force, I was thrown across deck. My hip clanged as it hit an edge along the ride. I felt the jackstay dig into my back as it obstructed my path overboard.

Impact over, I looked back at Dan, who grimaced. We were battered, exhausted and absolutely soaked through. We pulled our tired bodies back onto our seats and rested for a few minutes, collecting our thoughts.

```
11:36 Jon:
Seasickness has gone, actually. I've gone full
pirate, just need a parrot! How's Boxing Day
going?

17:09 Emily:
Haha, yes. You need a parrot companion for the
trip! You're still going the right way in a
straight line with four boats less than 50nm
ahead! Is the weather improving?

21:04 Jon:
Sorry, I won't be able to ring tonight. I'll try
tomorrow if that's possible! Yeah, hopefully we
will be able to take them! I think we're about
1/4 the way through now :) Weather is ok but we
spend most time in our coats because of the
spray and random waves. No idea how people row
naked. It must be freezing!

21:15 Emily:
How are the blisters? I listened to a live
interview with the Atlantic Ladies earlier; they
sound like they are really struggling. One is
still seasick! Team Antigua haven't got a fuel
cell and have to hand steer half the day as not
enough power. How is your power situation?
```

# SURFING

## Day 10: December 27th

I sat in the aft rowing position, keenly observing the waves before me. The pattern unravelling like a puzzle. Medium-sized waves surrounded us, the type that had enough oomph to give us a boost, but not enough that was terrifying. The early morning light still had the golden-hour glow, and the air felt crisp. The shift had just started. Blood pumped readily through my arms and legs. This was exhilarating.

'Now!' I shouted to Dan.

We executed an immediate sharp and strong heave of the oars. Driving our feet into the footplate, leaning back to give the boat a tiny boost, then immediately keeping our oars in the air to avoid any resistance.

Whooooosh!!

We had caught the crest of the wave perfectly. The energy of the wave and our oar stroke acted in unison, and we surfed down the incline.

In the hollow between the waves, we slowed down as I scanned around for our next wave. We were now getting used to seeing wave patterns and could understand which wave would be best for surfing.

'Skip this one. There's one immediately after that's better!'

Oars ready. Whooooosh! It happened again. With our oars in the air, we glided down the next giant slide in the middle of the ocean.

Each time we caught one, we reached over 10 knots for a few brief but brilliant seconds. If we missed the timing, there was immense frustration at a lost opportunity. Every caught wave took us closer to Antigua with less energy expended.

It became a game. Before us lay a patchwork of waves. Each one had the potential to add momentum to our crossing. How to row the most efficiently became a puzzle to be worked out as we scanned the oncoming waves for the best ones to attack.

```
13:02 Emily:
You've been smashing it over the last 24 hours,
think that's your best day yet! 60nm and in a
perfectly straight line, keep it up! If you
average that speed over the entire row, you'd
finish in 43 days.

16:12 Jon:
Needed to hear this. That's pretty good. Didn't
think we were doing that well, to be honest.

16:28 Jon:
Awesome, so they have predicted ETAs on the
site? What's our min and max? How are you doing?

16:30 Jon:
43 days would be nice.

16:45 Emily:
Yeah, it said 31st Jan at lunchtime, but the
ETAs change every four hours and I don't
understand the logic! How's your backside? Is
it looking like a pizza yet?!
```

# EXHAUST FUMES

## Day 11: December 28th

I opened my eyes. I could feel sweat on my face as I rolled my head over on the mattress to get my bearings. I was on an off-shift and asleep in the cabin. The fuel cell hissed in the background as it let out insufferable heat and fumes. A fuzzy weight was in my pounding head and I had a horrible feeling of dizziness and nausea.

We didn't realise until we were at sea, but with the rush in La Gomera, the exhaust pipe for the fuel cell had been installed to vent inside our cabin. Removing oxygen, and adding carbon dioxide and heat to the small cabin atmosphere, the cabin quickly became insufferable when it was in use. The manufacturer's website came with this message, which I found out after the row:

WARNING: ALWAYS LEAD EXHAUST GAS OUTDOORS. INHALING THE EXHAUST FUMES OR DRINKING THE WATER IS HARMFUL TO HEALTH.

The heat and humidity were now unbearable in the cabin. I had to do something. I sat up. Light from the midday sun crept round the edges of the foil on the cabin hatch, leaving a square outline to direct my efforts at. I thrust the cabin hatch open and fresh air came rushing in. It was a slight relief, but not enough. With only one hatch open, there wasn't that much air flow. The whole cabin needed ventilation.

'I need to vent it,' I complained to Mark, who was rowing in the aft position just a metre from the open cabin hatch.

'It's intolerable.'

I'd reached desperation point. My head was thudding and the queasiness now taking the lead role in my decision making.

I clambered back to the top hatch above the tiller and cracked it open. Mark remained rowing but now, crucially, kept one eye on the waves. With both hatches shut, we protected *The Nutilus* from sinking if we capsized. The air in the water tight cabins acted as floats, and with a bottom-heavy boat it would, in theory, rotate round. With the top hatch open, a wave could come in and ruin this system. We wouldn't just capsize. There'd be a good chance that I'd sink half the boat.

I was now opening both the cabin hatch and the top hatch. A direct route ran from the very back of the cabin, all the way through to the front, where the aft rower sat. Blissful fresh air funnelled through the openings.

The sea was relatively calm; it was worth the risk. We had done this a few times now, desperate to work out a solution to the fuel cell issue. Whoever was rowing in the aft position would watch out for waves and would shout it if they saw any incoming. The person in the cabin would hold the top hatch ready to shut it at a moment's notice. We had to keep the cabin dry, but it was unbearable without fresh air.

Wonderful fresh clean air soared into the cabin, taking with it the humidity, fumes and heat. If only we could row all the time with cabins vented like this, or perhaps even have air conditioning.

I clung to the handle of the top hatch, holding it open only a few centimetres so I could shut it quickly. Without being able to see the sea and with no call on waves, I assumed it was calm. I dared to open it just a little more to get even more air through.

'Wave!' Mark shouted.

I slammed it shut and held the hatch firmly closed. Without rotating the handle and locking it, it was only my arm keeping the ocean outside of the boat. The boat sank down with the wave and then water plummeted onto the cabin roof. The sound echoed off the walls.

The boat rose, and I opened the hatch once more. Feeling more assured in our system, I felt a beatific smile spread across my face. A wave slapped into the side of the cabin. I rocked sideways and a slight spray came in through the top hatch. A little spray was no big deal. We'd already brought dampness into the cabin every time we'd clambered in wearing our wet weather gear. A little fine spray was no problem at all.

Suddenly, the nose of *The Nutilus* dipped downwards. We were diving into another trough of a wave.

'Waaa...'

It was too late. Water poured into the cabin. I immediately closed the top hatch to stop the flow, but the damage had been done. About a bucket of water had entered the cabin.

I locked the top hatch and assessed the situation. Water was everywhere, soaking the mattress cover and running all over the cabin floor. I clambered to the front of the cabin and exchanged looks with Mark and Steve that didn't need accompanying words. It had happened before and it would probably happen again.

They drew the oars in as I passed the mattress out to them. It would never dry in the cabin; the humidity was too high. Images of sleepless shifts on a damp bed swam around my brain. Getting enough rest was hard enough, but trying to sleep on a wet mattress would be beyond uncomfortable.

I began mopping up the water in the cabin. The wet, hard cabin floor dug into my knees, as if I needed a reminder of what a nice comfortable dry mattress was like.

I sat in the cabin looking out at our bedding being held by Mark and Steve on deck. I sat there, annoyed at myself. Fuming. If only I'd have anticipated the movement of the boat better. I stared at the fuel cell in disgust. It hissed as it continued to spit exhaust fumes into the cabin. I couldn't help imagining that it was enjoying our fruitless shenanigans.

With not much else to do but wait while the mattress dried, I idly stared out at the guys on deck. I was conscious the mattress was in an even more vulnerable position. Hopefully, it wouldn't get soaked again.

I averted my eyes to the water maker on my left. The tube diameter looked like the right fit for the fuel cell exhaust. We had metres of the tube and we didn't need it. Would this really work?

I grabbed the escape knife next to the cabin hatch, cut off a section, and shoved it onto the hot fuel cell tube. It fitted!

I grinned as I opened the top hatch, just slightly, to vent the cabin. Maybe I could just leave it open and risk some water getting in. It seemed to be fine, so I routed the adapted exhaust pipe out through the narrow gap.

Free at last, I leant back on the hard cabin floor. My body ached. My head pounded. I was more tired than when I'd crawled into the cabin after rowing.

The mattress was starting to dry, and my time off the oars was running down. I'd be back out on deck soon.

```
09:13 Emily:
Good progress overnight! You are at the exact
location Oarstruck were at 48 hours ago, and
they are 120nm ahead. Continue like this and
you'll be one day behind at halfway and overtake
at 3/4 of the way!

14:05 Emily:
2038nm to Antigua. See if you can get to under
```

2000 by the end of the day! Only 4nm off overtaking Damian. You should do that before the next update at 4pm!

18:02 Jon:
Awesome, I'm just refreshing now but takes a while! We're hoping we're in a good position as we are slightly south of Oarstruck so may have better wind. Damian is bossing it! He's such a machine! We are doing the whole of Harry Potter from start to finish, currently at the end of the Tri-Wizard Tournament. What have you been up to today?

18:11 Emily:
Awesome, I didn't realise you could see where the other teams are. You look like you're in a really good position at the moment. Quite jealous of the HP!

21:51 Jon:
Nah, we can't, but I got Mum to send through everyone's positions so we can map them out.

# THE SUPER YACHT

## Day 12: December 29th

The ocean shone in every direction as it reflected the sun. It glittered like a sea of scattered diamonds. The water was a turquoise blue against a clear blue sky. The sun flared down on the deck where there was little protection from the elements other than our clothing. The weather had completely died down, and with it, our efforts increased. Flatter seas combined with a searing sun took the difficulty of rowing to another level.

The bigger weather, which our weather router had suggested would hit us, hadn't come to fruition. My hope and anticipation had given way to frustration.

With the sea not lending any help at all, every stroke of the oar was hard and heavy. I felt like my oar was stirring porridge I'd left on the hob for too long, turning from a fluid mixture, to a thick, repulsive mass, impossible to stir.

Monotony had kicked in. The usual ridiculous, superfluous, uplifting conversations didn't distract us, never progressing past the first few exchanges. It was as if our brains were being fully utilised to win this mental battle.

BEEP, BEEP, BEEP! The AIS alarm shrieked. A wailing alien sound against the silent, calm environment. The Automatic Identification System had detected a ship on a collision course with us.

I rushed to the cabin hatch, opened it and burst in, scanning the navigation screen for information, only to learn the name of the ship and that it was on a direct course. I stepped back out on deck, put my hand to my forehead, and stared at the horizon in the direction indicated. The boat gently swayed beneath my feet, as if it was in deep relaxation compared with my frantic state.

I couldn't see anything, just empty ocean in every direction.

Slowly, a white dot appeared on the horizon directly in my line of sight. It gradually increased in size as it progressed closer until we could make out the features of a super yacht.

I snatched the radio in my hand to make contact. No response. We'd been warned about this. There was no guarantee of making radio contact. For larger tankers, it was probable that either the person on deck would be preoccupied elsewhere or, most likely, asleep. Either this or the waves could be higher than our boat and the signal simply wouldn't reach the oncoming ship.

The yacht continued on a direct course to hit us, getting larger and more foreboding by the second. With no radio contact, they wouldn't even know we were there. Maybe no one was on deck after all, and they hadn't even noticed their AIS alarm.

Time was ticking, and with no contact, we decided we'd have to row away from imminent collision. I entered a northerly waypoint. The autohelm adjusted the rudder and steered us against the current.

The heat raged. Our oar strokes were short, rapid, and frantic. Rowing against these flatter, more docile waves was so much harder than anticipated. The current was an unstoppable, slow-moving force marching against us. It felt as if we were turning round in a crowd of people. The force from people slowly moving in the same direction had been unnoticed until turning round. Fighting against the flow was impossible.

The yacht was upon us. I could make out faces on deck, maybe 50 metres away. We eased off the oars. The yacht was on a parallel course to us now.

It turned and then pulled up right next to us. The vast, imposing metal box towered down. On deck were about 20 people, looking relaxed, drinks in hands, music blaring out. This was a party yacht.

'What are you doing?!' they shouted down.

What do you think we're doing, I thought to myself? Rowing this ocean and trying to recover from what we thought was an inevitable collision with your huge, bloody yacht, that's what!

'Rowing the Atlantic!' Dan and I replied in unison.

I couldn't quite believe we were having a conversation with strangers in the middle of the ocean. What a bizarre situation! Only a few minutes ago, this object was the enemy. Now we were talking as if in a pub. They were on a direct course with us simply to say hello.

'Are you having fun?'

Dan and I looked at each other. I imagined their journey to this random spot in the middle of the Atlantic. I guessed it had been very different to our week-and-a-half slog.

'Of course!' I replied.

'Well, we won't keep you. Enjoy your row!'

Just as quickly as they had arrived, the super yacht sped off into the distance.

Relieved and morale-boosted, Dan and I grabbed the oars, the black rubber handles hot from the radiating sun. Our minds had been distracted by the events of the last 20 minutes. The mental battle against the conditions lifted. The usual ridiculous, carefree escapist conversation returned.

On we went, but this time with smiles on our faces.

# Chasing Horizons

07:44 Emily:
You've done 981nm, so close to smashing the 1000 mark! Have you cleaned the boat yet?

15:23 Emily:
1990nm to finish now and level pegging with Damian, who is also on 1990nm, he has a burst of speed every now and then. See if you can overtake by 4pm!

15:38 Jon:
He's such a machine! Love the stats. How are Oarstruck doing?? What's our predicted finish? Bit worried this is going to take forever!

16:04 Emily:
Oarstruck are 1868nm from the finish so about two days ahead of you - 24 44.94N, 29 23.61W Can you compare that to your location? You are going 0.3kn faster at the moment. The winds aren't in your favour today. ETA is into the start of Feb based on current speed. Mum said the wind should be back to pushing you in the right direction on Sunday though, so you'll be able to make up for it then. ETA literally changes all the time, so it's not worth worrying about!

16:11 Emily:
Just spotted you've overtaken Damian! You're 2nm ahead. Next up is Team Remolon, 9nm ahead of you. (He's a professional sailor, which might explain why he's in front of Damian!)

20:40 Emily:
It looks like Carbon Zerow have been on para-anchor all day to clean the boat and do some repairs. They're still a way off at the moment, but if they don't get things fixed, you could overtake sooner than we thought! Another of the Pure fours.

# POWER

## Day 13: December 30th

'Weren't the waves facing the other way before?'

My head bobbed as I fought to stay conscious and focus on the glowing orange navigation display in the darkness. The clock seemed stuck in time the more I stared at it.

It was the early morning graveyard shift. Everything in my body told me to shut down and sleep. My eyelids were heavy weights, slipping uncontrollably down the surface of my eyes, only to bounce up momentarily when I was aware they'd fully closed. I was trying to convince myself that sleep wasn't inevitable, kidding myself that I had some control.

The bluey-black sea and sky merged into one as I struggled to distinguish features that would have been more obvious if I were in a state of alertness. Waves sloshed around, rolling the boat back and forth, rocking it like a baby's cradle. Silence enveloped the deck as we focused all energy on staying upright.

Smack!

I could feel a cold, hard, wet surface against my face. I

looked around. I could see my oar rest centimetres from my face.

It took a moment to realise that I was lying on the deck. I'd fallen asleep at the oars. I dragged myself groggily back onto my seat. I had to carry on rowing.

We were in an odd micro current that added to the immense disorientation. It was as if the sea and my mind had teamed up against me. I was drifting in and out of consciousness, while the sea continued its gentle rocking.

I tried to focus on Dan's question. Were the waves coming at us from a different angle? Confused, I wasn't sure what was right. My mind swam in and out of hazy consciousness. In this state, I didn't know if I was delirious or if we really were off track. Were we going round in circles? Were the waves really the other way? Is the navigation wrong or am I wrong? Disorientation and exhaustion overwhelmed.

I turned back to get Dan's opinion. He'd fallen off his seat again, but was now fully asleep. Having fallen backwards, he lay on the deck with the odd wave splashing on him, unaware and dead to the world.

I was not far off myself. I let him sleep.

The navigation system must be wrong, I decided, so I shut it off and attempted to steer manually. Clasping the wet ropes, which connected to the tiller arm through holes in the cabin walls, I began rowing for a few strokes and then steering a little. I reset the display countless times. The little craft meandered on the screen, drawing a large zigzag, as I constantly adjusted our heading. Yet I was sure we were just going round in circles, sometimes against the waves, sometimes with them. The dark, cold night had my mind.

The sky changed colour as time crept by. The beginnings of a sunrise blossomed. Lighter blues spread across the horizon, then the top of an orange circle began to rise. The temperature increased incrementally and hope flooded my body. Despite understanding the concept of time, I never really believed this shift would end.

I didn't know if we'd made any progress, and it didn't matter. The anticipation of succumbing to gravity, being horizontal and allowed to sleep was tantalising.

The more the sun rose, the more the light restored my mind. Mark and Steve were just clipping in.

'It was a tricky shift,' I mumbled.

Once in the cabin, out of the elements and into safety, I began the washing and eating routine as quickly as my tired hands would allow to get the maximum time asleep.

Tap, tap, tap.

The cabin hatch opened. They'd only been rowing for 20 minutes! It wasn't time to change, surely?

'The current is awful, mate. Let's switch it up and get the power down.'

My mind recoiled. It would mean all four of us taking it in turns at the oars every 30 minutes so that we could push through this turbulent sea. Getting back out into the cold darkness was against everything my body screamed at me, but it was the right thing to do. It would be hard, but it could mean the difference between spinning in circles and making forward progress.

The sun was now up, bringing with it its energy-giving warmth. Sweat ran down my face as I took to the oars once again. My tiredness quelled from the beaming sun and fraught, intense exercise. Still, I craved bed. My quads and arms burnt as I pulled the oars against the tricky current, powering through.

Both power and stroke rate increased, and we maintained that intensity for the 30 minutes. Then a blissful 30-minute break. Then back on. We could only maintain the higher intensity for short periods.

After a few hours of these sprint sessions, the boat seemed to settle. We were out of the strange current.

I collapsed on the mattress; rest was finally here. Time seemed to have shrunk and stretched at the same time. I felt as if I was already halfway through the day, yet it was still the middle night. My mind was a mixed-up blur.

## Chasing Horizons

09:54 Emily:
Morning! Did you know your bearing changed overnight? The last week you've been between 251 and 257, but at 8am you were showing at 269, which is virtually due west.

12:31 Emily:
Back to 250 at the 12pm update, looking much better! Oarstruck look like they have decided that they were too far north so are now at 218 degrees. Looks like that'll just add extra miles. You've done 14nm more than them in the last 24 hours and in a straighter line.

13:12 Jon:
Awesome! We had a few issues in the night. Ended up manual steering but were so tired we were all over the shop. No wind at all at the moment, it's so calm, which makes progress so slow. It's hot too.

14:42 Emily:
You didn't look all over the shop, only a slight change, so we wouldn't have guessed you were manually steering. Watch out for sunstroke if it's hot! Think the winds should pick up soon.

22:42 Jon:
We all got a bit done in by the sun today.

# BROKEN SEAT

## Day 14: December 31st

Darkness surrounded us as we swung and rolled in the turbulent sea. Only the sound of the waves accompanied our rowing. I concentrated on my form, staring at the lit-up deck from the navigation light.

Thud!

The deck hit me hard. Water cascaded down over me. *The Nutilus* swayed in the inky-black sea. I scrambled back to my seat, drenched and disorientated.

Something was wrong. The seat wasn't moving. I looked down. The seat wasn't in line. I assumed a bolt had come loose or something, but looking more closely, it was worse. The entire frame had sheared, and the part that the wheels secured to had completely snapped off. My heart sank as I knew the spares for the seats were right at the bottom of one of the deck hatches. Fixing this in rough seas at night would not be pleasant.

Borrowing Dan's head torch, I dived into the deck hatch head first. The beam from the torch flickered over various objects, lighting them up momentarily as I scavenged around in what felt like a cave. Hauling other parts back over my head and onto the deck, I finally located the spare seat frames and wheels. I jostled my torso out of the hatch, conscious that a wave could fill it up at any moment.

Closing the hatch, I sat back against the jackstay and looked at the piece in my cold, wet hands. I was exhausted, mentally and physically, and not in the mood to replace these parts. I'd lost all motivation.

Waves crashed around in the darkness, the boat rocking gently as silence filled the void. Dan leant on his oars, patiently waiting for me to get going. Repairs at sea, especially at night, were extremely difficult. I knew this and had no motivation whatsoever to get started. The boat rocked sideways, and the jackstay dug into my back.

I huffed again. Maybe I could just sit here forever; staring at the tools glistening in the light of my head torch; hearing the waves lap against the hull; feeling the cool spray on my face. Maybe I could delay the job for all eternity. Maybe this was it and they'd find us weeks from now, floating along in the ocean, me still sat here in my wet weather gear, staring at my tools and a broken seat.

The water on deck glinted in the light. I let out another long sigh.

Dan listened to my mutterings and calmly waited whilst getting hit by the odd wave.

'You've got this,' he said.

He could sense that there was a fine line between me throwing a wobbly and just getting things done.

I looked into his eyes and could feel his support. I wasn't alone in my exhaustion. We were here, we were together, and this needed to get done.

Searching deep within myself for the focus and patience that was seriously lacking, I got on with the seat repair. I needed to get this job done without loose parts getting swallowed by the sea. I swore at every wave that smashed the boat, scattering the tools from wherever I had placed them on the deck. This is the part no one tells you about.

## Chasing Horizons

You don't see this on the promotional videos; the repairs in the middle of the night when the sea is pushing you around like a punch bag; when your fingers are numb from the cold; when your muscles are screaming from the constant strain; when all you want to do is sleep.

After several minutes of frustrating work, the seat was back in position. I ran it forwards and backwards to check it worked and gingerly lifted myself back on. We continued through the night.

```
00:07 Emily:
```
Have any of you been in the water yet? Have you seen any marine life? We've got Storm Dylan this weekend. I'll send him down your way! You've still had a good day compared to the boats around you.

```
09:37 Emily:
```
Awesome night behind the oars. Only 95nm behind Oarstruck now!

```
11:18 Jon:
```
Hey, that's excellent news. I'm not getting used to the nights at all! Other guys seem to be a bit better, but I need my sleep! Haven't been in the water yet sadly. We really need to!

# SUNRISE

## Day 15: January 1st

Bang, bang, bang!

The cabin hatch vibrated, waking me for my shift. It felt as if a pickaxe was being dragged across my brain. The cramped cabin was dimly lit from the blue light emitting from the navigation display, and there was, as always, a sharp humidity in the air.

Bang, bang, bang!

'Five minutes Jon!'

The five-minute warning, I was sure I hadn't fallen asleep after the 10-minute warning!

02:55 the clock read. It was correct. My shift was the 03:00 to 05:00, the worst of the lot, the time where my body craved sleep the most. My brain didn't understand why we had decided to go through the torture of sleep deprivation. The cumulative effect of the two-hour shifts meant that my already fuzzy head pounded when being woken. A trance-like state overtook that felt like an instant insane hangover whilst my brain struggled to get a grasp of basic cognitive functions.

I'd already wasted a minute trying to orientate myself. Four minutes remained to ready myself for the shift.

This shift was the worst. I felt I could just about make it through every other hour of the night, but between 03:00 and 05:00 my brain needed to shut down and I had no control over it. I was powerless. I couldn't fight against the circadian rhythm; the millions of years of evolution with the sun. I could drag my body onto the deck though, even if my mind wasn't functioning.

I sat down, grabbed the oars, and began. Cold air struck my face like a slap. Stunted conversation took place as Dan and I struggled to wake up. Our otherwise vacant bodies were moving automatically in a rowing action, but nothing more.

Time passed at a glacial pace. Darkness seemed infinite. But there was hope in the back of my mind. The sun would rise at the end of this shift.

A faint glow emerged on the horizon, making our surroundings more visible than before. It was still dark, but we could now make out the waves once more. The character of the sea was more tangible and the horizon now a clear line in the dim light. Slowly, a deep orange crest peaked out from the horizon, adding more warmth and light. The circular edge of the sun shimmered and blurred against the sea, making the line between them hard to distinguish. Darkness was being hunted down and banished.

A full disc now welcomed us into the day, as the sun had crept above the horizon. Pastel colours flooded the sky; pinks, oranges and yellows against a hazy light blue morning. The sea turned a lighter, less fearsome blue. As the sun rose, we gained a new lease of life, warming us like a raging pub fire after a long walk in the rain. Relief poured into my body. My soul felt like it was being replenished. With the sun, we were warmer, dryer, and felt safer. Everything would be ok.

My muscles relaxed. My brain felt different too, like I'd had an injection of caffeine. The sun had literally woken me up, as if it had taken away a portion of the sleep I required, lifting me out of the dark early morning hours. It wasn't long before I was too hot, frantically stripping off layers, revelling in this moment of warmth.

We looked at each other and stopped rowing. Grabbing a chocolate bar, we took a minute to sit and gaze at the sunrise as the boat bobbed peacefully on the waves. An uninterrupted view of the sun across a vast empty sea welcomed us.

Very few people experience this. Very few people are lost in the peace of a sunrise in the middle of an ocean. I must remember this feeling, I thought.

I'd never seen sunrises as consistently spectacular as this. It seemed like every day was more stunning than the last; as if I was seeing the sunrise for the first time each morning. It was mine to own and to savour, and it felt good. The life-giving sun gave us an unparalleled boost to morale. It was the anti-dote to our exhaustion.

The environment had been transformed, and with it, so had we. We grabbed the oars with enthusiasm. Daft conversation filled the air, and we attacked the remainder of this sunrise shift.

```
09:46 Emily:
You're smashing it! You've overtaken Team
Remolon and Oceanomads since yesterday! (You
overtook Oceanomads before and they snuck past,
those pesky Aussies!) Team Noble next, who are
11nm away. Then you'll be past all the Pure
pairs. I feel sorry for Atlantic Ladies. They
are so far back now.

10:57 Emily:
The last 24 hours are the best you have done so
far. Have you been working harder or is it
because of the wind?
```

# SHOCK

## Day 16: January 2nd

My eyes tracked a bird in the sky. It had been darting around in close proximity for days. It swooped right down next to the boat and then up into the sky again before sitting and resting on the waves. I hadn't expected to see birds out at sea. They lunged and whizzed round the undulating waves like fighter jets through the hills. I was grateful for this, but also eager for more wildlife. Apparently, Steve and Mark had seen an entire swordfish leap out of the water!

Steve and Mark were on their off-shift, but awake and chatting to everyone as we slowly rowed.

'Shall we get in then and give the boat a clean?' asked Mark, 20 minutes before they were due on deck.

We needed to give the hull a scrub. The waves were medium-sized, not too big, just consistent hills in one direction but they were pretty quick waves. I was eager to jump in at some point, but today there was no way I would get in. It was far too choppy for me.

Without hesitation, the other two were on deck, getting ready to take the plunge.

# Chasing Horizons

*The Nutilus* glided up and down the waves as they sat on the side of the boat, their feet dangling in the water.

'Remember to take some pictures of us!' Steve said.

Splash!

There was no dithering. They were both in.

Without holding onto the boat, Steve was immediately flung back a couple of feet alongside the boat. He grabbed frantically at the side, fingers scrabbling along the hull.

Eventually, he got hold of the grab line that looped around the boat. We looked down at him from the deck. Steve's eyes were wide, his face radiating shock.

The current was stronger than any of us had appreciated. We'd been only a metre away from the sea at all times while on deck, yet we had no idea what its temperament was like. If they had jumped in without their harness strapped onto the jackstay, they would have been swept away in an instance, unable to swim back. Although the sea was nothing as violent as we'd experienced before, it was a stark reminder of the force of the ocean.

```
12:07 Emily:
Hello there! You're doing so well, even better
than yesterday! ETA at this speed is Sun 28th
Jan which is 6 weeks total.

13:36 Jon:
Just had another huge wave come into the cabin,
which was pretty depressing. In other news,
Steve and Mark went into the water this morning!
How are you doing today?

13:45 Emily:
Have you had time to write much? Bad news about
the wave, is the equipment ok?

17:59 Jon:
Not that much time, but I'm making a note of any
major things that happen. I usually write
something every other day. Thing is, not much
happens for long periods!
```

## Chasing Horizons

```
18:17 Emily:
You're smashing it on the tracker, faster each
time I look!

20:20 Emily:
You've just hit 70nm in the last 24 hours! Yes!
```

# THE TROPICS

## Day 17: January 3rd

09:52 Emily:
Super speedy again overnight!

11:01 Jon:
Hey, having charging issues with my phone, same as Mark's, but mine hasn't totally packed in yet thankfully! Hopefully, we can keep this pace up! If we do 65nm a day, we finish in 43 days.

12:58 Emily:
Still a fab pace, only 1nm off Team Noble now.

22:41 Jon:
We are gaining on Oarstruck which is good. I think it's day 17. So eager for Antigua. Just going to eat everything and sleep.

23:13 Emily:
You're in the tropics now. According to Google, the surface temperature is at least 26.5 degrees. That's lovely and warm for swimming! Oarstruck and Carbon Zero have headed further south. Not sure if that's a good plan?

The weather had changed today. The sea was calmer, more settled, like a lumpy blue mattress as far as the eye could see. We'd headed south and were now in the tropics. The temperature had risen drastically. The sun, having been our life-giving force for so long, now draining our energy with its unrelenting rays.

The midday shift had been hard fought, the heat inescapable and the ocean flat and energy sapping. It had dragged. Each oar stroke lasted longer than it should have. It felt like the next stroke required more energy and the water felt denser. Sweat ran into my eyes and down my nose. My hands stung from gripping the oars. This was such a contrast to the earlier weather we'd had. Back then I couldn't imagine coming off shift in anything but wet weather clothing. The faff of taking off all that soaking wet gear in a tiny cabin whilst shattered, was huge. Now I was in shorts and a t-shirt and simply fell on the cabin mattress.

Finally, the shift ended. I shut the cabin hatch. Every muscle in my body instantly relaxed. A sloshing, watery noise accompanied my rest, along with a wobble of the cabin and an overwhelming sense of quiet. I had switched to the forward cabin and what a difference it made. In comparison, the aft cabin was unbearable, being unable to lie down properly, condemned to the heat of the fuel cell and noise of the drive unit, whilst feeling the brunt of the waves.

Now that we were in a hotter environment, we had devised a shift pattern rotating round the two cabins to ensure it was fair and everyone got a decent rest. I was dreading being back in the aft cabin, but for the moment at least, I could enjoy the relative luxury of the forward cabin.

I rotated my head to the side. The Tupperware of now hydrated porridge waited and rested against the spare oars that span the length of the cabin. The plastic of the Tupperware box had a slight orange tarnish on it from absorbing tomato sauce from the other dehydrated meals.

I loved the porridge we had with us. The other guys weren't so keen, so I'd been exchanging other meals for it and now had a few days' worth of the stuff.

I hadn't anticipated this beforehand, but since being so tired at sea, I hated chewing. It took time and effort. Porridge had a fair few calories and was easy to get down your neck. This was way more important than just convenience; we were all under-eating and weight was being shed.

After virtually drinking the porridge, I washed it down with some Ultra-Fuel. At the beginning I hated the powered drink, but now my tastes had changed and I loved the convenience of the nutritionally balanced food supplement. The vanilla tasted just like custard, and again, there was little chewing or faff.

I cracked the top hatch and cabin hatch slightly. A cool breeze rushed through, along with sunlight. The reflective foil on the hatches kept the worst of the heat out compared to the direct sunlight outside. I immediately succumbed to lying down, fully stretched out, and stared at the roof of the cabin. My view wobbling slightly as my body rocked with the movement of the boat.

My mind drifted to what was going on back home and what we'd do when we got back. Three weeks in and I was craving home comforts. I got lost in an imagined alternative seeing family, friends, countryside, trees, fruit and Chinese takeaway.

It was important to remember why we were here on a tiny boat in the middle of the Atlantic. I wanted to see as much of the world as possible in the time I had, and challenge myself to see what I was capable of. I knew that, as soon as I stepped off the boat and the journey was over, I would crave the excitement again and would look for my next challenge.

My mind continued to wonder. I felt relaxed. Switching to the forward cabin was a mental game changer. It was like a different expedition up here. The constant hum of the drive unit had been replaced by the peace of the ocean gently washing against the hull. Relaxing was easy. It was as if I was on a mini spa break compared to the noisy furnace of the aft cabin. I closed my eyes and drifted into a peaceful sleep.

# DEBT

## Day 18: January 4th

My hand rotated the latch on the cabin hatch as I secured myself in for my off-shift. At last, I could let my aching limbs relax for two hours. My hands grasped the netting on the side of the cabin as I subconsciously reached for my phone. My tired fingers got caught up like a fish in a net, but eventually I held the phone in front of my tired eyes.

```
08:16 Emily:
You've done 1180nm. You are past Team Noble now!
Next up are the Pure fours. Oarstruck first!

20:20 Emily:
Hey! How is it going? Do you still need money
to ship the boat back or is that sorted now? Do
you want me to start a 'Get Nuts Home' campaign
or whatever you want to call it?
```

It was true. Despite being on the expedition after two years of work, we still needed to do admin and more fundraising. Even when we reached land, it wouldn't be over. We needed to sell the boat.

Before embarking on the expedition, we'd looked at various options, such as storing *The Nutilus* in Antigua, to sell remotely from our homes in the UK. Back in La Gomera, I'd asked Team Antigua if they knew of anyone with some land where we could store our boat while we tried to sell it. Although trying to help, nothing came of it. We thought of selling it to a team immediately after the race, but this was unlikely to happen. With storage costs starting a few days after we touched land, we needed to ship it back.

We had shipping reserved, but didn't have the money to pay for it. Once we sold the boat, we would have some cash flow, but that might not happen for some time. We were rowing into the unknown.

Despite this, I wasn't as hyped up by it all as I had been on land. Back then, I'd had a driving force, a deadline, a target to aim for. Out here on the ocean, I only had one focus: get to the finish line. I didn't even want to discuss this over text despite this being a massive help and certainly needed. I selfishly wanted the texts as escapism, not as a reality check.

We were having the expedition of our lives and had worked hard to get here. In this environment, I felt so far removed from finances. They seemed much less important than the immediacy of battling the waves, huge weather, and simply enjoying the moment. I knew it was important. I had just lost the enormous sense of urgency to solve the problem. The expedition, in some ways, was the easy bit. The bit in the middle of two great big financial admin book-stops.

Before we left, we had set up a crowdfunding page. People could pledge anything from a few pounds for a shout out on social media or clothing such as buffs, to larger sums for tailored speeches. We thought that a smaller specific campaign for this labelled 'Getting Us Home' may be more tangible and have more emotional connection.

Unfortunately, this had got nowhere. The word wasn't spreading. I don't think people realised we were struggling.

## Chasing Horizons

The reality was we were massively in debt and in the middle of the sea, sat on our only asset. If we couldn't get the boat back, it was looking like we would have to sink into more debt.

22:44 Jon:
Yeah, we really need to do this. I changed our crowdfunding to this before we left and sent a few emails about it. I'll speak to the guys and we can sort it out tomorrow. Thanks though. Massive help!

22:46 Jon:
1200nm completed. Smash!! We celebrated with the surprise halfway chocolate, even though not quite halfway yet! Glad you made me put that on board in La Gomera. Eager to get halfway now. Hopefully, it will be in the next few days, then the countdown begins.

# FAILED INTERVIEW

## Day 19: January 5th

The cabin walls surrounded me as I lay on my stomach, scuffling along towards the nose of the boat. With every inch I moved, my surroundings closed like a funnel. To the side and in front was spare equipment. There was room to store things in the front of the boat, and it helped to weigh it down so the boat stayed level.

My arms stretched out in front of me with the para-anchor. We'd been at sea for a while and eaten a lot of food. This had affected the trim of the boat; the stern was now rising out of the water. I shuffled down the forward cabin to shift the para-anchor as close to the front as I could to add some weight. Finally, I dropped it. It felt pretty heavy at this odd angle, and with the closeness of the funnel-like compartment, it was extremely humid.

I turned my head to assess my horizontal backwards retreat as the cabin hatch opened. Dan stuck his head in.

'Ready?' he said, trying to feign enthusiasm.

'Ready.'

Today was the day we had our Bristol Radio interview.

## Chasing Horizons

Our friends and family were looking forward to it and it had taken a lot of organising. Communication home was often slow, and trying to arrange a specific time for something to happen on board was difficult. Apart from the troubles with the signal, it was hard to predict the weather. We never knew what was going to happen.

Steve and Mark continued to row outside. Dan extended the aerial of the sat-phone and pointed it out of the top hatch at the sky. The weather was calm. The hatch was fine being open. Signal was good. This might just work.

We dialled the number and waited.

We needed this. This would bring awareness. A tired voice on the ocean sounds real and brings home the enormity of the task. This phone call might be the piece of the puzzle that leads to a little extra funding that would enable us to bring *The Nutilus* home. Maybe someone would hear the interview and feel moved enough to donate to our crowdfunding campaign.

However, our slumped bodies suggested otherwise. We'd just rowed for two hours and were giving up this off-shift, this prime sleep time, for this interview. We were exhausted, hungry, and tired. The last thing we wanted to do was talk to an upbeat radio DJ on the other side of the world.

We continued waiting.

This wasn't the first time we'd had trouble with arranging this interview and our pessimism had grown. It would mean a huge amount to our friends and families. It would be worth it... if we could get the call to work, that is.

We'd waited long enough. I pressed the hang-up button, and the call ended.

I could only imagine people at home being frustrated. The interview hadn't happened, despite all the efforts that had gone into its organisation. We'd waited a long time, but for whatever reason, it didn't come off. Despite my lack of drive, we genuinely needed this. We had funding issues, and although I didn't want to think about it, it was necessary.

I opened the cabin hatch to tell the guys.

'We rang and waited for an age, but nothing came of it.'
'What?!'

They also felt annoyed. We needed this. All our significant others had worked hard on this one.

Dan and I gave each other a tired glance before climbing into our separate cabins to make the most of the little time left of our off-shift.

```
19:15 Emily:
Ok, just give me the go ahead and any log in
details I need! Is it £6,000 for the shipping?

19:17 Emily:
I forgot about the chocolate! Have you cracked
into the hobnobs yet? You're making such good
progress. Halfway in no time!
```

# INTO THE BLUE

## Day 20: January 6th

The ocean had relaxed into a gently undulating surface of tranquillity, covered by a sky so clear and blue it looked like it could go on forever. *The Nutilus* bobbed around on the waves, softly dipping up and down as it rolled over the ocean. The only sound was the gentle lap of water against the hull and the singing of the Jetboil as it reached optimum temperature. We had taken a break from rowing to get some admin done, so the guys sat on deck idly chatting and drinking coffee. It was very peaceful.

Or it should have been. I wasn't feeling peaceful at all.

We were three weeks into this expedition, and the bottom of the boat needed cleaning. Gooseneck barnacles grew on the hull of the boat and caused unwanted drag. Every time we powered through the water, the collection of crustaceans on the underside of *The Nutilus* were acting like a mass of tiny brakes slowing us down.

I was eager to get into the sea. It was now calm after all, and I had volunteered to be the next in after Steve and Mark's attempt a few days before.

But the reality was now before me, a reality that involved leaving the safety of our boat for the first time, in the middle of the ocean. Although tied on, I had to physically let go, and rely on the harness. My eagerness for a swim had vanished. It all felt very different. Eager curiosity stripped back. I felt scared.

My rigid, quivering body edged towards the side of the boat, naked other than my harness. I grabbed the jackstay with both hands and stepped over it, the lip on the side of the deck digging into my feet. I stayed there, motionless, anticipating some sort of courage that resolutely failed to materialise. I didn't know why I was so nervous; I was tied on and the jackstays had more than proved themselves in some extreme conditions. The weather was completely calm, but my heart was racing a mile a minute.

Finally, I had no choice. I crouched down and placed one foot forward and plunged in, my fingers keeping a firm grip on the side of the boat. My pulse raced as warm water rushed around my body. My senses heightened as I clung to the boat. I could taste the salt on my lips, hear the thump of the waves against the hull, feel the water running across my legs and chest, and it all felt amplified somehow.

After a minute or two, I became acclimatised, and my breathing relaxed. I felt my pulse slow, and I settled. I became used to the rhythm of the boat and sea riding up and down. Everything was fine.

For the first time, I could stretch out and felt refreshed from the confines of the boat. My body was liberated from the cocooned cabin. I extended my limbs to their full reach, my joints creaking with the unusual movement. It felt amazing to have so much freedom of movement.

I put my head under water and stared into the depths of the beautifully clear turquoise water. I stared at my feet dangling above the abyss. Below them were miles of water. I could see clearly for quite some way, maybe 10 metres, and then suddenly, darkness.

I was swimming in the middle of the Atlantic Ocean!

What a thing this was!

Steve passed me the scuba mask and scraper. With no lanyard to tie it to my hand, I clasped the scraper with a firm grip. I didn't want to lose it to the depths.

There was work to be done. Like an astronaut tethered to their spacecraft during a spacewalk, I dived under the boat. The hull was covered in barnacles, taking advantage of *The Nutilus'* smooth surface as somewhere to make a home. I began scraping, digging the scraper into the crack between the shells and the hull, but I could only manage a couple of swipes before rushing up for air.

I removed my harness from the jackstay and had both clips now on the grab line to get to the extremes of the boat. After scraping the forward end, I traversed to the aft.

At the back of the boat, I was out of sight from the guys on deck. I suddenly felt isolated. I could have been out here all on my own. I looked towards the horizon. There was nothing between me and land, except miles and miles of ocean. I felt tiny.

The aft cabin slapped on the water with a fearsome whack. As the boat rose, the rear of the cabin went in the air, something I had no idea about when nestled inside the cabin. Then, when the boat reached the trough of the wave, it slammed down on the top of the ocean and continued below the waterline for a foot or more, depending on the wave. I had to time my scraping with the ebb and flow of the sea, being careful to get my breathing right.

With the scraping done, I took advantage of the moment to wash my hair and body. I would be salty after, but it was more refreshing than wet wipes and alcohol gel. For the first time in three weeks, I'd felt water on my skin. Not the pummelling we regularly received at the oars, but a full body soak. It was the best spa treatment in the world. My brain felt cleansed.

Drawing in a deep breath, I took a final look directly down at my feet and the dark depths below, trying my hardest to take a mental picture of this unique experience.

I grabbed the jackstay and landed one foot on the grab line. I hauled myself up onto our island in the middle of the ocean, tipping the boat slightly. With my other foot now on the boat, I rotated over the jackstay. Not having thought this manoeuvre through, and unable to master my limbs as they shook, searching for stability, I fell on deck, nearly landing on Dan. I lay there for a minute, soaked, naked, as the guys just stared at me in disbelief.

'We've been out at sea for three weeks now, Jon, and you still haven't found your sea legs!' said Steve.

They were all laughing, but I didn't care. Getting in the water in the middle of the Atlantic Ocean was one of the best experiences of my life. Hopefully, *The Nutilus* would be incrementally quicker for it.

```
18:49 Jon:
Yeah, halfway is 225nm away and then we have
1500 to go! Bit of a slower day today but
still making good ground!
```

# THE NUTILUS

## Day 21: January 7th

*The Nutilus* edged us closer to our distant destination. Cruising steadily and strong like a tank, gaining experience with every wave. We had now been acquainted for three weeks. Before embarking on this journey, neither of us, the human crew nor the plucky little boat, had any ocean rowing experience. We were both growing and settling into the long expedition. Just as I was battling with sleep deprivation and finding my sea legs, *The Nutilus* also had some quirks to overcome.

I sat in the forward rowing position and grabbed my right oar. Through experience, I knew it didn't sit square in the gate. It was something that, at first, seemed manageable. But after three weeks of adjusting our rowing technique, it had become an issue. Forcing the oar into position and then holding it for two hours was difficult. The extra muscles that were being used to hold the oar square ached. Intense concentration was needed to keep position. When concentration lapsed or there was a mistimed stroke, the oar would get dragged into the sea and rock the entire boat, upsetting the rhythm of both rowers.

Looking down the deck, I saw our skewed rowing positions. The rowing seat and foot plate were closer together in the aft position than in the forward position. The footplates were a problem because they weren't perpendicular to the centre channel of the deck, so our legs were pushing at an angle. We had ditched these footplates and rowed with our feet on the deck, whilst we made some makeshift plates to push against.

Between the two rowing positions, in the centre of the boat, sat the life raft. The life raft was heavy and so it made sense to have it located here to create optimum balance and trim. It was also in between the two rowers, meaning that, in the event of a capsize, it was easily accessible. This position had been a last-minute change and not thought through. Water filled this section of the boat and the life raft swam in a pool, making it even heavier and sodden.

Finally, my eye was drawn to the aft cabin. The dungeon of the boat. Entry to the cabin was via the perilous cabin hatch. When the aft rower was at the catch, the most forward point of the rowing action, they were closest to the aft cabin. The opened cabin hatch would clash with their knees. At night, this had caused countless shrieks during shift changeover. The cabin hatch would be flung into their kneecaps just as they threw their weight at full force into the stroke. Aft position changeovers were always a dance that could go either way.

On top of the aft cabin was a huge cut out rectangular shape. Once thought of as a suitable position for the life raft, this abandoned cut out had unforeseen repercussions. A large section of the cabin was completely unusable due to the area of lowered roof. Consequently, the living space was so much smaller than it needed to be.

The water maker ran through the aft cabin, making it the only place to fill water bottles. Looking at the boat now, I wondered why they hadn't placed a pipe in each cabin, allowing easy access to water with less disturbance to the person in the aft cabin.

We were learning to live with *The Nutilus'* abnormalities. Things which should have been designed out, or noticed and fixed on practice rows - that hadn't occurred. Despite these oddities, *The Nutilus* felt formidable and resilient, and was settling into the ocean, just as we were. We'd battled through some rough conditions together.

I looked back at the boat. Despite all the issues, I felt a certain pride. Even with regular knockdowns, where *The Nutilus* would roll on its side and throw us across the deck, we hadn't capsized.

A Pure boat, although slower, was so far proving to be a fine choice. With a deeper keel, we were steadier. I wondered how many times we would have capsized without the deep keel in the conditions we had faced. There had been so many other teams in peril, but although it had been a rocky ride, we remained unscathed.

Nothing had gone so terribly wrong that it had put our crossing in jeopardy.

Nothing so far.

# FUNGAL INFECTION

## Day 22: January 8th

*The Nutilus* rocked unexpectedly. My backside slipped sideways on my seat. I grimaced as pain rocketed across my nether regions.

It had become progressively worse over the last few days. The sea was relatively calm, but even the small waves that slapped up against the boat were causing issues. Despite the glorious sunshine, I felt that the day was tarnished. The blue sky above with the cotton wool clouds did nothing to lighten my mood. I put the oars down. Enough was enough. I had to do something.

Over the last few days, I'd developed an infection in the groin area. Because of our close proximity, the whole team had become infected, but I was most definitely patient zero. At first, a few unsuspecting white spots appeared, but they rapidly flourished into a dense population. The constantly wet, damp, humid conditions were a breeding ground for this stuff. It was having a great time. I was not.

We'd all been trying various coping strategies and updating each other on progress, but so far, nothing worked consistently. We didn't know what the infection was, but we knew we wanted it clean, so we tried alcohol gel. As I slapped it on to the infected area, a warm sting warmed my groin. The heat steadily rose in intensity to an all-consuming burning sensation, as if my groin was on fire. After a minute or two, the pain subsided.

Another small wave side-swiped *The Nutilus*, and pain once again raced across my groin. I screamed in agony and frustration.

That was it! I'd had enough! The current remedies weren't working, and it was time for drastic measures.

I stood up, grabbed the escape knife from the side of the hatch and started hacking at my foam seat. I jabbed the blade at the seat with unconcealed aggression, whittling away a cut out at the front. The hope was that it would eradicate the friction and ease the pain. In fact, we'd been advised to take foam seats with us for this very situation. Our individually labelled seats were now individualised further, each with its own specific carving.

Laying the knife aside, I gingerly sat down. The pain was still there! The instantaneous burning sensation returned with a vengeance. There was no escaping it. Even the simple act of sitting down caused unbelievable discomfort. Staying still was fine, but any slight movement caused clothing to brush against the rash. Undressing had become even more difficult as my shorts stuck to the infected areas. Doing anything was painful. Manoeuvring around was such a challenge.

I applied varying amounts of Sudocrem and Vaseline. My shorts were heavy with a thick, never-drying layer of Vaseline, which clung to my inner thighs. It was painful to wear anything from the waist downwards. We didn't know what would cure it, or if we'd even be able to cure it this far from land. The only sensible suggestion was the rejuvenating power of fresh air.

We were all naked from this point on.

Free at last, I grabbed the sat-phone and called the doctor.

'It's a fungal infection. It's common, painful and there's not much you can do about it. It's the environment you're in. Take some painkillers and the anti-fungal tablets in your med kit. It will clear up in 24 hours after arriving on land.'

I understood the concept. The rash needed fresh air, to be kept dry and washed in clean water. But this was something I didn't want to hear. Clean water was in short supply and our boat was perpetually damp. There was no relief in sight.

My shift ended. I scrabbled into the forward cabin, crawled down to the end, and retrieved the medical kit. In it were endless sachets of tablets that scattered onto the deck the moment I opened the box. I rifled through them, searching for the ones I'd been prescribed.

I gathered together all the relevant medication. It fitted in one hand.

'Lads, we've got a problem.,' I said tentatively. 'There are not enough pain killers for one each per day, and the athlete's foot medication won't last long either.'

```
08:39 Emily:
Wight Lightning just shared the photo of you in
the cabin with this message: 'Nuts Over The
Atlantic, whilst retired from the race, are
still continuing to Antigua and are doing
amazingly well. Admiration goes out to them.
Great effort.' Everyone is behind you! :)

12:16 Emily:
You're only 49nm behind Oarstruck now! At this
rate, you'll overtake them next week!

13:21 Jon:
Yeah, hope so! Cleaning the boat seems to have
worked, though. So hot in the cabins, on the
verge of melting. Not long until Antigua now :)

13:32 Emily:
Haha, I think they might be fishing too! That's
good about the clean boat!
```

20:20 Jon:
Keep doing maths on when we will get there. Unfortunately, we haven't had the best winds in the last few days, so progress hasn't been the best, which is frustrating. Really don't want to this to drag to 50 days! 45 would be ideal.

# FLAT WAVES

## Day 23: January 9th

Catch and drive.

Everywhere I looked, the sea was flat, a mass of blue that reflected the heat of the sun like a mirror. The air was still, as if our surroundings had frozen in time. It was far from freezing, though. The temperature had risen and sweat dripped down my face as I got lost in the never-ending pattern of rowing.

Catch and drive. We craved the cooler, bigger weather we had at the start of the trip. The enormous waves not only gave us speed but meant the seascape constantly changed and made the entire experience exciting and vivid. We had now passed through the mountain ranges, through the foothills, and had stepped into the desert.

Catch and drive. Monotony had struck. This shift seemed to have no beginning or end. I glanced around in all directions, wistfully hoping to see something other than the flat, glistening, heat-saturated ocean before me. Without getting thrown around and battling the waves, it became a mental struggle.

Catch and drive. I stared at the navigation screen, willing the numbers to get smaller, the distance left to the waypoint to have decreased. With nothing distracting me from the rowing, I focused on the miles we were slowly ticking off. Metre by metre. One by one.

Salty sweat ran into my eyes, mixing with sun cream, making them itch and sting. Tired muscles resisted another stroke but were too entrenched in repetition to stop.

Catch and drive. We had somehow edged our way across the Atlantic and were close to halfway. I couldn't grasp how we'd actually managed this. With each day rolling into one and no landmarks to gauge the distance, it didn't feel like we'd travelled that far. And yet the miles had reduced each day. Apart from the heat of the tropical sun, the numbers and charts on the screen were our only marker of the distance we'd covered. We'd been at sea for 23 days, unbelievably. I felt like this was our life, as if this would never end. It certainly felt like that in the heat.

Catch and drive. I stared at the miles to the waypoint. 63 to go. We'd be there in around a day at this rate. With the weather still, this was our only marker of progress, the only thing changing in the motionless sea.

We rested the oars, time to call our weather router. Steve opened the hatch and grabbed the phone. I was grateful for the rest. The boat seemed to sit perfectly still on the flat ocean, as if we'd parked up.

A new waypoint, a slightly different heading but virtually the same, 430nm away. My heart sank. My arbitrary reward system based on waypoints meant I felt as if we'd failed. In reality, we were never supposed to reach them. They were far enough away for us to head in that direction until we needed to change direction, with a new waypoint. Yet I couldn't help but wish we'd make one, at least once, and see the distance run down to zero.

I grabbed the oars, my sweaty hands slipped on the handle as I attempted to get back into the rhythm. My muscles ached, but psychological relief crept in. As we approached halfway, it meant that we would soon be closer to Antigua than La Gomera. In this half, we didn't have to learn about the boat or get used to the sea, so it should, in theory, be easier.

Catch and drive.

```
20:06 Emily:
You're 50nm away from the halfway point!
Huzzah!! You've done 57nm in the last 24 hours,
so should hit it tomorrow afternoon! Smashing
it! Super proud of you!!

20:46 Jon:
Yeah, should hit it tomorrow! Conditions have
been so slow the last few days. It's a bit
annoying. Our next way point is 430nm away.
Conditions should remain the same, so will be a
slow seven days. Then it should be fast and
we'll boss it to Antigua in two weeks!

21:03 Emily:
You're consistently faster than Oarstruck, so
doing something right!
```

# WATER MAKER

## Day 24: January 10th

I sat in the aft cabin, hatch open, light and heat flooding in. I'd just finished my rowing shift and was settling into my rest. I grabbed my water bottle, put the water maker pipe in, and pressed the start button on the control board.

Nothing.

I tried again. Still, nothing happened.

Not the water maker! We can't lose the water maker!

I did a cursory check of the water maker motor and wiring; nothing seemed unusual and still it didn't work. Surely, such a vital bit of equipment couldn't be broken. If this went, we'd be down to hand pumping water. The manual water maker made one litre of water with one hour of pumping, with no breaks. Water would be at the expense of sleep.

It had to be something simple. Only a couple of days ago, a pipe had come off the water maker itself. Luckily, it didn't take too long to diagnose, and I ended up going head first into the deck hatch to stick it back on. My waist upwards above deck, with my legs flailing around in the air, like a failing handstand attempt. It was awkward to get to anything in that hatch and anything significant needed your head in there. The humidity of the enclosed area and head-rush from being upside down was unbearable. I didn't want that again.

'The water maker seems to be playing up!' I said to Mark, who was rowing in the aft position.

'Not again!'

I checked again for anything obvious. My eye ran along the length of wire from the motor to the control board. There was nothing wrong. I had a check of the motor and it didn't seem damaged. All the connections were in place. Mark checked the water maker itself in the hatch, and again, everything seemed connected.

'Maybe we should check the continuity?' I suggested.

Steve, who was in the forward rowing position, delved into the deck hatch next to him to retrieve the tools.

'If we're stopping, I'll switch out the wheels on my seat,' he said.

The bearings in the seat would rust and disintegrate from the salt. The wheels then wobbled and grated with every movement of the seat. Changing them made the world of difference. The seat would, once again, travel in a straight, firm line, smoothly and quietly. Steve took the tools he needed and passed the bag to Mark and then to me.

I unzipped the canvas bag and sighed. Why had we chosen a canvas bag? In La Gomera, we'd noticed most teams had a sealed box. Ours, being canvas, had let water in and the tools were already pretty rusty. The drill chuck was looking quite sorry for itself.

I took the multimeter out, unravelled the wires and checked the electrics. All was ok. Holding my breath, I pressed the start button.

EERRRR

The water maker was back on! What a relief. Perhaps it had just overheated. It had been out for half an hour, and with nothing obviously wrong, I was worrying. Hand pumping water in this heat would have led to a rather gruelling second half of the expedition.

00:33 Jon:
They've caught a tuna!? Nice! Well, I caught a flying fish tonight, a proper sized one. It flapped a lot, then it went straight back in the water! Nights are hell, to be honest. I can't describe how bad they are! But it will be over soon! Things are much better when the sun comes up.

07:10 Emily:
You'll have slightly longer days as you go further south. What about the stars at night, impressive?

20:30 Jon:
Stars at night are incredible, actually. Shame they won't come out in photos. Antigua couldn't come fast enough! Still slow going here, but hopefully, only for a few more days.

21:31 Emily:
Yes, smashed halfway!!! Closest bit of land now is Antigua! I bet you'll never see the sky like that again. Must be amazing!

# RADIO INTERVIEW

## Day 25: January 11th

Another night was drawing to a close, and I'd just stopped rowing 10 minutes before the end of our shift. I drew in the oars and leant against the jackstay. Steve and Mark sat perched on the sides of the deck right by the aft hatch. Inside the cabin, just at the end of his off-shift, was Dan. The sun hadn't risen yet, and I felt the chill.

Our radio interview, that had taken some arranging, would be within a few minutes, and we'd all huddled together in anticipation. Mark grabbed the sat-phone, extended the aerial and dialled the number, then waited on hold for our slot.

Interviewer, 'We go live now to a small boat where we're joined by Mark, Steve, Dan, and Jon. Hello mid-Atlantic. Can you paint a picture of what it's like? Has the sun even come up yet where you are?'

Mark, 'It hasn't come up, no. It's been a pretty cold night and the sea is calm. We've seen the stars, and it's been pretty peaceful, to be honest.'

# Chasing Horizons

Interviewer, 'You've said in your reports that you've had 40-foot waves, you've had calm days, you've had all kinds of weather, your progress has been fast and slow.'

Mark, 'We had a week or so of really quick 40-foot waves and started making great progress and since then it's been up and down. We've had days being battered from the side and made no distance. We've had days where we've made 80 miles, and we've had days and nights like last night, which have been incredible. We feel very privileged to be here.'

Interviewer, 'Thanks Mark. Now going to Jon Lakin, one of the four-man crew. Jon, are you currently rowing or resting?'

Jon, 'The whole crew are actually resting at the moment. It's a welcome break in our regime, so thanks!'

Interviewer, 'You guys still sound chipper. There was a little laugh there. Is it possible that what you're doing is completely bonkers and totally amazing at the same time? Do you still feel that's the case, or are you now in another state, another place?'

Jon, 'Yeah, definitely in another state! We're constantly in this battle between an epic gruelling challenge, and at the same time, there are moments that are absolutely fantastic. You get to see the clear skies at night, that few people will ever see.'

Interviewer, 'I was going to ask you about the money you've raised so far for Movember. I was also thinking about asking you about the bilge pump you've lost, but the question we really want to ask is, is anyone on board a Bristol City fan?'

Jon, 'I'll pass you to Dan.'

Interviewer, 'Hi Dan! How are you?'

Dan, 'Very well, thank you. I've just had my two-hour break.'

Interviewer, 'You sound fresh.'

Dan, 'Exactly.'

Interviewer, 'Are you a Bristol City fan?'

Dan, 'Yeah, yeah.'

Interviewer, 'They're doing rather well, just to let you know.'

Dan, 'The season's been going very well for them so far, and it's nice to see a Bristol team really cracking on and showing what we can do.'

Interviewer, 'Let's talk about what you can do, though, Dan. You've had problems with the boat. One wave, it says here, flung Jon to the side of the boat and the metal brackets under the seat broke off. What you're doing is dangerous, isn't it?'

Dan, 'Incredibly dangerous, and we've also had some real problems with our jackstays, the safety lines which we clip onto, and obviously, if they go then we go, and well, that's it. It's scary. So, it's very dangerous. We're doing all we can to keep it together to get across to Antigua.'

Interviewer, 'We'd like to ask how people can support you, because what you're doing is amazing. You've raised over £20,000 for Movember already. We want people to give more money to the cause, especially when you still need £6,000 to ship the boat back from Antigua. How can people help you?'

Dan, 'People can help by visiting our social media. You'll find our crowdfunding page, so people can donate to get the boat back. If they want to help raise money for Movember, they can go onto our website and through that they can donate.'

Interviewer, 'Thanks Dan, now let's go to Steve. Steve, what's next on the agenda for today?'

Steve, 'Well, after this call, we'll do a shift change over and get back to rowing. Although cold, the sea is really tranquil, so it should be a cracking shift, and distract from the tiredness.'

Interviewer, 'How is the tiredness? Is that the hardest bit, because two hours on, two hours off sounds pretty intense?'

Steve, 'It's not great! But we've all got more used to it

and there's not that much time to question things, and the highs make it worth it.'

Interviewer, 'Thanks guys, I won't delay you any more. Best of luck, and I wish you a safe passage to Antigua!'

Steve looked up at us and then pressed hang-up on the sat-phone. It was done! Finally, the radio interview had been completed, and it was a success. We'd even managed to plug our crowdfunding campaign.

```
20:19 Emily:
Awesome interview on the radio this morning. So
good to hear your voice.
```

# LOST ELECTRICALS

## Day 26: January 12th

I put my food down to the side of the cabin and laid back on the mattress. Every muscle relaxed as the weight of my body seemed to plunge deeper into the soft foam. I was tired, but I also wanted to text Emily.

My phone was stashed in the netting, where it had been stuffed in the last mad rush while changing shift. I grabbed it and tried to unlock it. It was out of battery.

'Dammit!'

I relied upon these small moments for boosts of mental strength and sanity. It was my window into normality; a reminder of the world we'd left behind and the one we would return to. Texting people off the boat was not only helpful when I was low, but it was just great speaking to people who weren't on the expedition. It lifted my spirits.

I grabbed the phone and plugged it into the USB charging point. Communications home were now getting harder. We hadn't had much luck with phones. One phone had been dropped in the ocean, and the other two weren't charging properly, perhaps due to the humidity. This meant we were down to my phone being shared between the four of us. On top of this, the charging points didn't seem to work that well either.

There were also logistical issues. The signal in the forward cabin was terrible, and besides, all communication ran through the aft cabin anyway. This meant that if you wanted to send or receive a message, you could only do it from the aft cabin. Combined with the shift rotation between cabins, it could be a job to sync texting home with being in the right cabin at the same time with a phone that was charged.

On many occasions, I was just too exhausted to text. Even though I promised myself I'd text back on the next shift, sleep was almost always the greater priority. I'd end up texting three or four shifts later. Time seemed to play tricks. It felt as if I had texted just a short while ago but, in reality, it had been ages since. Time out on the ocean seemed to stand still, and yet also be infinite. It was as if I had lost all sense of real-time.

Even when I managed to grab the phone, everyone could see everyone else's messages in the common inbox. I found this hard. Unable to confide my feelings, I kept a lot of things locked up in my head that otherwise would have been more useful coming out in a healthy venting session. Stored in my brain at sea, the negative thoughts stewed somewhat. I felt I couldn't raise all my grievances with the other lads. I didn't want to be the one bringing down the morale.

Conversations home lacked depth. My ability to express my worries and concerns, frustrations and annoyances took place only at the surface level, and this had a compounding effect. My introspection got worse, and the petty frustrations grew out of all proportions. I hadn't realised how much I leant on the emotional support of loved ones for strength, until now.

With the phone now on charge, my mind drifted to earlier in the day. The sea was flat and tranquil, barely a ripple for miles around. Steve, rowing in the aft position, spotted a group of sparkling fish of multiple colours, skimming beneath the surface right next to the boat.

'Jon! Get the GoPro! Quick!'

I enthusiastically handed out the tiny camera. We'd attached it to a hollow metal rod so that, if it fell in the water, it would float and we could retrieve it. Unfortunately, neither of us noticed the loose screw.

Steve grinned as he lowered the GoPro towards the water. This would be an incredible shot to show our family just what it was like rowing across the middle of the Atlantic.

Suddenly, with an undramatic plop, the GoPro slid off the end of the metal pole. Steve and I watched open-mouthed, as it began its descent into the deep, deep water.

Fortunately, the camera didn't have any footage on, but it was a distinct loss. Without it, we'd have even fewer ways of recording our journey. It wasn't anyone's fault, but it was extremely frustrating. We weren't having much luck with electrics.

I glanced at my phone again as it sat in the webbing above my bed. At last, it had some juice. I grabbed a handful of dried nuts and hurriedly texted before I succumbed to the palpable, overwhelming urge to sleep.

```
00:04 Emily:
Only 25nm behind Oarstruck now! Could overtake
as early as Sunday! Hope the night-time rowing
is ok tonight.

17:49 Jon:
The night wasn't great, but another day done!
I'm pleased we're over halfway now.

18:06 Jon:
Just heard as well that, when we get to our
southerly waypoint, the winds won't be very
good. This could take longer than expected! It's
so infuriating!!
```

## Chasing Horizons

```
18:36 Emily:
Yes, just keep crossing off the days. That's
what I'm doing!
```

# FLOOD

## Day 27: January 13th

The shift had been passing without incident, just idle chat, the pulling of the oars and relatively calm weather. I rowed in the forward position; my right arm fixed in place because of the odd oar setup.

Crack!

I fell back heavily in my seat, the fungal infection once again sending searing pain through my groin. In front of me, Mark leant on his oars and breathed a sigh.

'What was that?'

I pushed myself carefully to the side and inspected the port rowing gate. It had snapped, fatigued through constant wear.

I cursed. We had already been through a couple of rowing gates, and only had a few spares left. My heart sank. My muscles ached. I just didn't have the motivation to fix it.

If it was possible, it needed to be repaired instead of replaced with a new one. We didn't know how many more would break.

'You alright, buddy?' asked Mark.

'Yeah,' I sighed. 'I've got this.'

I poked my head into the deck hatch to retrieve the tool kit and spares, and grumbled as I set up.

On the horizon, a well-defined column of grey rain channelled down from the sky, in contrast to the light blue surroundings. Around me, the wind changed character to a more threatening nature, as if warming up for something special. A squall was heading for us. It was Sod's Law. The sea knew I was about to fix something off the side of the boat and was preparing to give me its worst. It was the perfect opportunity to drop things into the sea.

The waves picked up, white spray wisped off the crests, and *The Nutilus* jolted around violently. Our environment had changed drastically in an instant.

I grabbed the hand drill and began attempting to make a hole through the gate to put a cable tie through and secure it.

With nothing to push against, the gate flexed even more. The rusted drill slipped precariously in my hands, the handle damp with seawater as the boat rocked with the sea, which lapped at the gate.

We were now side-on, making the ups and downs more violent. I wedged my foot against the lip on the side of the boat and tried hard to steady myself whilst leaning far over the side.

Rain pelted down so fast I could hardly see. It hit the ocean as if someone was shooting it with a machine gun. The sea looked like it was boiling, as turbulent white water overtook. Dropping either the drill, spanner, nuts or washers felt inevitable. Everything was grey, hazy, wet, and chaotic. I tried desperately to maintain my position, but with my body weight shifting all over the place, it made everything difficult.

The drill wasn't going to work. It was too rusted and too difficult to get through the thick plastic. I wrapped cable ties round the gate and drew them tight until it felt secure.

At the exact moment that I sat back in my seat, exhausted, battered, and fed up, the unpredictable ocean changed. The sun came out. Heat evaporated water from our bare skin. Calm was restored, as if Mother Nature knew that we had finished the repair.

I looked at Mark, who just shook his head in bemused astonishment.

Shortly after we had got back on the oars, the sun left us again and the weather changed once more. The chaos returned. Rain bombarded the deck, and the unpredictable waves shook us around once more. We kept our heads down and rowed.

Time was nearly up. Soon, we would switch shifts, and although it would be a horrible changeover for Steve and Dan, I was looking forward to the cabin.

They came out, grimaced at the conditions, and clipped on. I grabbed the cabin hatch, and with muscles depleted, I collapsed in the cabin. Now horizontal, I rocked from side to side, listening to waves crashing on the cabin, and wondering what on earth it was like out there.

Boom! A wave thundered into the boat, shuddering through my soul. The noise was like having a bucket on your head and getting whacked by a baseball bat. I could instantly feel that this one was different. The force felt prolonged and on another scale. *The Nutilus* was instantaneously shunted forwards and down, by what felt quite some way. The monstrous wave crashed on top of us, tonnes of water plunged onto the boat, forcing it downwards into the sea, with an almighty rage.

Suddenly, a torrent of water came flooding through the cabin hatch. I had neglected to shut it properly. I'd left it half-open, hoping to relieve some of the humidity in the cabin. But with the hatch open, there was nothing to stop the sea from rushing into the cabin. If the cabin was filled with water, this half of the boat would sink for sure!

The boat rotated sideways, and water began flooding in from the top and side of the hatch.

I launched myself across the tiny cabin. Frantically, I grabbed the handle of the hatch, pulling it towards me, desperately trying to shut it. Cold water gushed over my hands.

In my panic, I'd forgotten to rotate the handle. Water continued to pour in. This was it. This is when we capsize and it was all my fault!

Finally, the influx of water ceased. The boat rotated the other way, the torrent stopped, and the boat rose to the surface.

It lasted for what seemed to be an eternity, but must have been around 10 seconds.

Without hesitation, I immediately flung the cabin hatch wide open. The guys were still on deck. I had to see if they were alright.

'Are you ok?!'

They looked like they'd seen a ghost. They just sat there completely drenched and motionless.

'The boat... it was... half of it was under the water. Your cabin was... it was just gone!'

It was usual for the aft cabin to get pummelled by waves, but we'd not experienced a complete submersion of half of the boat before. The brothers seemed a little shell-shocked but, to their credit, they got back to rowing, regardless of the waves and weather.

I ducked back into the cabin to assess the damage.

To say the cabin was wet would have been an understatement. Water was everywhere, and a tonne of it was in the footwell. Having had our bilge pump accidentally go overboard in the first week, I spent the next two hours bailing out the cabin using a 500ml water bottle. Everything was soaked, but we were alive.

```
18:12 Emily:
Hey, how's your day? So, I hear you know that
the race was won today. Don't let it get you
down. You are doing it in a Pure rowing boat and
you won't regret that when you look back after
the finish. The videos from Antigua look
incredible, and I just can't wait to see you
cross that finish line. It's going to be sooo
good!! You're picking up speed again and clocking
up the miles!
```

21:33 Jon:
Needed this! When we get our next waypoint, we get three days of more slow weather, which is frustrating! Luckily, the current should be stronger tonight, so we should make some ground. It's annoying we didn't leave on the correct date, as the other Pures apart from Oarstruck are getting great winds! Just found your Xmas card!

21:37 Jon:
Oh, we're also down to using my phone! Everyone else's has broken!

21:43 Emily:
You might get better winds later on and catch the other Pures. You never know! I wondered if you'd opened that card! Not good about the phones! Hopefully yours holds up for the rest of the trip!

# FLYING FISH

## Day 28: January 14th

A jovial atmosphere accompanied Dan and I as we rowed through a balmy afternoon. As usual, discussions revolved around what was the best cake or if you could only have five items in a fry up, what would they be. We conjured up a myriad of plans for what we would do when we met up back home. The chatter of a podcast gently added to the background noise of the relatively calm sea. Waves were around us but very small, only about the same height as the boat, gently pushing us along, enough to keep us entertained. At least today it wasn't completely flat and sweltering like it had been.

'Hey! Look at that!' said Dan, breaking through a conversation about who would play us in a film of our adventure.

I followed his pointed finger towards the horizon, where a spectacular rainbow arced across a clear blue sky. The ends of the rainbow dipped into the sea, with each colour clearly defined. I don't think I'd ever seen such a perfect rainbow. It was magnificent.

A few glistening flying fish leapt out of the sea nearby. They reached a couple of metres above the water before they extended their fins and glided effortlessly for what seemed forever. Every time they reached a wave, they looked as if they would fall straight into it, however they almost always flew over the crest and kept going.

The silvery, aeronautical fish were a constant companion over the next few days, darting out of the sea like arrows in a medieval battle. We'd been told about this from previous ocean rowers, but nothing could have prepared us for how frequently they flung themselves into the air. The big ones were around a foot in length, with precariously thin wings, translucent and gossamer-thin.

Looking back, I find it hard to believe how quickly I became normalised to this bizarre scene. I didn't think twice about seeing a few fish darting through the air and gliding across the waves, sometimes for hundreds of metres.

Whack!

Dan's stroke timed impeccably with a flying fish and smashed it for six. Connecting perfectly with his oar, he sent the poor fish flying several metres into the distance.

'Oops!' said Dan, genuinely guilty for his accidental fish battering.

```
15:52 Emily:
Hey! How's Sunday? You've rowed over 1,800nm
now. That's further than the distance between
my house and Marrakech! Pretty impressive!!
Looks like you'll soon smash the 1,000nm-to-go
mark! It will go quickly, so make the most of
it. No matter how bad it might seem now, in a
few years' time, you might be sitting behind a
desk wishing you were back out there!

21:26 Jon:
Yeah, cannot wait to get under 1,000nm to go or
within a week of Antigua. I think you're right
about the desk thing, but it's definitely a type
2 fun!
```

```
22:04 Emily:
So how is boat life? The Duty Officer said you
have sore rears! How is your body holding up?
```

# NIGHT THEATRE

## Day 29: January 15th

The ink black sky draped above us like a stage curtain about to open. The humid air was warmer than usual and the calm sea rippled and glinted in the moonlight. My legs pushed wearily against the footplate and gently eased the boat through the waves. To my left was an electric blue shimmer, about a metre under the water.

Two dorado fish had been keeping us company for about a week now and danced around our oars. They were more visible at night as they seemed to glow in the water. Dazzling turquoises leapt off their metre-long bodies. Easily keeping up with the boat, they would then speed off and hunt in the open sea, then come back and glide next to us. They were both so agile compared to *The Nutilus*, accelerating effortlessly and darting around. We were a cumbersome whale in comparison.

Thud!

I couldn't see it, but I was now familiar with this sound at night. Another flying fish had hit the cabin. Flying fish continued to litter the air throughout the darkness. There would often be a second thud if the fish landed on deck, followed by a chaotic flapping. But there was only a splash, so I knew this one had gone straight back into the water.

I wondered what it must be like to be gliding along effortlessly without a care in the world, and then to suddenly smash into an alien craft the size of a house. Dazed from the impact, I expected it would land back in the water, feeling a little under the weather and extremely confused. It was probably why these two dorados were keeping us company, for the easy pickings from disorientated flying fish.

Flying fish frequently landed on deck or hit the cabin during shifts. It was always tricky to get them back in the sea as they flapped around. One of us would have to stop rowing, clamber over the seats and grab the distressed fish. Touching its slimy skin as little as possible, we would fling the fish over the side where, more than likely, it became a tasty midnight snack for the hungry dorados. It was never a pleasant experience.

Whack!

Something smacked into my neck. I lifted my arm to my skin and felt a horrid slimy texture. I sniffed the gooey fluid between my fingers. It stank.

'Eugh!'

'What's up?' asked Mark.

I looked down between my feet where a fish was madly flapping around on the deck.

'I've been hit by a flying fish!'

I stood up to scoop it up back into the ocean. The fish launched into a huge panicky flap as soon as I got near. I carefully picked it up by its wings and flung it over the side.

I was glad I got that one. Some days, there would be an unbearable stench emanating from the life raft. After careful searching, we'd find a dead flying fish that had got stuck there unnoticed, and was slowly decomposing. Chunks of dead fish would float around in the hollowed-out compartment.

Having rescued the fish overboard, I glanced out towards the open sea. A zap of light filled the darkness for a fraction of a second. The entire surface of the ocean lit up, transformed from black to a dark blue, revealing the contours of the water as far as I could see. Distant cloud formations became clear for an instant as another lightning fork lanced across the sky.

My eyes were glued to the horizon. The air remained still. There was no wind or rain where we were, only the incredible view. Flash after flash continued as we watched from our unique viewing point. With the electric blue of the dorados dancing around our oars, we sat and watched the duration of the storm.

```
13:57 Jon:
Yeah, it's painful to sit. I have more of a
groin issue! Haha! How did you know? Lots of
heavy rain lately. How's home?

20:10 Emily:
There are updates on all the teams on FB every
week or so. Sore groin doesn't sound good!

21:13 Emily:
How much weight do you think you've lost?

22:31 Jon:
Is it that obvious already?? Our weather update
wasn't great again. Going to be slow for a while
and think it may be a 50-dayer.

22:35 Jon:
Also saw dorados today, which was awesome. And
we found a squid on our solar panel.

22:47 Emily:
You look thinner in the latest photos. Good
beard too! Oarstruck have covered three miles
more than you in the last 24 hours, which is
unusual.
```

22:58 Emily:
Dorados sound awesome! Just googled them. I had no idea there are so many different types of blue fish!

# NEW MOON

## Day 30: January 16th

Black soot painted the roof of the sky, and with it were more stars than I could possibly comprehend. Wherever I looked, stars littered the sky. A cool breeze made me aware of the exposed skin on my hands and face. A new moon was here, and with the lunar disk not detracting from the view, the stars were at their finest.

The night was still and tranquil. I stood up, stretching my legs and back, cracking my sore joints. My gaze was drawn to the endless sky above. It felt different, closer almost. With no light, the usual feeling of separation from the sky and earth seemed to have blurred; the stars and sky and sea felt closer.

I stared at single points, clusters of bright stars in the inky blackness, and then tried to gaze everywhere, my eyes trying to gorge on the view as if they'd been starved. Looking at the stars was like trying to look at all the grains of sand on a beach all at once. Countless fairy lights on the ceiling against an intensely dark, infinite backdrop. I felt as if I was looking at a photo of space. It was magnificent.

## Chasing Horizons

I leant into the cabin, careful not to wake Dan, and switched off our navigation light. I closed the hatch and leant against the cabin. As my eyes adjusted to the darkness, I could see even more stars. A hazy, thick line ran across the sky, full of pinks, purples and blues. The Milky Way. I was in a trance, pacified by sight. I just gazed, lost, forgetting I was even on a boat, as the stars filled every corner of my eye's view. In the background, Stephen Fry's voice was still updating us on the goings on of Harry Potter, which only added to the moment.

Earlier on, we had agreed to have one of our emergency rations each day as a morale booster. We had plenty of dehydrated food leftover to get us to the end of the crossing, even if we had a massive disaster on the way. Our emergency rations were sticky toffee pudding. We had nothing like this in our daily ration packs. It was a massive treat.

I cracked open the deck hatch, leant over, and delved in. The wet packaging felt slimy as my hand searched for the pudding in the dark. Ripping it open I was immediately struck by the sweet smell. Without hesitation, I devoured the contents.

Taste buds danced in excitement as the saccharine sweet flavours swirled around my mouth. The sponge itself was like a brick but the sauce was sticky and sumptuous. My veins were pulsating with the sugar-rush, almost feeling dizzy with the dopamine. It was a welcome change to the monotony of dehydrated meals, to say the very least. We saved these wonderful delights for the worst shift, the early hours of the morning. The sweet treats would be a reward for the first hour of rowing.

What a different experience this was to the terror of the night, back at the start, when we were blind to the towering cliffs of waves that were about to strike. The ocean was calm, and I was relaxed, gorging on sticky toffee pudding whilst star gazing.

I stared up. The only objects moving were shooting stars and satellites. If I knew more, I'd be able to identify the constellations and name the planets. I'd be able to spot the International Space Station that glistened somewhere in the sky above our heads. I might have even been able to tell you the names of the astronauts aboard the space station at this very moment. I wish I could have. These were most likely the closest human beings to us in the entire universe.

Despite this distant proximity to the human race, I didn't feel isolated. I wasn't lonely out on the waves. Maybe it would have been different if I was completing this row as a solo.

In that moment, the incredible galaxy spread out in the cosmos simply captivated me. I didn't want to be anywhere else in the world.

```
14:43 Jon:
The dorados followed us all night, though, which
was cool. How's your day going??

14:50 Emily:
Wow, that is cool about the dorados! Sure they
weren't dolphins? ;) You do seem to have slowed
down quite a bit. Hate to tell you that Team
Noble have overtaken you and they are further
south. You might have some better winds coming
though? Atlantic Campaigns have released some
ETAs. They haven't said yours yet, but the
others are faster than the ones on the tracker,
so that's positive!

21:09 Emily:
Sorry if the last message got you down. You're
still doing really well. Just think positive
and keep on rowing. Atlantic Campaigns said
it's too early to confirm your ETA and said,
'Your boys are rowing machines!' I'm not
making this up. You're doing really well! Dig
deep and keep pushing on!
```

# AUTOHELM DISASTER

## Day 31: January 17th

Dark, weary, and wet, I eagerly crawled into the aft cabin for some rest. It had been a tough night shift. The boat was regularly side-on, and I was ready to lie down after a battle of a shift. I said bye to Steve, closed the cabin hatch behind me and collapsed on the mattress.

'Jon!' Steve shouted, banging on the cabin hatch. 'We need to turn the boat. We're side-on and it's impossible!'

Not now, please! I just wanted to rest. But if I didn't help, they would be stuck side-on all shift, and I would roll around in the cabin, failing to get to sleep.

I dragged myself back off the comfortable mattress, and opened the cabin hatch so I could communicate with Steve and Dan, who were at the oars. The boat rocked violently under me as wave after wave smashed at the sides. As I looked over to the guys, I could see they were rowing with one oar, desperately trying to turn the boat. As we plummeted into the trough of the wave, they dug with their oars, like spades into mud, and heaved with all their might. Reaching the peak of the wave, their oars sprung from the black cement of the ocean with intense force, water spraying through the beam of their head torches.

The guys hurried me on. Swaying precariously with the boat, I grabbed the tiller.

Something was wrong. It felt different in my hand. I effortlessly swung it forwards and backwards. It had no resistance whatsoever.

Wide awake now, my eyes traced each part to check for immediate issues. Then I saw it.

The rod which pushed and pulled the tiller had completely sheared! My heart sank and my muscles tensed. This wouldn't be a simple fix.

'It's snapped!' I shouted from the cabin.

'What?! What's snapped?!'

'Get in here and look!'

Steve drew his oar in and poked his head through the cabin hatch. His expression immediately sank. We had a problem.

Having been advised on what to bring with us, we'd bought a spare autohelm but our boat builder had failed to bring it to La Gomera. Here we were, mid-Atlantic, broken steering, knowing we had forked out hundreds of pounds for a spare and no way to get it.

The intense darkness was giving way to a dim early morning light, and Mark and Dan had made their way to the aft cabin. We discussed our options.

'What do we do then?' Dan said with a heavy sigh. 'What are our options?'

'We could manually steer,' I suggested. 'Lots of other teams do.'

'Do you mean that one of the rowing pair would steer and row?'

'That's not going to be easy. We'll get knocked around a lot by the sea. The autohelm has done a great job of keeping us on a direct course so far,' said Mark.

'Maybe,' I said. 'Or we could have one person steering while the other two row.'

Even as I said it, I knew this would be a terrible option. It would mean we'd need three people awake all the time. We'd have to rearrange our routine to three hours on, one hour off. This would leave only one hour for rest for the fourth member, not a prospect that appealed to any of us.

'What about fixing it?' asked Steve.

It was definitely an option, but fixing it would require a lot of work, with no guarantee of success.

'But the push rod is now shorter from the break, so we'd have to move the drive unit,' I said anxiously.

'Yeah', agreed Dan, 'and then we'd have to reattach the rod to the tiller, and then recalibrate the autohelm. Easier said than done.'

'Let's have a go at fixing it,' said Mark. 'If we can get it fixed, it'll be better in the long run.'

To do this, we had to figure out a new position for the drive unit and, as a consequence, the fuel cell. All equipment would need new mounting holes, which meant drilling more holes through the cabin deck. Space was tight. Moving things around would further compromise our space, so every inch mattered. Our measurements, however, were rough. Accuracy was impossible

Steve pulled out the toolbox and passed the hand drill down a chain of hands to the aft cabin. I took the drill and attempted the first hole. It was like hand-drilling into concrete. The drill bit just spun. I applied more pressure but only made the smallest of indent. Thud, a wave hit the boat and my sweaty hands slipped off the drill. Our unpredictable world never stopped moving. Repairs were never easy. I picked up the drill, another wave hit, my head jolted into the corner of the navigation screen. This repair would be relentless.

'Jon, we don't even have the right size drill bit, do we?!'

I looked at Mark, exasperated.

He was right. After checking every spare on the boat, we'd realised this in La Gomera and failed to hunt down a drill bit for this unlikely scenario. We'd need another way to make the holes.

'Let's try the needle file and just slowly file them out.'

We began shifts on filing out 16-millimetre mounting holes in the carbon fibre. Sweat dripped off my nose as the exertion continued. The heat felt like a new level of intensity. The cabin was always hot, but without a break to get out on deck, it was unbearable.

Filing through carbon fibre meant that loft-insulation-like fibres and dust went everywhere. This, when combined with the moisture of the cabin, stuck to every surface. The incredibly itchy fibres clung to my sweaty skin like iron filings to a magnet. It was all over our bedding, rendering it useless. I grabbed a water bottle and poured it over my skin. Nothing would get this stuff off.

Exhausted, I sat back for a moment's rest. The cabin was chaos. Equipment was everywhere. Tools littered the cabin floor. The drive unit and fuel cell rocked on our mattress to the undulating waves. The broken push rod abandoned like a dead snake in the corner. All other daily items such as food were rammed as far back as possible. The only space in the messy, hot cabin was where I was sitting, and this was being used in rotation with Mark to continue the repair.

Hours slipped by. We were working long into the night, filing holes with a hacksaw blade. Steve and Dan had stoically stayed on deck. They were manually steering to keep us roughly on track, trying to avoid the side-on position that would make us more susceptible to rolling. Night shifts were always brutal, but they were out there on their own, without a break. Resourcefully, they'd tied screwdrivers to the steering rope to use as makeshift handles. Instead of rowing, which would have kept them warm, they used their oars to keep us in a straight line. They were getting pounded by waves and carrying on, regardless.

Eventually, between us, Mark and I got the holes cut. We mounted the drive unit and fuel cell in their new positions and attached the shortened rod to the tiller. It was time to recalibrate. Our eyes glued to its every movement.

The navigation system sent its signal to the drive unit, setting the cable and push rod in motion. But the rod kept pushing beyond its maximum, causing the drive unit to pull away from the deck, bending the deck in the process. Once the deck had bent a certain amount, the cable spilt out of the drive unit, twisting so much that it was at risk of snapping the rod again. We had no idea why it was going over its maximum. We couldn't afford the rod to snap again. All that work for nothing!

After rowing two hours on, two hours off for around a month, this 24-hour period of intense, relentless work had left us all physically and mentally exhausted. My body was now covered in carbon fibre, which itched my skin like a terrible rash. My muscles ached and the tiredness in my brain made it difficult to think. And after all this, we hadn't even fixed it.

We sat in a heavy, dejected silence, taking in the enormity of our problem. There was no other choice. We'd have to revert to the three hours on, one hour off shift pattern that none of us had wanted in the first place. We were already exhausted and the thought of even less sleep over the coming weeks was devastating.

The future did not look good.

# MANUAL STEERING

## Day 32: January 18th

I sat down in the cabin, and stared at the navigation screen. In my hands were the screwdrivers tied to the steering ropes which I'd routed through the cabin hatch. The bright navigation screen felt harsh on my tired eyes. It was night, hard at the best of times. My torso rocked gently with the boat and the cabin was eerily quiet without the autohelm. The waves were now a clearer background sound without having to fight against the noisy drive unit.

The autohelm had us accustomed to very accurate navigation with very little variance from the waypoint line. With waves constantly battering the boat, veering off path would now happen frequently. We experimented with locking off the steering, setting it on a course, and manual steering, but we doubted the accuracy.

Perhaps we were getting obsessed with the details. Going off course by these small margins, ultimately, didn't matter, as long as we were going in roughly the right direction across this vast ocean. But for us, it felt like it mattered. We had become used to the autohelm. We craved the accuracy. It felt like any energy spent even slightly off course, was energy wasted.

With no entertainment other than keeping on the correct path, I stared at the image of the boat on the navigation screen. I desperately tried to keep it within the boundaries and remain on track. It was like an odd computer game. Without being able to see outside, the screen was all I had to steer from within the cabin, and it was my entire world for one hour in every four. But it was clear when it was wrong. The waves rocked the boat violently.

The boat swayed to the right. I pulled the rope and corrected it, but as usual with an overcorrection, it went over centre and again I corrected it. Constant, miniscule adjustments were needed.

My eyelids were beyond heavy. I was desperate to stay awake, knowing every mistake I made affected my friends on deck. Every careful adjustment I made to the steering would prevent them going round in meandering sweeps, or getting smashed by side-on waves. I daren't lie down. But I'd found Steve lying down on his steering shift; maybe I could too. I lifted my legs out of the footwell and assumed a horizontal position. I could still see the screen; I could still steer.

'You're asleep, Jon!' Steve blurted out, whilst thrusting open the cabin hatch.

'No, I'm not!' I responded, lifting my head.

'You bloody were! We keep going off course and ending up side-on!'

'You lay down while you steered!' I replied defensively, jerking myself bolt upright.

'Yeah, but I didn't fall asleep.'

I had no idea I had fallen asleep. I genuinely thought I'd been awake the entire time. I looked at the screen. We were clearly in the wrong position. The little image of the boat was perpendicular to our heading.

Steve gave his usual forgiving smile and quickly went back out to re-join Dan at the oars. I desperately tried to refocus, but I kept thinking about Steve and Dan. I'd let them battle the sea side-on to the waves, without having control of steering. I'd let my teammates, my friends, suffer out in the cold darkness while I was dozing away in the cabin's warmth. I felt terrible.

This shift pattern was already proving brutal and unsustainable… at least for me.

# MISINFORMATION

## Day 33: January 19th

I sat on the side of the boat, clipped in, excited. The sea was serene, a restful lapping noise of the water gently rocked the boat. Everyone was on deck making use of the hour down-time we'd given ourselves to get some admin done. With our weather router promising stronger winds in the coming days, we were advised it may be our last opportunity to clean the boat before Antigua. With the prospect of improving the speed of the boat, it was an opportunity not to be missed.

I had readily volunteered for the swim. With two dorados swimming around the boat, I think the others were less than keen. I didn't mind. They didn't look too menacing.

I looked out at the horizon. A vast blue awaited. However far I could see, it would be deeper beneath my feet. It was strange to think that the horizon was closer than the seabed beneath us. It almost felt like we were floating in space.

This time, I was eager to jump in. All fear had dissipated

since the first experience and I couldn't wait to stretch out and wash off in the warm water.

I plunged in. My body felt instantly refreshed and liberated. A deep turquoise blue surrounded me. I was immediately relieved to be off the boat in a different environment and able to stretch my body out.

I looked down at my feet, this time knowing what to expect. It was still amazing to see my feet dangling into a few miles of deep ocean.

Turning my head sideways, I saw a dorado. I was now in its habitat, looking it in the eye. It swam around the boat, but never came too close to me, staying a wary few metres away. This was the first time I'd seen one from this angle, only now could I see they were a yellow colour underneath.

I tracked it as it swam by. To my amazement, there were not two but five dorados round our boat and they were pretty big. We hadn't realised this many had been around us; we simply had not seen them all at once.

I grabbed the scraper, took a deep breath, and dived under the boat. Leading with the scraper, I went straight for the centre of the hull and got stuck in. Directly in my line of sight, on the other side of the boat, a dorado swam around and lurked close by.

Boat scraped, I took the opportunity to wash in the ocean and then clambered, typically ungraciously, back on board.

With all that had happened in the last couple of days, none of us had had a chance to text home to let everyone know we were alright; our pace had dropped dramatically. It must have been worrying to watch our slow progress on the tracker, wondering what was going on in the middle of the ocean?

```
07:58 Mum to Emily:
Hi Emily wondered if you'd heard anything
recently? I sent a text a while ago but haven't
had a reply. They're going very slowly. Hoping
all is OK.
```

## Chasing Horizons

```
08:02 Emily to Mum:
```
Hi, the last message I received was on Wednesday evening. I think they might be having problems with the phone.

```
10:12 Emily to Mum:
```
Becky had a call from Steve last night. She said he was a bit down and shattered. Apparently, the rudder is broken, so that's why they are going slow. No one can sleep as they are constantly trying to fix it and someone has to steer all the time. Doesn't sound good, I hope they can fix it.

```
10:42 Mum to Emily:
```
Oh no……

```
10:43 Emily to Mum:
```
She said he was talking about drilling holes and cutting poles, so think they are trying to fix it

```
12:04 Mum to Emily:
```
OK!

The unfortunately mistaken news that our rudder had broken meant Dad was in a huge state of worry and panic. In La Gomera, he had been instrumental in installing the rudder. We wouldn't have managed it without him.

It must have been awful at home, not being able to help, living by four-hour updates on the tracker, wondering if it was something we did in La Gomera that had caused this. Luckily, it wasn't the case at all. I had no idea this sense of worry was going on at home. Although the new regime was gruelling, we were ok.

```
15:10 Jon:
```
Been a tough day. Our autohelm broke. We worked round the clock to fix it with no sleep. So onto hand steering and a fairly brutal regime. How are you?

```
15:15 Emily:
```
Sounds brutal. Is there any research I can do

online to help or have you tried everything? Probably a stupid question, but can you tie it in place and take the risk that you might not go in a completely straight line but at least you can have two people on the oars? Hope you're ok, so good to hear from you.


15:21 Emily to Mum:
Sounds like it's the autohelm, not the rudder, so that isn't as bad!

15:34 Mum to Emily:
Thank goodness it's not the actual rudder.

15:35 Emily to Mum:
Yes, I know!

# WHALES

## Day 34: January 20th

I crawled out of the cabin and onto the deck, desperate for more than one hour off the oars, dearly missing the two hours on, two hours off regime from earlier in the row. I never thought I'd miss that. At the time, I thought it was gruelling, but it was paradise compared to the exhaustion we were feeling now. Dan was already in his seat, getting his water bottle ready and strapping his feet in. I traversed the short couple of steps to my position and eased myself slowly down to minimise aggravation to the more sensitive areas of my body. The sun beamed down. The sea was calm, and the beginning of our shift was subdued.

Three hours on, one hour off was not sitting well with me. I was desperately trying to come up with another solution. We all were. If we couldn't fix the autohelm, then we needed to work out another shift pattern, as the current regime was not sustainable.

We were all constantly doing mental arithmetic to work it out. We wanted a solution that enabled a two-hour break every so often to get a decent sleep. But finding the right balance between rowing, steering and sleeping between all four of us in a 24-hour period was difficult given the sleep deprivation. We couldn't work out the maths.

We also wanted one person dedicated to steering most of the time. We had tried locking off the steering and keeping a waypoint, as other people did, but when we tried this, the boat seemed to meander. We wanted to maintain our direct, straight line.

It was obsessing me. I was going mad trying to work this out, but my brain was just not functioning. Worst of all, I knew that if I was at home, having had a good night's sleep, I was sure I could have cracked it.

Eventually, I thought I'd worked it out, and I explained it to Dan.

His forehead crinkled in confusion.

'Mate, that doesn't quite add up,' he said. 'But don't worry. I'm working on it.'

He gave me his usual reassuring grin.

Later in the day, he came out of the cabin and announced that he had worked it out. Steve and I listened intently. The maths worked. It comprised of sprint sessions lasting 30 minutes with rotating partners, and then two hours on, two hours off, and then back to more sprints.

This was helpful at night, too. Doing sprints was far more preferable to the long, drawn-out shifts where we relentlessly battled the enveloping sleep. We reasoned that as long as we approached them as sprints and put the power down, we could make up for the additional lost time in changeovers.

It sounded like a plan.

However, this sounded like the plan I had explained to him just a few hours earlier. It infuriated me, a ridiculous reaction, I know. It must have been the sleep deprivation, but I was disproportionately angry. A dark cloud of fury raged around my mind.

'This was my idea!' I ranted to Steve once Dan had

ducked back inside the aft cabin.

Steve said nothing, but had a warm smile as he sat on deck looking at me.

'It's ridiculous!' I continued from inside the cabin.

I felt tense, unable to let go.

Steve just sat silently listening to my angry ranting, calm, clearly able to see the bigger picture.

'But it was my idea!' I said, blind to reason.

The negative thoughts whirred round in my brain over and over like a terrible storm. The next shift passed and with each stroke of the oar, the thought that I was right cemented itself further into my mixed-up brain, blocking out all sense.

When the shift ended, Steve turned and smiled at me. I wasn't sure if he was just humouring me, or if he agreed and didn't want to speak too loudly. In fact, it took multiple shifts for me to work out that Dan was right all along. Mine wouldn't have worked at all and his was the correct choice. I had to apologise to him now for reacting so poorly.

'I'm sorry about the schedule. You were right. Mine obviously doesn't check out. I'm just finding it difficult to think straight at the moment.'

'That's alright, mate. I knew it wasn't you anyway!' Dan said, slapping me playfully on the shoulder and flashing me one of his winning smiles.

I thought back to some advice we'd been given before the row. The smallest things can blow up into something catastrophic. For several hours I was livid about this tiny, insignificant problem. It was entirely irrational, but in the moment, it felt completely rational. Even if I was right, even if Dan had taken credit for my idea, it didn't matter, as long as we worked together to make the crossing as quickly and as safely as possible.

I was glad we were back to it, working together as a united team. And with this new schedule, I was looking forward to a two-hour rest.

```
09:34 Emily:
You're still going in a super straight line.
Most teams are drifting about. You're back to
being faster than Oarstruck, so catching up
again! What food are you craving?

17:33 Jon:
Awesome! I guess the other teams must be locking
off their steering so they don't have to
constantly adjust it. We are back to rowing so
I'm glad to hear we are quicker! Wind is still
bad but hopefully will pick up tomorrow and
we'll smash it to Antigua. Craving all sorts.
Basically, fresh fruit and anything with sugar.
Also cheese!

17:49 Emily:
Yeah, you're faster than Oarstruck and Noble
again, which are the closest to you. Wind looks
like it'll pick up, so you'll be smashing it
again then! You can have all the food in
Antigua. I bet the fruit there is amazing!
```

Most of the shift had passed, and joyful, ridiculous conversation had resumed, putting my mind at ease. Small waves rolled around us as our oars ploughed through the surf.

Then, to my utter surprise, a dorsal fin sliced through the water. A small crest of a huge, grey animal surfaced in an arching motion to the aft port-side, about 20 metres away.

'Whale!' I immediately shouted.

'Whale?!' Dan replied.

Cabin hatches flung open; eyes glued to the ocean. The shift had been forgotten, and a captivating silence gripped us all.

Lazy waves lapped against the hull. The ocean continued undulating all the way to the horizon – empty.

'You're hallucinating, Jon. There's no whale!' Mark said, breaking the peace.

Maybe he was right. I looked around. All I saw were

regular waves rolling around in every direction. It hadn't resurfaced, but I knew what I'd seen.

'Whale!' Dan shouted. 'There's two of them!'

Two dorsal fins came momentarily out of the water, and their bodies arched across the surface. It really was happening!

After sussing us out, they edged closer to the boat. They were enormous, about the same length as *The Nutilus*, and moved with a graceful, effortless gliding motion through the ocean. As they got nearer, I could see a white stomach on the underside and a large black body through the couple of metres of clear water around us. Were they killer whales?

The pair of whales slid up right next to our boat, running perfectly parallel to it, as if measuring themselves against the hull. These weren't killer whales, but they were most definitely whales.

Quiet euphoria struck the entire boat. Oddly, none of us felt intimated. It was clear these gentle giants were inquisitive; they were just saying hi. Despite their huge size and immense power compared to us, there was no fear on either side. A strong sense of trust exuded from each species, humans and whales alike. It felt amicable.

This was the most calming and tranquil moment of the entire row. The whales were literally within touching distance for around 20 wonderful, glorious minutes.

They swam languidly away and circled round, coming in close for what seemed like a last look at us each time. With each swim out and back, their shadowy outlines just below the surface were clear for quite some distance, dorsal fins popping up and down every so often.

We can't be sure of the type of whale we saw, but with a bit of research we are fairly sure that they were minke whales.

When they finally left us, we were all buzzing. All tension left my body, all negative thoughts had disappeared. It was as if the whales had come along at just the right time to provide precisely the distraction I required.

As I went into the cabin for my off-shift, I collapsed on the mattress, replaying the moment over and over again in my mind. After a pretty rough week, this was exactly the boost I needed.

# SLEEP DEPRIVATION

## Day 35: January 21st

```
08:50 Emily:
That must have been incredible, I'm so envious!!

19:01 Jon:
The whales were magnificent. They came so close
to the boat as well. They were huge!

19:09 Emily:
That's so awesome about the whales! How's your
day been? Are you still hand steering all the
time? You look like you're still going very
straight!
```

I awoke in the cabin. It was time for my shift. I checked the clock on the navigation screen for the second time. Six minutes until I needed to get up. I'd obviously slept through the first call. I frantically readied myself, threw on a t-shirt, then scrabbled around for my harness.

Two minutes until I was on. Panicking that I would eat into their rest time, I opened the cabin hatch, thrust myself on deck, and clipped in.

'You've done it again, Jon!'

I stared at Mark, bleary-eyed. What was he talking about?

'Get back in the cabin. You've still got another hour and a half rest.'

'Wha…? I'm sure I'm meant to…'

I stared at the clock, the digits blurring in my sleep-deprived vision. I didn't understand it. They were right. I'd hallucinated again. I looked down, I didn't even have my t-shirt on this time.

This had gone beyond funny. I felt like I was losing my mind. It had been happening on and off for ages now. I'd wake up after just 10 minutes of sleep, and panic that I was late for my shift. I'd stare at the clock to double check the time, confirm it was time for me to be up and I would get ready. Then, when I'd got on deck, I would find the guys just starting their shift. The worst thing was that it was interrupting my sleep, the one thing I needed to fix it.

With no further conversation, I resigned myself back to the cabin and lay my head on the mattress. This couldn't keep happening. I couldn't keep having these hallucinations.

The sun lowered with an orange glow on the horizon, the last fragments of light glinting across the water. I clambered towards my rowing position, this time for real. Swaying with my weight on the jackstays, I sat down on the damp seat, put the oars out, checked to see if Dan was ready, and then began.

We got into a steady routine, chatting endlessly about food and things we craved. A breeze brushed my face. The air seemed colder than usual. Tiredness was kicking in. I put my coat on for comfort, finding security in its protective shell.

That's when I sensed it. My eyes felt like they were rolling back in my skull. A hazy, fuzzy weight came over me. My head felt like it was dipping, but I wasn't sure if it was. The peak of my hood was in line with the horizon, creating a zone in my vision that my brain couldn't quite work out. Now that I was used to it, I could feel it coming. I knew the signs.

Suddenly, the world rotated 90 degrees, and my

perspective was shifted. With no change in the situation, we were suddenly rowing vertically up a wall of sea. Even though I was sitting on the boat, I felt myself looking down on *The Nutilus* as it climbed the watery tower, as if we were rowing up the wall of a skyscraper. Gravity and logic seem to have been thrown out of the window.

I continued rowing, aware that my world had flipped; aware I was seeing things that couldn't possibly be real; aware that I was hallucinating and this was not reality. I seemed able to have this contradictory vision, this gravity defying hallucination in my mind and still hold a conversation and row. I knew I'd fall out of it sooner or later. If I could just keep rowing, I'd be fine.

Sleep deprivation had now been an issue for a while, with frequent oddities happening. The lens through which I experienced the world had fractured slightly.

There were other, more obvious signs that I was sleep-deprived. Falling asleep while rowing was now a common occurrence. I'd have no idea it had happened until I'd wake up with a thud as my body hit the deck, or a spine-shuddering crack when my rowing partner's oars collided with mine. The vibration sent a chilling reverberation down our spines.

The previous night had been so bad that I kept falling asleep multiple times in one shift, oars crashing against each other frequently. I tried my best to fight it, but it was futile. I ended up accepting it and lying down in the centre of the deck, waves crashing over me, for about half an hour.

Eventually, I came out of the hallucination and back to reality. The world resumed its normal horizontal equilibrium, and I carried on rowing.

Around us, the undulating waves rose and fell like a familiar set of hills in the countryside.

In fact, they looked too familiar.

'We were here a few days ago!'

'What are you talking about?' said Dan from the seat behind me.

'The waves, they're identical to the ones we saw a few of days ago!'

'Sorry? What?'

'Look at the waves. We've been here before. To this exact location! Don't you remember?!'

'Remember waves?'

'Yes! Come on! You must remember! We've seen these waves before! They're exactly the same height and pattern as the ones we saw two days ago!'

'I think you need to get more sleep, mate!'

I argued my case for a few more minutes and gradually came to my senses. The waves were days apart. It was impossible to see the same wave twice. Even if we were in the same place, there was no way that the waves would have been identical, they were constantly changing.

At least it was a proper conversation. Other times I'd grumble and talk to myself, thinking the other person was fully engaged in conversation with me. I later found out that they'd just been sitting there listening to me mumbling away to myself.

After suffering from the effects of sleep deprivation for quite some time and being the only one to suffer in this way, Steve began to show signs. I would knock on the cabin hatch to tell him it was his turn to come out, and he'd say something unrelated, or ask a question that had nothing to do with anything. Other times he'd claim he had already dressed and was ready to come out when in fact he had no clothes on at all and was still asleep. It was odd seeing it from the other side, and I knew how he felt.

We all needed proper sleep, and it would only come when we hit Antigua.

# FRIGATEBIRDS

## Day 36: January 22nd

I stared up at the crystal blue sky. Wispy streaks of cloud interrupted the otherwise perfectly clear scene. Large black angular shadows soared and darted around, as if someone was playing with a kite on a nearby ship.

These were frigatebirds, Antigua's national bird, a welcome distraction from the calm monotony of the open ocean. With a two-metre wingspan, black plumage and long, deeply forked tails, they were huge objects in a vacant sky. These giants soar for weeks on wind currents and spend most of the day hunting.

There were a few high above us, circling round and round, riding the thermals and scanning for fish, covering vast distances with no effort at all.

Beneath the surface of the ocean, silvery shimmers flapped and accelerated through the water. Suddenly emerging like bullets, with fins extended into wings, they soared across the sea. The flying fish were desperately trying to escape whatever danger lurked beneath.

Immediately, the frigatebirds dived down. The calm

persona they had shown while riding the thermals and scanning the ocean vanished as they went into attack mode. Wings arched in two half-moon shapes. They caught the air, suddenly changing direction like fighter jets in a dogfight. Their flight path was angled directly at the poor flying fish.

There was a sudden splash. Out of nowhere, a dorado leapt out of the ocean, snapping its vicious jaw at the flying fish.

The flying fish were stuck between a rock and a hard place. They were being attacked from above and below. Carry on flying through the air and they were at the mercy of the frigatebirds. Sink below the surface and the dorados were sure to devour them.

With the flying fish either eaten or lost beneath the waves, the frigatebirds flapped their giant wings and rose up to their scanning position in the sky. Their beady eyes constantly on the lookout for more food. Again, flying fish launched out of the sea, this time from the other side of the boat and yet again the frigatebirds dived down. The dorados jumped up to snatch the fish, and the cycle started all over again.

I sat back and watched. What a cinematic scene! I felt like I was in a wildlife documentary, but it was happening only metres away. We'd heard stories of whale and dolphin sightings, but nothing at all like this.

We were all on deck, in silence, watching this play out, witnessing the life and death battle that was a perpetuity out here on the ocean. Very few people get to see this.

I noticed my shoulders relax. I hadn't looked at the navigation display in quite a while. Instead, my eyes had been glued to the stunning battle at sea; the aerobatic display from the frigatebirds; the mad splashes from the dorados and the desperate fight for life from the flying fish. My mind was distracted from the exhausting emotional turmoil of the autohelm fiasco. I was once again in silent awe of this incredible environment. Enjoying the experience, rather than thinking about the challenges we were facing and wallowing in frustration.

Suddenly, I remembered why I was here. It was about the adventure along the way.

```
11:50 Jon:
We're still hand steering all the time, but
we're trying different shift rotations to see
what works. Basically, we have to sacrifice
sleep.

11:56 Jon:
It's good that we're still going straight. Our
weather router said we may only have 10 days
left but no idea what he's been taking! How was
your night then?

12:17 Emily:
I want you to finish as soon as possible, but
don't kill yourself with lack of sleep! You
might be better using that energy to row, just
a thought. 10 days sounds optimistic, but not
impossible if the wind picks up. That would be
an average of 77nm per day and your best day was
72. What's he said about the weather?

17:20 Emily:
Don't fall asleep at the oars, haha! Definitely
sounds like sleeping is a better use of time to
me! I don't reckon you'd go far off course in a
couple of hours.
```

# AUTOHELM FIX

## Day 37: January 23rd

The end of our 02:00 to 04:00 shift loomed. Our navigation light glistened on the black water, and despite the time, and two hours of rowing, Mark and I were upbeat. We had been discussing a plan the last few days and decided it was worth a go. The reward was too great not to have another shot. Not even the darkness deterred us.

We desperately missed the autohelm. Manual steering, combined with extreme lack of sleep, was incapacitating. Although we had attempted to fix the autohelm by repositioning the drive unit, the holes we had made were too big. Without washers the drive unit wobbled precariously, flexing the deck, and making it impossible for the autohelm to hold calibration.

The original mounting bracket for the drive unit was still attached to the side of the hull. We had the right drill size for the original bolts, meaning we could easily secure the bracket to the deck. The downside was that someone would have to hang off the side of the boat to undo the bolts to retrieve it.

## Chasing Horizons

My stomach tightened. After the last experience of cutting out holes, I was apprehensive. Was this was going to be another hellish 24 hours, ending up with yet more itchy carbon fibre on our bodies? I still wasn't free from it from the last attempt.

I grabbed the adjustable spanner, lay down on my back on the hard deck floor and wriggled down the footwell of the cabin, like a caver, to where the mount was. My shoulders pressed against the sides. There wasn't much room to get my arm in the right position.

'Ready!' I shouted at Steve.

I was glad I didn't have the job on the other side of the bolt. Mark clung onto the cabin roof, his feet resting on the lip of the deck getting wet as they dipped into the sea with each roll of the boat. His head torch lighting up the bolts in the dark, one hand gripping the spanner, the other gripping a bolt. Mark braced himself, desperate not to drop either into the ocean.

'Ready, bolt one!' he shouted at Steve, who was acting as the communication between us whilst trying to keep the boat perpendicular to the waves to prevent it from rolling.

'Bolt one!' Steve shouted down to me.

We'd labelled the bolts so we could tell which one to work on. Mark placed his spanner on the bolt to stabilise it. I put my spanner on the nut and began turning.

It worked. We progressed through the rest.

'Bolt four is done!' I said, as I caught the bracket in my hands.

Mark then clambered round the cabin and back on deck.

'What do you think, then?'

'Let's get the drill out and begin on the holes.'

I grabbed the drill, pressed it into my shoulder for extra force, and began rotating the handle. It bit; this was working!

Four holes later and we proudly sat the drive unit on top and bolted it down on the mounting bracket it was intended for. It was secure. There was no way the deck would rip up this time.

After fiddling with it for days, we understood the autohelm more. We adjusted the cable to get the correct tension and recalibrated it, this time using smaller maximums for the rudder rotation. It would mean that we wouldn't be able to turn as sharply, but hopefully it wouldn't get close to ripping the drive unit from the deck if it went wrong.

I looked at Mark and Steve and crossed my fingers. Time to switch it back on. I could feel the tension in the air.

I hit the switch.

The familiar whirring noise began instantly. The push rod engaged with the tiller to move the rudder, adjusting it to the pre-programmed setting. It was working, and it wasn't ripping through the deck!

The difference was immediate. We weren't getting battered all over the place, and we could get some more rest. Relief washed over me like a wave. I could feel my muscles relax for the first time in days. A relieved smile spread across my face.

Moments later, I collapsed on the mattress and slept. The buzzing of the drive unit was suddenly a lullaby compared to the noisy annoyance it had been just a few weeks before.

```
07:06 Jon:
Only gone and fixed the bloody autohelm!!

07:09 Emily:
YES! YES! YES!!! That's awesome! Well done!! You
get to sleep again!!

07:20 Jon:
Haha yeah! There's been a lot of falling asleep
at the oars, which isn't great! Also, a lot of
sleep talking... So pleased about autohelm.
Hopefully, it will buy us a day if it holds.
What've you been up to?

07:28 Emily:
Such amazing news about the autohelm!
```

# Chasing Horizons

22:08 Emily:
You're smashing it again. Fastest boat in the last 24 hours! Here's an update on the numbers:1955nm covered, 1045nm remaining. 15nm behind Oarstruck and Team Noble. 73nm behind Nomads. Nobody is close behind you. 250nm before the rest of the fleet. Have you got any insider knowledge on ETA? It looks like you could overtake Oarstruck, Team Noble and Oceanomads! It could be a tight finish with the four of you so close... you can take them!!

# FLIGHTS

## Day 38: January 24th

I stared at the navigation screen, obsessively zooming in and out, as if it would affect the distance somehow. I zoomed in on the boat, to a few metres with just blank sea all around. Then, by each increment, I gradually zoomed out until the vast Atlantic engulfed the small screen and I could see how far we'd come.

I had religiously stared at this screen for weeks now. At first, I couldn't comprehend how we'd get to the other side, and it astonished me when we made it to the middle, and now we were clearly on the other side of the ocean.

Yet it still didn't feel real. It was just an image on the screen. I couldn't see land; I could only see the sea in every direction. It seemed impossible that we would reach Antigua in a couple of weeks.

I felt tired. We'd been at sea for ages, yet the picture on the screen wasn't relatable. I almost didn't believe we were that close, or that it was even possible that we could be that close. With no landmarks to gauge progress, numbers had become our world, our only measure of our crossing.

## Chasing Horizons

Throughout the expedition, we had been tracking our daily averages, and estimating the total time. At the start, it was just the vast time in front of us. Now, it could be less than two weeks and, if we got lucky with the weather, it could even be 10 days. Mentally, things for me would change when I knew there was a high chance of having under 10 days left. This felt attainable. After so long at sea, having less than 10 days would be a huge milestone, we'd be in single figures.

Early on, our families were reluctant to let us know our predicated ETAs for morale. They probably didn't know it was a constant thought that swirled around our heads and filled many of our conversations. They were probably right; it probably wasn't good for morale. We should have stopped worrying and just carried on doing the best we could. The outcome would sort itself out.

However, this forced ambivalence about our ETA needed to change. Flights needed to be booked for the finish and timing that was difficult. There were so many variables such as our speed, weather, flight prices, negotiating maximum time off work, but not leaving too early. There was also the added complication that flights were selling out. If we didn't time this right, our loved ones wouldn't even be in Antigua to greet us when we arrived.

```
13:14 Jon:
We really want to beat Nomads. In terms of
finish, we are aiming for 60nm days (last night
we had a cross current so was hard). On
Saturday, the wind should pick up again and
we're hoping for a few 70s. So, all being well
around 10 days!

18:38 Emily:
10 days is so exciting! Think we are booking
flights tonight!

21:04 Emily:
I think you'll hit 2000 miles later today.
You're on 1979! And that's nautical miles, of
```

course, so you've done 2277 normal miles! Based on my original calcs plus the delayed start, I was expecting you to finish 5th Feb, and your ETA is 4th Feb! I'm not lying when I say you're smashing it!!

22:05 Emily:
Flight is all booked :) :) So in one week, I'll be on the plane! Ahh, so excited! Should arrive a couple of days before you, unless you speed up. Just don't go faster than 80nm per day or you'll arrive before we do!

# CAPRICE

## Day 39: January 25th

```
08:29 Emily:
999nm TO GO!! Yes! Smashing it!!

11:45 Jon:
Awesome! I reckon it could be an early morning
chocolate sesh tomorrow, which would be great.
```

Towering, angry, mountainous waves surrounded us everywhere I looked. It was night, but the full moon wasn't long away, so I could see the aggressive seascape in the moonlight. The navigation light highlighted the spray being violently thrown at us in the darkness. Floods of water crashed onto the cabins whilst the hostile waves roared around us.

'Hold tight and look after yourselves for the next 24 hours,' our weather router said.

He'd warned us that this would be a tough and hectic period. It was delivering on that promise. Keeping the cabin hatches firmly shut was paramount to avoid capsize. To add to this, we were back to manual steering. Despite all the effort of remounting the drive unit onto its original mount, the autohelm still wasn't working properly. For some reason, the cable tension was wrong; it was constantly going over its maximum. Consequently, the two rowers not only had to battle the aggressive waves, but one of them had to steer.

So far, it truly was one of the toughest periods of the entire crossing, an absolute blur and raw battle against nature. Brutal and relentless waves battered our small boat as we clung on to the oars and continued powering ourselves forward.

Our weather router told us that, even though we were still far away from Antigua, we were lining up for the finish. He warned us that this 24-hour period could push us far south, making a straightforward route to the finish impossible. We needed to hold our line. This was now simply about riding the waves and avoiding a capsize. We were trying to hold our position and stay on course despite what the ocean was trying to do to us.

Our group mentality was now like a tag team between shifts. Looks of exhaustion exchanged between getting in and out of the cabins said more than any conversation.

Go out.

Do battle for two hours.

Get drenched.

Retreat into the cabin for two hours.

Collapse.

Get up and repeat.

Around us, all-encompassing waves engulfed our world. With the monstrous waves attacking us from the side, this war of attrition was fought mainly rowing with one oar. It was a constant battle to keep the boat straight.

I gripped the oar and dug it straight into the water, trying my best to time it with Mark in these horrendous conditions for maximum force. We were in the trough of a wave and side-on.

'Now!' Mark shouted.

We pulled with everything we had. It felt as if the oars were at breaking point. But we hardly moved; the current was so strong against us.

We rose to the top of the wave, and about three quarters of the way up, I stared at the white water breaking and tumbling down towards us. I instinctively grabbed the jackstays and braced for impact.

The wave roared as gravity pulled the gigantic volume of water back towards earth. It hit the boat, shunting it sideways. I got launched into the jackstay, but I held on. My oar caught beneath my knees. It dug into the skin and levered my body upwards off my seat.

The wave passed, and I collapsed down, water dribbling from my hood, my cold fingers splayed out on the deck.

I heaved myself back onto my seat and looked round at Mark. We were being smashed all over the place. Almost every wave was a side-on knockdown. It was horrendous.

Mark's face was set. He didn't need to open his mouth to communicate. We knew that we both had to carry on. Despite the atrocious waves, we had to continue. We didn't want to lose position and get flung south of Antigua.

I grabbed my oars and dug them back into the waves.

But it was too late.

The next wave was already descending towards us.

Bang!

*The Nutilus* was cast aside as the wave smashed into it. I got launched across the deck, disorientated in the rushing seawater. Cold water poured over me, engulfing me, swallowing me whole. I was swirling around in a washing machine, hanging on to the jackstay. I felt my life truly depended on it at that moment.

I'd experienced harsh impacts, but this was different. The violent power of the wave was on another scale.

The water abated, and I was able to look around. I was horizontal on the edge of the boat, staring into the depths. Mark, who had also landed in a precarious position, lay at the other end of the deck.

Both of us had survived…

But the boat…

It wasn't righting! The starboard side was level with the water and the port side was high in the air. Still, massive waves pounded into the boat, holding it at this steep angle.

Then I noticed. It was side-on to the oncoming waves. If another wave hit us, we'd capsize for sure.

Desperately, I flung myself over to the other side of the boat, hoping that my weight would shift it.

It didn't work!

I glanced across at my oar. It was resting vertically in the sea. Straight downwards. The gate was completely smashed. The power of the wave had ripped the oar right out of the gate in one hit. Nothing stopped the oar from being washed overboard except a flimsy lanyard.

Mark was in a similar situation. He was sprawled across the deck, disorientated, but ok. He gave me a pained nod. I knew he was ok.

But the boat was at a steep angle. Another gigantic wave was bearing down on us. Without doubt, we were going in the sea.

I had to retrieve my oar. I stood up, head spinning, and grabbed it with two hands. It was like trying to pull something out of cement. Gritting my teeth, I hauled the oar upwards. I couldn't move it sideways, only vertically out of the dark, violent ocean.

The three-metre-long oar went straight up above my head. I felt like a knight unsaddled, wielding the heavy lance above my head as I stood tired and broken on the ground.

I knew that this was it. As soon as that wave hit, I would be thrown into the water. I stood, precariously holding the giant oar up. My muscles ached. My heart was hammering in my chest. The inevitable wave was about to strike. I was done for.

But, as it did, *The Nutilus* suddenly righted itself. The keel did its job, hauling the heavy craft back into position. My sea-legs, developed over hundreds of miles at sea, kept me steady as the wave passed under the boat.

I carefully put the oar down on deck and collapsed onto my seat, exhausted. I was completely spent.

These 24 hours had been the toughest yet. We sat there, done. The sun would be up in a couple of hours. Its rays would replenish our broken minds. It would represent the end of one of the hardest nights and bring a sense of safety.

Waves crashed over the deck. We would fix the gate at sunrise and regroup. But not yet.

We only had 10 minutes left of our shift, so we dug some chocolate out of our ration store and sat there, feeling miserable but alive. Despite our best efforts, sometimes we just couldn't beat the demonic sea.

As I chewed the sweet chocolate, I gazed around at the stricken craft. We had no autohelm and now we were temporarily one rowing position down, the oar gate a shattered mess on the side of *The Nutilus*.

Shortly, Steve and Dan came out.

'What happened? What did you do to our boat?' asked Dan.

We explained what had happened, and they nodded their understanding. We were all tired. There was no point in making a situation out of it. No one was at fault and it wasn't the end of the world. We would fix this in a couple of hours, when it was light and warmer.

We were alive; we were relatively safe, and we were still heading in the right direction. That was all that mattered.

# NEAR COLLISION

## Day 40: January 26th

Another long night stretched out before us. This was completely different to yesterday's battle against the demonic sea. Its angry temperament had given way to a relaxed mood, so we returned to our shift pattern of two hours on, two hours off, with the 30-minute sprints.

The calm of the ocean and stargazing were the themes of this shift. The night sky never ceased to amaze us. There was one red star near the horizon, in particular, that we kept debating.

'That's Mars,' I said. 'I'm sure of it.'

'No. Look. There look, it's twinkling. That's definitely a ship's light in the distance.'

'If it is a ship's light, we better keep an eye on it.'

Seeing one light is fine because there's a different coloured light on each side of a ship. If you see one colour, you know the ship is parallel to you but if you see both, then it is heading directly towards you.

The red light that we'd been tracking for the first hour of the shift was now accompanied by a green light of equal size and brightness against the dark sky.

# Chasing Horizons

The worst-case scenario was true. It was coming directly for us. I looked at Mark. Even in the dim glow of our navigation light, I could see the concern in his eyes. My posture unconsciously changed. I suddenly sat more upright as a heightened sense of alertness struck me. Mark ducked into the aft cabin and picked up the radio.

'Calling unknown vessel. Calling unknown vessel. Calling unknown vessel. This is *The Nutilus*. This is *The Nutilus*. Over.'

No answer.

'Calling unknown vessel. Calling unknown vessel. Calling unknown vessel. This is *The Nutilus*. This is *The Nutilus*. Over.'

Still nothing.

We kept trying, but it wasn't working. Every call was answered with dead radio static. We both looked at each other. We knew what to do.

'I'll get the flares,' I said.

I opened up the hatch. Dan was asleep, naked on his back.

'Alright mate, what's up?' he groaned away.

'Nothing. Don't worry. Go back to sleep.'

There was no point in alarming him. Reaching into the hatch, I got the flare container out, wishing we had practised this. I unscrewed the top, and then a noise.

'SSHCRR. This is Cargo Ship.... SSHCRR.'

The radio had kicked in. Mark waved at me urgently before responding to the radio call. I lowered the unlit flare as Mark finished the call. The huge vessel diverted its course, and we watched it for the next half an hour as it faded back into the darkness.

Relief washed over me like a warm bath.

We'd survived another night.

```
08:39 Emily:
Over 2/3rds of the way now! Boom! You're only
5nm behind Oarstruck! Based on current speed,
you'll overtake them this evening!
```

# SARGASSUM

## Day 41: January 27th

For the last few days, a never-ending line of yellowy brown seaweed had accompanied us for as far the eye could see. Sargassum. The yellow-brown colour contrasted hugely to the deep blue ocean, making the wriggly trail easy to see all the way to the horizon. It was like a pathway leading us to Antigua.

I looked to my left. There were multiple lines of it snaking along in the same direction. It was as if we were in some huge running track and the seaweed were the lane markers stretching for miles. I lifted my oar. Beneath was a vast, tangled, floating forest. It surrounded the boat as we pushed ourselves through this huge seaweed mass and out the other side, back into our familiar seascape.

```
19:25 Jon:
Hey, my phone didn't switch back on for a while.
We thought we were down to zero phones, but we
are back in action! So chuffed that it's under
1000nm to go. Don't think we can make a 70nm day,
unfortunately. The winds haven't been as good
```

as predicted, so at the moment we are hitting around 55. I think it will be another 8 days.

19:31 Jon:
What food is in Antigua?

22:55 Emily:
I'm mostly looking forward to the jerk chicken and rum cocktails! But I've read that the fish is really good and lots of things with sweet potato and plantain. The national dish is fungi, similar to Italian Polenta. Caribbean food is one of my favourites! I'm sure anything will taste amazing to you!

# SUNTIKI

## Day 42: January 28th

I looked towards the horizon. I was sure I saw a small outline of something different and stared at that point for a few minutes. A mast peaked up. It slowly rose in the distance like a meerkat on the savanna. Rising further, looking like it could pierce the clouds on the horizon, the outline of the yacht became clearer as it sped towards us. The yacht was on a direct course for us, and we were looking straight at it.

The brilliant white yacht was now within shouting distance. We recognised it as Suntiki, the support yacht. At the stern was Thor, the race doctor who had helped tow us back to La Gomera on our first, and only, practice row.

'Channel 72,' he yelled, beaming at us with his traditional wide smile. 'We'll do some loops.'

Suntiki danced round us, harnessing the sea in one direction, then in the opposing direction. Effortlessly going against the waves. The hull slapping down on the waves with a crash each time. The yacht had a far superior command over their trajectory than we did and nimbly glided round. It looked unforced, like being out here was the most natural, carefree thing to do in the world. There was room to move around on deck. It looked more stable and their body language suggested they were relaxed and having a great time. It looked more like a scene out of a music video, confidently chatting on the radio one-handed whilst negotiating Suntiki on the waves. It seemed completely different to our sweaty, exhausted expedition.

'Gentlemen, did you know your AIS is off?!' Thor asked over the radio.

No, it wasn't, we thought to ourselves. Dan poked his head in the cabin and checked the Automatic Identification System. It was on. It was definitely on. But Thor reiterated he couldn't see us on it, which was worrying. Other ocean traffic wouldn't be able to see us on their navigation screen. It had certainly worked when the super yacht had visited us, but maybe that's why the cargo ship the other night came closer than we'd have liked. Apart from our navigation light, we would have been completely invisible to it.

We now had to be vigilant about any ships around us.

'Get the guy with the fungal infection off the oars. He needs to rest,' said the doctor.

Dan picked up the radio receiver.

'Err... that would be all of us!'

Thor leant back and paused before laughing his head off.

'You better row faster, then. Get to Antigua sooner.'

We laughed with him, but the reality was true. Without enough painkillers for one a day and without it healing, getting to Antigua as soon as possible seemed like the best option.

'Well, good luck with the last leg, gentlemen. I'll see you in Antigua!'

Just as quickly as he'd arrived, he sped off across the ocean, Suntiki effortlessly slicing through the waves.

It was great to see a familiar face out here in the abyss. With spirits raised, we cracked on.

10:47 Jon:
Yeah, I'm also looking forward to endless jerk chicken and a cold beer! Bet you're eager for snorkelling?

17:21 Emily:
Oarstruck have just posted a photo of their backsides! They're not pretty! Haha! They have, however, managed to do an extra 4nm in the last 24 hours, so maybe their competitive edge is coming out now. It's getting close! You're only 10nm behind and have the same wind conditions so you can catch them!

# OUT-VOTED

## Day 43: January 29th

```
09:02 Emily:
Hey! How's it going? Still tough without the
autohelm? You're on a more southerly bearing. I
think that's a good idea to go with the wind.
```

Antigua drew ever closer. Its call reeled us in. Relatively, it felt as if we were almost there, so close but still with a considerable chunk to go. Having completed the majority of the expedition, we were all too aware that we were in the latter days of the journey. However, the unrelenting side-current made it impossible to predict our finish day.

We were 300nm east but critically only had 35nm to play with before we were south of Antigua. It was now all about holding our latitude as much as possible whilst still making westerly progress. We didn't want to mess this up. Lining up the finish had to be considered days ahead of arrival. If too far south, it would be a struggle against the current to get north and there would be a risk of missing the island altogether.

The monotonous side-current had got to us all. There was a constant stream of waves slapping against the side of the hull causing the boat to roll. It meant that we couldn't get into any rhythm when rowing and were constantly battling against the current.

A wave smacked against the boat, and my oar painfully dug into my shins. With each wave that struck, I shifted on my wet seat. It was only about a centimetre at a time, but with my fungal situation, down there was excruciatingly painful.

It seemed as if I was sliding round on my seat so much more than earlier in the row. Maybe I was just noticing it more because of the pain. The pain was constant; a background feeling that accompanied my every movement. It felt like I'd suffered an intense burn that just wouldn't heal.

I looked out over the surface of the water. It undulated softly. I longed for the huge waves that we soared along before, that powered us forward to 70 and 80nm per day. With the sea as flat as a slightly wobbly pancake, I felt we were making very little progress. Combined with the heat, the aching fungal infection and the fact that we were so close to the finish, we were all desperately hoping that *The Nutilus* would pick up speed and carry us to the finish line faster.

Sat on deck, the morning rays continued to pierce down on our weathered skin. I looked around at the others. They'd all changed so much since the start of the race. Beards had grown impressively. Skin had darkened. Lips were cracked. We were now a rugged bunch.

We'd been discussing the autohelm for a while. If we could figure out why the cable tension was wrong, and get it working properly, we'd be able to ditch the 30-minute sprints, get back to our original shift pattern of two hours on, two hours off, and power it home to Antigua. But I thought fixing it would require at least half a day of faffing around, which seemed a waste as we were so close to the finish line.

'Let's have a vote then,' said Mark. 'All those who think we should fix the autohelm, raise your hand.'

Mark, Steve and Dan all raised their hands.

I didn't.

Even though I agreed it was possible to fix the autohelm, I didn't want to use precious time messing with it when there was no definite outcome. We could spend the day adjusting and readjusting it, but it would be a day lost. Our current shift system seemed to work ok, and we were making good progress. It seemed a shame to potentially waste a day, rather than use it to get home sooner.

Three to one it was. I grimaced internally. A vote was a vote. This was a team, after all, and I had to go with the majority. And, besides, it may work. We could fix the autohelm and have an easier ride for the last few days.

I drew in a deep breath and reluctantly clambered back into the humid aft cabin. We were quietly confident, although nobody wanted to admit it for fear of cursing it. I tightened the cable and rod to what we thought was now a good tension. Next to calibrate the system. Instead of holding the tiller, we locked the steering off and set the maximum rudder angles to slightly less than before. We would have even less of a turning circle, but that didn't matter at this stage.

The noonday sun was beating down when I finally put the tools down and looked at Mark. With nothing left to do but try it, there was a reluctance in the air. If we switched it on and it didn't work, a whole morning's rowing would have been lost for nothing. All our hopes were held in Mark's hands as he pressed the button.

The familiar whirring began as it adjusted our course. Things were looking good. But the real test would be if the cable tension held at the maximum settings.

It buzzed round to the far right.

And held!

We'd fixed it! Finally! And in a few hours too. It was completely worth the time spent. I was glad I'd lost the vote.

We stood up, arms held high and cheered in the middle of the sea. Relief and joy could be heard in our happy voices. The tension and aches from working in a hot confined area vanished in an instant. Grins couldn't be contained and fists were thrust into the air. The boat was an island of pride and excitement surrounded by endless miles of open ocean.

We were on the home straight, and nothing could stop us!

Despite fixing the autohelm, we kept the 30-minute sprint shift pattern to avoid the heat. Even though we were getting less sleep, we all felt more awake. The fixed autohelm would help us keep our latitude, and without having to steer, our minds would be freer. Now to crack on and cross the last bit of this ocean.

As long as the autohelm survived, we would be ok.

```
22:37 Jon:
We fixed the autohelm today so we're back on
track and trying to put some miles down! Yeah,
we think Oarstruck and other teams are in a bit
of trouble as they have to row into the wind to
get north! Didn't you fly today??
```

# LETTERS

## Day 44: January 30th

```
05:54 Emily:
Amazing news on the autohelm! Well done!!

10:02 Jon:
Of course, you're flying today! For some reason,
I got confused on the days and thought your
flight was yesterday!

10:21 Emily:
Haha, it must be difficult to keep track of the
days! Just waiting to board the plane now. Have
a good day on the oars!
```

I lay down on the cabin mattress and stared at the white roof above me. My hands rested on my stomach, my body rolling slightly with the movements of the boat. It was calm out there. I was calm too. We were nearly there, and it was starting to sink in.

In the netting to my side was the yellow book my family had given to me before I left. Inside, it was stashed with photos, memories, quizzes, trivia, and messages from family and friends. I'd dipped into it from time to time on off-shifts as a pick me up. It immediately transported me home.

At the back of the book were sealed letters from Emily, Mum, Dad, and Charlotte – these were to be opened when I was at my lowest; when I was in dire need of a mental boost; to remind me of the big picture and to keep me going. These had been written without knowing the situation in which they would be opened, written to rebuild their loved one's mind in a potentially treacherous situation in the middle of a vicious ocean. It could have been after a capsize, cold and wet, shivering, in shock, terrified and desperate. The time when I had hit rock bottom and had nothing left mentally.

Despite everything we'd been through, I hadn't opened them.

We had faced some incredible situations together as a team and battled through monstrous waves and equipment failures. I thought back to our first few days in this alien environment. It had now been my life for over six weeks and I had changed with it. The sea couldn't be bigger than we'd already seen. We'd fix anything that broke. We were almost there. Hopefully, we wouldn't have anything worse than we had already faced. Even if we did, I'd have the experience from the expedition to work through it and the motivation of family and Antigua so close.

The letters called to me. It was day 44. When was I going to open them? With the autohelm fixed and being so close to the finish, it was time to tear them open.

I opened Mum, Dad's and Charlotte's first. I wanted to save Emily's for last. I shook with tears. My face became a mess of liquid. After a few minutes, I calmed and had a huge overwhelming feeling of peace. Unexpectedly, I broke down when they said they were proud of me. It was an odd realisation this far into the journey, but for the last two years I had assumed they thought I was nuts and a bit mad. It hadn't occurred to me they were proud of this project, and me for being part of it.

I remembered when I'd brought it up for the first time. We were travelling in the car when I turned to her.

'I'm going to row the Atlantic, Mum.'

'Err...ok...,' she cautiously replied, trying to sound enthusiastic.

Looking back, I was so obsessed with the concept of rowing an ocean that I couldn't see why people wouldn't want to do this. For me, it was an instant yes, without question or any need for details. The end result was simply so enticing it dwarfed all worries or obstacles along the way and became an instant singularity of immense focus in my mind. For so long, my brain had been rammed with the enormity of how to get this project off the ground and how to get across this ocean. I didn't have the mental capacity for much else.

I hadn't allowed myself to open the letters until I'd reached my darkest point. But not knowing when that would be, I had kept them in reserve. Even though I'd faced so much hardship at sea, the waves, fungal issues, sleep deprivation, emotional and technological challenges, I didn't know if it would get any worse. I had knuckled down and did the best I could, willing myself to get through each difficulty until I could see the sunrise again on another day.

Opening the letters now signified that I had been through the hardest moments of the trip. With finishing looking more and more like it was in the bag, I knew it was time to see what they held. Now that we'd nearly completed the crossing and were almost safe, my brain was allowing room for other things.

A weight lifted from my shoulders as pride and acceptance rushed in.

```
19:38 Jon:
Hey, how's it all going? It's quite tough here
at the moment. Heat is intense. Annoying being
so close, but so far. I think it could be another
six days at this rate. Very jealous of your films
and G&Ts on the plane! Can't wait to see you.
```

```
19:40 Jon:
Opened your letter. Helped so much, thank you.
Definitely made me cry. We'll get there :)

20:06 Emily:
Hey there! Just landed. It's so hot here. It
must be so sweaty on the boat! Six days isn't
much longer, really. I think it'll go quicker
soon. That's good that you saved the letter this
long. Glad it helped! I'm so excited to see you.
It feels so good to be here! Keep on rowing and
counting down the miles!
```

Bang, bang, bang! The cabin hatch rattled as someone struck it. My eyes wearily opened and adjusted to the light. It wasn't time for my shift yet. I craved more time asleep, valuing every minute.

'Jon! Get out here!' someone shouted.

Something must have gone wrong. I hastily sat upright, leant forwards and pushed the cabin hatch open.

My eyes were met with Steve, Dan, and Mark's. They were grinning, standing up and pointing at the ocean. I followed their pointed fingers.

'Look, there!'

A small grey dorsal fin sliced through the water.

'Dolphins!'

Four Atlantic spotted dolphins had come to say hello, rolling around just off the forward cabin, only a metre or so away. They messed around, playing almost within touching distance.

The world seemed to stop. The sea was calm, a gentle breeze brushed our tired faces, and the sun was shining, adding to the serenity of the moment. There was no rowing, and all four of us were on deck, something that rarely happened.

The dolphins continued to play, their distinctive spotted complexion resembling over ripe bananas. They weren't in a hurry to go anywhere and seemed to be like us, inquisitive and in the moment.

## Chasing Horizons

We had heard reports and watched countless videos of ocean rowers seeing dolphins at sea. We had seen little wildlife, just the flying fish, the birds and the dorados, but we now had these dolphins and the whales.

We stood and watched the dolphins for an hour as they gallivanted just off the forward end of the boat. It was great to just relax in the sunshine, chatting happily, and enjoying the sights of the open ocean. It was a special moment and gave us another boost to battle the unrelenting heat on the last stretch to Antigua.

```
22:41 Jon:
Amazing work! Where are you now then? I couldn't
be more jealous! The flight ok? Yep, not far and
you're right, it will go quickly. We saw
dolphins today :)

23:07 Emily:
Yes to the dolphins!! So, so jealous of that!!
I've just seen the photo. Absolutely awesome!! :)
```

# FULL MOON

## Day 45: January 31st

10:19 Jon:
Yeah, the dolphins were great! Well, we are still rowing…… How are you doing?

10:39 Emily:
You're doing twice the speed of Oarstruck and Noble!

21:39 Jon:
Oarstruck are stuck in the current we are in but are obviously south of Antigua so have to row north whereas we just have to use the current and stay in the same line. Great weather routing! How's it all going then? We think we will get in around Tuesday. I feel like we are basically there, but still a few more days!

21:53 Emily:
You've overtaken Oarstruck and Noble!! Awesome work!! And you're in a better location, so should hold the lead!

I sat at the oars on another 02:00 night shift. This one,

however, was a joy. A full moon had joined us for the occasion, shining brightly in the sky, shedding silver light across the gently rippling ocean. In every direction, water glistened, and the calmness of the sea filled the crew with serenity. These nights weren't as cold as at the start; the ocean radiated the heat from the day. I felt relaxed, such a contrast to the mayhem at the beginning of the trip.

The huge, white disk of a moon shone brightly, the features and craters of the surface showing clearly. Wire-wool-like clouds dabbed darker textures here and there in the sky.

Water glistened like a shining oil slick in front and behind us. A path of bright moonlight shone directly down onto the sea, illuminating a silver road for us to row along, guiding us through the night to Antigua.

Stephen Fry's comforting voice boomed out of the speakers on deck. Having accompanied us throughout the trip, we were on our second run through of the complete set of Harry Potter. With the full moon in the night sky, listening in the middle of the ocean was taken to another level.

A gentle breeze brushed by. Every now and then, there was the sound of a flying fish striking the cabins and splashing back into the water. When I'm back home dreaming of this adventure, these would be the nights I'd miss.

# ALMOST THERE

## Day 46: February 1st

14:23 Jon:
Still have another few days of heat in this travelling aquatic prison!

14:33 Emily:
Only a few days though. You've already done 45 days! Travelling Aquatic Prison? Haha! You should have named the boat that!

# SLOW PROGRESS

## Day 47: February 2nd

15:51 Jon:
Progress is slow at the moment. We are going across the current and constantly trying to keep the boat on track!

16:44 Emily:
Yeah, we noticed you were slower. The tracker is updating every two hours now you're under 200nm away! Is it forecast to improve?

18:11 Jon:
Unsure if it will improve, it's such a struggle. Can't really explain it but difficult to stay in seat and row. Anyway, we will get there!

18:35 Emily:
Sounds brutal. Hopefully, the winds will improve.

21:25 Emily:
The family briefing was good. He warned us you might start rowing in your sleep and push me out of bed!

21:41 Jon:
I'm eager to finish. We change our bearing at 06:00 as the winds change, so hopefully things should get easier then. Literally can't get there soon enough. Can't wait to see you, sleep for 24 hours, get dry, fix my groin, wear clean clothes, shower and scrape a layer of salt off me! Cold beer and a clean bed, too. Beds are rank here.

22:16 Emily:
Good news about the bearing change at 06:00, you've got faster though!

# COUNTDOWN

## Day 48: February 3rd

01:52 Emily:
My Mum said: 'The forecast is for the wind to increase and come from a more advantageous direction.' Hope she's right and you have some waves to surf!

18:09 Jon:
Yeah, it's changed and we're on the home stretch :) It's so hot! We should have less than 100nm to go in a few hours.

19:04 Emily:
Yes! Not long now!

21:50 Jon:
We are now down to double figures - the countdown is on!

22:05 Emily:
Yes to double figures!! That means we can see your location every hour! Enjoy the last few miles!

# NECESSITY

## Day 49: February 4th

I stared at the orange numbers on the navigation screen on deck. I couldn't get my head around it – less than 100nm to go. We had virtually crossed an ocean.

Emily's mum was right. Finally, the weather was in our favour. We had picked up speed and were cruising towards Antigua. These were some of the best conditions we had experienced on the trip. Strong, predictable waves, perfectly aligned with our boat, smashing us towards land. Spirits were high.

I had mixed feelings. On the one hand, I was dreaming of the immediate joys. I wanted to step on dry land, see my family, sleep for as long as I could and eat different and vast quantities of food.

Even more pressing was our fungal issue. The race doctor had prescribed fresh-water showers combined with getting 100% dry. After weeks of being constantly wet, our infected areas hadn't had a chance to heal. Once on dry land, they would clear up in no time. I couldn't wait.

However, there was also a part of me that was dreading

getting to land. There was the lingering realisation that normal life was about to kick in. I quite liked life being simpler. Being at sea was liberating.

For nearly two months, all I had to do was sleep, eat, and exercise. I had lived a very basic life, a rare opportunity in today's world. I had a large quantity of sunlight every day, not fierce artificial office lighting. I had exercised a lot compared to being sedentary. We had solved real-life problems as a team, instead of individually staring at spreadsheets. It felt like a few of my basic human needs had been met and I was in tune with the raw elements. I didn't crave modernity. My brain felt settled and still.

Perhaps an element of this had urged me to row an ocean. I wanted to do a huge expedition, but maybe I hadn't noticed how much these basic human needs were off track in my day-to-day life, and that was what was pushing me. Soon I'd have a flurry of messages to reply to, people to talk to, and the prospect seemed quite hectic. I hadn't missed the world of constant communication.

There was also the feeling of achievement. Every day I felt like I'd worked and was tired, and the distance to Antigua had dropped slightly each day, showing progress against a very clear goal. Reality wouldn't be like this. With so many goals and people demanding time, it would be difficult to experience this feeling of progress. I certainly hadn't felt as physically worked as I did now. Physical graft felt more rewarding out here.

The real world was drawing closer, though, and I would step on land. The overwhelming joy of seeing my family was at the forefront of my mind. I couldn't wait to get there.

# THE LAST TWENTY-FOUR HOURS

## Day 50: February 5th

11:35 Emily:
So excited that you're just over a day away!

13:21 Emily:
Your ETA is now showing as 04:00 tomorrow (local time) or 09:00 GMT. Sunrise is at 06:47.

16:33 Jon:
All sounds amazing! We are having a bit of an admin day to get sorted. So hot still! We are less than 50nm away now!

16:42 Emily:
Can't wait for tomorrow morning!

20:17 Jon:
Under 40nm to go! Conditions are great. If only we'd had a few more days like this!

20:37 Emily:
Conditions sound perfect! Oceanomads hit an unexpected current on their approach, which delayed them by a few hours. Hope you don't have

that! You might be able to see the lights on the
island once it gets dark!

20:45 Jon:
Haha, yeah! I know how they feel. Our food
requests are Pringles, chocolate Hobnobs,
crisps and stuff. Basically, a tonne of junk
food! Yeah, hopefully we'll see it around 10
miles out. My beard is quite large, by the way.

21:15 Emily:
Haha! Ok, we will get some junk from the
supermarket now! I brought Hobnobs; they
travelled inside your walking boots so they
didn't get squashed. Hopefully, they don't
smell! The Duty Officer said you might see the
lights from the airport at 40nm and the island
from 20nm. Your beard is huge! It must be so
hot! Think you might win the beard race!

23:46 Jon:
Awesome! We are 27nm away but can't see lights
yet. Cannot wait for land! Haha beard is ok. I'm
eager to take it off though. Let's see what you
think! We have music on loud, coffees on the go
and looking out for lights.

I sat on the deck with Steve, pulling slowly on the oars. It was our last night shift. The next time we would be on the oars, the sun would be up on a new day, our last day at sea. Tomorrow, we would hit land.

The air was warm, and the sea was well lit from an almost full moon. The waves were pushing us in to Antigua, and *The Nutilus* was flying. With a decent pace being made, we decided to have a coffee and take in the last moments of the expedition.

We sat there, feasting on snacks and sipping our coffees, watching the stars above our heads and listening to the soft wash of the waves against the hull.

We'd divided up what was left of the emergency snacks between the four of us and had decided to eat only these in the last 24 hours. I was more than happy not to eat another dehydrated meal ever again and wolfed down a sticky toffee pudding.

Over the forward cabin, a dim glow sat low on the horizon. At first, it was a faint radiant light on a point which could have been a cloud. It grew horizontally and then raised slightly further above the horizon. We questioned if it really was Antigua, but as the light grew stronger and larger, it became undeniable.

It was land!

The finish line was in sight!

The realisation that the journey was nearly over began to sink in. I had spent so many hours staring at the navigation screen, wobbling around in the cabin, obsessing over the distance. Constantly playing arithmetic games, trying to estimate when we would get to land, watching the distance to Antigua gradually reduce. But now, to see the light from land made everything more real than numbers on a screen. We were going to make this, and it was going to end. We finally were here. We were actually here!

Steve and I became reminiscent and considered. Obviously, we both wanted to get off the boat and have a shower, but it was an odd feeling. This was the last time we would sit on the boat, staring at the night sky. We'd miss these moments of peace and tranquillity.

Every now and again, we glanced over at the glow on the horizon, checking we hadn't been hallucinating. Antigua still sat there, glowing happily, welcoming us in.

'Thanks for asking me on this journey,' said Steve suddenly.

He was looking at me over the top of his mug as he sipped his coffee. There was a deep contentment in his eyes.

'It's been quite a journey, hasn't it?'

A moment of comfortable silence passed between us.

'Do you think we'll ever see stars like this again?' I asked.

Steve followed my gaze into the heavens.

'Of course!'

# JOURNEY'S END

## Early morning: February 6th

I reached forward for the cabin hatch and pushed it open. Warm daylight struck my face, greeting me and making me feel alive. The waves had died down but were still in our favour. I stood up, energised, proud, unconsciously standing taller than I had for years, possibly for my whole life, and twisted round to see how Antigua looked now.

It was huge compared to when I'd gone into the cabin in the small hours of the morning. I could make out clear features of civilization; trees, cliffs, and houses dotted the coast. It was an enormous contrast to seeing the sea every day. It looked out of place and cumbersome after over seven weeks of staring at an empty horizon.

I breathed in the fresh sea breeze. It filled my lungs. Today was going to be a great day. Nothing could go wrong this close to land.

Smiling, I turned to greet Dan and Mark on the oars. Then I saw their faces and my smile dropped away.

'What's up?'

'We just had to call the tanker to avert course,' said Mark.

'It was right on track for us!'

My eyes immediately looked aft, beyond the boat. The giant, formidable metal ship sat lurking in the water. How had I missed this when I stepped out?! It was side-on to us, steadily moving away. We really weren't totally safe until we stepped onto land.

Again, I turned round and gazed over the forward cabin. Antigua was clearer now. The island was within our grasp. I could see a car skirting around the coastal road, disappearing between trees and houses. Even the mundane felt alien and enthralling to watch.

It was time to get ready for the finish. We had saved clothes after a wash a few weeks ago, specifically for this moment, and had stored them in a dry bag. It seemed odd that the finishing photos wouldn't represent our life at sea, wearing salt-ridden, filthy shorts and t-shirt, or absolutely nothing at all.

Antigua and Barbuda Search and Rescue (ABSAR) were now in contact with us over the radio to see us safely in.

'You need to hug the coastline by the cliffs. Not too close as it gets shallow and rocky, but not too far out as there's quite a bit of chop. The current could push you out to sea again and you'll miss the English Harbour.'

ABSAR sped towards us in their orange speed boat and were soon within shouting distance.

'Get the flares out!' they shouted, as the race photographer began taking photos.

I frantically opened the cabin hatch, fished out the box, and handed everyone flares. Four intensely bright lights suddenly launched from our hands.

This was it. This was the finishing photo I'd been staring at for nearly two years. Arms stretched upwards and cheers yelled out as the orange speed boat circled around us, taking shots at different angles.

Suddenly, I noticed that my hand had become increasingly hot. It felt like I was burning. Stupidly, I hadn't been looking at the flare. It was now finished and was close to scalding my hand. We threw them out, to be retrieved later, and then continued with the short row to the harbour.

As we made our way round the corner, the land parted and the entrance to the harbour revealed itself. With land on either side of us, we were sheltered from the ocean and the wind. *The Nutilus* slowly made its way further down into the harbour as if it was passing over a drawbridge into the safe confines of a castle.

Green, hilly land now surrounded us. Calm turquoise water was beneath our hull.

EEERRRRR!!! EEERRRRR!!!

A vast chorus of super yachts sounded their horns in celebration. A deep saturation of contentedness seeped in. This was surreal.

And now, in front of us, there it was. Two buoys on opposite sides of the water marked the finish line, the official end of the expedition, the point the clock would stop.

'Get some more flares on the go if you have any left!' they shouted from the speedboat.

We drew the oars in, grabbed the flares and drifted the final metres towards the line.

Clang!

As we crossed the line, an oar struck the buoy, knocking the light straight off the top. The oar was stuck against the buoy and the boat was pivoting around it.

The oar started to bend. I stood there, watching, my heart raced.

There wasn't much we could do. We couldn't draw it in further and there was way too much tension to lift it out of the gate, plus we had flares in our hands.

The buoy then toppled over, and everyone burst out laughing. It was later confirmed that no other team in the race's history had crashed into one of the finish line buoys!

We continued sauntering into the harbour, trying to soak up every second. Super yachts continued to sound their horns. We could hear crowds on the jetties and harbour walls, cheering us home. Sea birds wheeled in the sky above, cawing their own celebrations.

I was so proud of our little team. We are just four ordinary guys who'd had a dream about rowing an ocean, and who'd worked hard to make it a reality. And now here we were, crossing the finish line together.

The rough waves were now a distant memory as we drifted in the calm docks sheltered by the surrounding hills. I had watched so many finishing videos and now we were living it. We'd be in the inspiration for the next generation of ocean rowers.

I could make out people waving on the dockside. Then, as the metres ticked off, faces were visible in the crowd. I could see our families waving ecstatically, their faces full of pride and love. I couldn't wait to get up there and put my arms around every single one of them. All of them had supported us from day one and now they were here for us again, as we completed the biggest challenge of our lives.

The Atlantic Campaigns' rib guided us in until we ended up alongside the dock facing our families. Cheers roared in our direction. Champagne sprayed as we lit our last flares and rejoiced with the crowd. Smoke filled the air. It actually became hard to see, and it looked and smelled like a bonfire.

A welcome hand came to help us onto dry land. At 07:38, my foot touched down on solid ground. My legs felt like jelly. After weeks of adjusting to the ebb and swell of the waves, I could barely stand on the dockside. It felt safer on the boat. There was nothing in my legs, all the energy had wasted away over miles of ocean rowing. The wobbly first step felt like my leg would go through the floor. I desperately clung to the arm of Steve's dad, who helped me on land. I was now more stable on the boat, and it showed.

I didn't really know what to do. It didn't feel like reality being surrounded by people and noise. I'd spent nearly two months at sea with three guys on a 30-foot-long boat with nothing but the sound of the ocean and birds. The noise of a crowd of voices speaking and cheering all at once was overwhelming. I just stood there, bewildered.

I felt odd. This wasn't the instant relief that I had expected. We'd crossed the finish line. I thought I would be euphoric, but I wasn't. I was in shock.

It hadn't sunk in, but at the same time, I had had days to accept that we'd pretty much completed the expedition, so I'd already started processing the accomplishment. I didn't feel instant jubilation. It had been a simmering realisation that had slowly built, an extremely slow realisation. It wasn't like finishing a 100-metre race, where crossing the finish line was a defined point. Although there was a defined point, I'd been digesting the end of the expedition for a while now.

Stepping on land, for me, was a continuation of the process that, for the last few days, felt in the bag. For me, maybe even just going on the expedition was the victory. The finish was just one point along the journey, one of countless incredible memories. More than anything else, I felt more relief for being safe, not having to row for two hours on, two hours off, and seeing my family. Instead of an adrenaline-filled jubilant finish, I felt a warm pride.

Looking up, I saw them in the crowd. Emily, Mum, Dad, Charlotte.

Immediately, I went over to hug Emily. Tears ran down my family's faces as they beamed with pride. No words were needed as I hugged each of them. After all the messages and disjointed phone calls for nearly two months, here they finally were. They'd been there for me the entire way, from supporting the fundraising, which seemed a 100 years ago, to helping fix our boat on the start line.

All around us, cheers, claps, Champagne spraying and horns continued to fill the air with noise.

The Race Director announced our arrival.

'Ladies and gentlemen. We present, Nuts Over The Atlantic.'

He turned to look at each of us.

'Guys, you have a phrase on one of your oars saying, "Alone we can do so little, together we can do so much." I think you guys have shown true determination. You started later than the rest of the fleet, three days to be exact, and now you are here in beautiful Antigua. I am proud and happy to announce that you are here on the other side of the Atlantic Ocean in a time of……

'50 days, 20 hours and 31 minutes.

'Let's give a big cheer for Nuts Over The Atlantic! Well done, guys!'

Flags saying we'd rowed the Atlantic were thrust in our hands and more cheers boomed out of the crowds at the dock.

Shortly after the initial celebrations, we had an interview, but I'd lost the ability to have an in-depth conversation. I could barely walk the few metres required, let alone string together a coherent sentence. The overwhelming change in environment, the feeling of accomplishment, coming to terms with its ending, and just wanting to see my family, left me quiet. I was still. In the moment. Unable to articulate the experience.

With the interview complete, we walked over soft grass, which felt like medicine to my bare feet, to have our first meal. It was our first hot food in nearly two months, proper food, not dehydrated.

We had finally done it. Dry land. After 50 days at sea, we were now on a hot Caribbean Island with friends and family all around. We had rowed from La Gomera, to Antigua, across the Atlantic Ocean.

# PART FOUR

# THE AFTERMATH

# ANTIGUA

We sat in a bar at the harbour, *The Nutilus* in view, bobbing gently by the pontoon. The sun glistened on the water as it rippled gently in the protected harbour. Super yachts dressed the perimeter and green hills provided a spectacular backdrop against the clear blue Antiguan sky.

I couldn't wrap my head around everyone being here. All these people that I'd been thinking of for all this time and now here they were, right in front of me. I could talk to them without having to wait for a turn on my phone.

Being with my family on the other side of the world felt bizarre. I was aware I wasn't saying much. Although the physical transition from sea to land had happened quickly, I was still taking it all in, absorbing the new sensations, the voices, the laughter and the warm smiles, like a sponge. Yesterday, I'd woken to the news a ship was on course to hit us; now I was sitting in a bar with my family.

I put my drink down. It was time to go to the hotel. My bare feet gripped the textured road as we walked to the nearest shop. I didn't have any shoes, and needed flip flops before going to the hotel. As I entered the shop, the products on the shelves immediately bewildered me. There seemed to be so much colour and variety and choice. Why did we need so many things? Out on the ocean, I had got used to simplicity. We could only choose from the few things that we had in our cabins and store boxes. The minimalism had been refreshing. Here, the consumerism was overwhelming.

I grabbed the first pair of flip-flops I saw, and we jumped in a taxi to the hotel. The car accelerated away from the kerb. Immediately, I felt uneasy, like we were racing at 100mph.

'Do you guys think this is fast?'

'Yeah,' said Steve.

Dan nodded. Emily looked across at us, laughing.

'Guys, we're going 20mph.'

Trees, buildings, and people seemed to fly past the window. My brain was still adjusting. Everything was an assault on the senses.

We arrived at the hotel after a short drive and went up to our room. I couldn't wait to have a shower, and take some time out. I looked in the mirror, but hardly recognised the face that stared back at me. He was thinner, sun-tarnished, had long scraggly hair and a gigantic beard. It suddenly struck me. I hadn't seen my face properly for 50 days. I looked weathered.

Legs unsteady, I cautiously stepped into the shower. Fresh water rained on my skin, washing weeks of salt from my body. The hot, clean water felt like silk compared to the sea. It was pure luxury. It felt so easy, too easy, almost. Amenity felt effortless.

Once I was clean, I dried off and collapsed onto the bed. The mattress absorbed every muscle. My limbs felt like they were sinking, dropping into the warm softness. The sheets smelt divine. They didn't smell of musky sea salt for the first time in months.

I was so comfortable.

Maybe I'll just stay here for a moment and rest my eyes.

'Wake up!' Emily said, prodding my arm and laughing. 'You've been asleep for hours. I couldn't wake you!'

## Chasing Horizons

This nap had turned into an immediate sound sleep, my body craving the restorative repair of deep hibernation. I was so far gone that we were verging on being late for our evening meal with my family.

Despite my wobbly legs, we walked the short distance from the hotel to the restaurant in the warm Caribbean air. As we got close to the restaurant, my world started spinning. I had to lie down on a patch of grass for a bit and then walked on all fours to the restaurant to contend with my dizzy head.

The next morning, I woke with a start, looked round the room and shouted.

'Where is everyone?!'

I thought I was back on the boat, but none of the other lads were there. Well, at least I had it easier than Dan. Apparently, he had woken up every two hours, ready to row.

I lay back on my pillow and let my body relax into the mattress. The rowing was over. The adventure was finished.

# ONE YEAR LATER

I put my beer down on the table and looked across at Steve. We'd met in the pub for a catch up. Without one huge shared priority, normal life had crept in and it was difficult to get everyone together. I snatched at the chance for an impromptu pint with him. Around us, people were sharing an after-work beer and the low ambience of conversation buzzed through the bar.

Sat in our work clothes, we looked as we did when we first discussed the Atlantic so long ago. It had been a mad idea back then. We'd started out with no money, no boat and no rowing experience. But here we were, three years later, enjoying a pint with all that shared experience between us.

I looked over at Steve as he swigged his pint. He looked different to me now. I saw him as someone who had ridden the mid-ocean waves, someone who had fought for funding and battled all the way across the Atlantic. Here was a man who had been through the hardships of the rowing patterns, the sleep deprivation, the muscle ache and the fatigue, not to mention the fungal infections.

But he'd also seen the whales with me as they'd basked along the side of *The Nutilus*; watched dorados and frigatebirds fight over flying fish; seen the moonlight reflecting off an open ocean; watched dolphins frolic in the waves; sat and bathed in the starlight of an empty sky.

We had shared experiences; experiences that most people will only ever dream of. There were conversations that had been shared in the middle of the open sea that no one else would ever hear; sights and sounds that others would never experience.

Facing adversity together had forced us to grow, forged bonds and cemented life affirming memories. I glanced at Steve. The look between us said more than any conversation could. The shared experience transcended words.

A year on and life was back to normal. I'm not sure what I expected out of rowing the Atlantic. Perhaps I was looking for a profound change in who I am or a change in life direction. From the outside, I look the same. I have a similar job and the same friends, but on the inside, there had been a monumental shift.

'This time last year we were getting ready for La Gomera,' I said, breaking the silence.

'I know,' he glanced up.

I knew he knew. It's all I had been thinking about recently. I was certain he was thinking the same thing as me.

'I miss it, you know. Striving day-to-day for something I don't know is possible.'

He nodded sagely.

'I already feel like I'm coasting again,' I said. 'Like I'm slipping back into the old, comfortable ways.'

I thought about the experience daily, not just the row but everything that came with it – the training, the fundraising, the marketing. I missed the blind ambition, the challenge, the unknown. The expedition and build up had stripped us to our core. We'd found out things about ourselves that we couldn't test in normality.

I put so much on the row, my entire life, every waking second, every calorie of energy focused on a singularity. I had given no consideration to what would happen after.

What happens in the aftermath of reaching an audacious goal and getting back to reality? Life after the row felt slow and empty. Returning to meetings and daily life didn't really cut the mustard.

As clichéd as it sounds, there is something in the phrase, "It's about the journey". I had spent a lot of time living in the future, dreaming of what may be. But in reality, all we have is the journey, and the present moment. That we were sitting here reminiscing was proof that, with enough grit, determination and the right people, we truly can achieve great things. It hadn't scratched the itch; it had just cemented what was possible and with it, an even greater restless ambition. The world and my mind had opened up.

I found it difficult to remember, even though I'd learnt through a fairly extensive test, that happiness isn't a destination. Achieving goals wouldn't fix anything; the real joy of life is in the process of doing.

I missed the day-to-day graft towards a dream. Goals have their place, but it is wrong to rest happiness on their achievement. I felt proud, but not content.

'At least we've sold the boat, though!' Steve replied.

I nodded and sipped my pint. It had taken nearly a year. But he was right; at least we had sold the boat. We had negotiated shipping with the arrangement that we would pay the funds when we sold the boat. We'd sold it shortly after its arrival back in the UK to a new team of adventurers. *The Nutilus* would cross the Atlantic again soon.

I put my empty pint glass down on the sticky wooden table. It was time to catch the train home, home to Emily. I gazed through the window. Leaves scuttled past in the wind and a dark night sky rested above, reminding us of the incredible nights we'd had mid-ocean. I stood up and put on my coat and scarf, ready for the outside world.

'Until next time then,' I said, putting an arm around his shoulder.

'Until next time.'

# Chasing Horizons

# ACKNOWLEDGEMENTS

Writing a book is obviously a tremendous team effort. First, I'd like to thank all those who helped us along the way, getting the expedition off the ground and then supporting us during and after. Without the initial support, none of this would have been possible.

I'd like to thank my teammates, my friends Steve, Dan and Mark. Their unrelenting determination, tenacity and sheer stubbornness, not only got us to the start line and across the Atlantic, but picked me up and drove me forwards when I couldn't see the path.

I'd, of course, like to thank my family for their ceaseless enthusiasm and unwavering backing throughout the campaign and across the ocean. Now, as a father, I can't imagine what must have gone through their minds when I announced I was going to do this. Instead of worry, overwhelming support shone through.

Supporting the team were the incredible families and partners of Steve, Dan and Mark. An expedition of this size is a family endeavour, and we felt it every step along the way. Surrounding each team member was unparalleled support.

Thanks also to all my friends who supported and helped along the way, from asking employers for a meeting with us, last-minute prep for the black-tie event, graphic design on our sponsorship booklets and website, to last-minute panic-buying of tents when needed, and so much more.

I'd like to thank Atlantic Campaigns and staff members. Thanks, of course, go to all of our sponsors, without whom this project would not have got off the ground; for believing that despite everything, there might be a chance we actually pull this out of the bag. I'd especially like to thank Jon Lansdown. Bristol Sport went over and above what we had agreed. I'd also like to thank him for all the food and coffee at Ashton Gate stadium!

There are several people whose support made writing this book possible.

My thanks to Anna McNuff for spurring me on, and for giving me advice on the self-publishing journey. Thanks to Ben Saunders who kindly and humbly shared his wisdom, gained from years of polar expeditions.

Huge thanks to Jon Doolan for his wizardry editing skills. Book editing is no simple task, and he gave me the tools to turn a list of events into crafted story that I'm proud of.

I'd like to thank Simon Avery for the wonderful cover design, and to Ben Duffy for the magnificent photo.

Thank you to Mum for all the work she put into the final processes needed to get this book ready for printing.

Lastly, I'd like to thank Emily, whose unrivalled patience I struggle to comprehend and strive for. Thank you for becoming an instant member of the rowing campaign, without question, and giving whole heatedly. I am ever grateful for your support and believing in me, despite my rants during dog walks, as I figured out how to write this book. Thank you for enduring endless conversations on story, grammar and so many aspects, whilst always remaining helpful, reassuring and invaluable during the entire process.

# ABOUT THE AUTHOR

Jon lives in Cheltenham, UK, with his family.
When not dreaming of his next adventure, he's usually
found out on his bike, cycling around the Cotswolds.

www.ingramcontent.com/pod-product-compliance
Lightning Source LLC
Chambersburg PA
CBHW060550080526
44585CB00013B/513